Thank You For Having Me
A PERSONAL MEMOIR

Books by Maurice Lindsay

POETRY

The Enemies of Love
Hurlygush
At the Wood's Edge
Ode for St Andrews Night and Other Poems
The Exiled Heart
Snow Warning
One Later Day
This Business of Living
Comings and Goings
Selected Poems 1912–1942

The Run From Life: More Poems 1942–1972
Walking Without An Overcoat: Poems 1972–76
Collected Poems
A Net to Catch the Winds

PROSE

The Lowlands of Scotland: Glasgow and the North
The Lowlands of Scotland: Edinburgh and the South
The Scottish Renaissance
Robert Burns: the Man: his Work: the Legend
The Burns Encyclopedia
Clyde Waters
By Yon Bonnie Banks
The Discovery of Scotland
Environment: a Basic Human Right
The Eye is Delighted
Portrait of Glasgow
Robin Philipson
History of Scottish Literature
Scottish Lowland Villages
Francis George Scott and the Scottish Renaissance

ANTHOLOGIES

Poetry Scotland 1–4 (4 with Hugh MacDiarmid)
No Scottish Twilight (with Fred Urquhart)
Modern Scottish Poetry: an Anthology of the Scottish Renaissance
John Davidson: Selected Poems: with a preface by T. S. Eliot and an introduction
    by Hugh MacDiarmid
A Book of Scottish Verse (with R. L. Mackie)
Scottish Poetry 1–6 (with George Bruce and Edwin Morgan)
Scottish Poetry 7–9 (with Alexander Scott and Roderick Watson)
Scotland: An Anthology
As I Remember: Ten Scottish Writers Recall How for Them Writing Began (Ed.)
Scottish Comic Verse.
The Buildings of Edinburgh (with Anthony F. Kersting)

Thank You For Having Me

A PERSONAL MEMOIR

by

Maurice Lindsay

ROBERT HALE · LONDON

© *Maurice Lindsay 1983*
First published in Great Britain 1983

ISBN 0 7090 1173 3

Robert Hale Limited
Clerkenwell House
Clerkenwell Green
London EC1R 0HT

The Publisher acknowledges subsidy from
the Scottish Arts Council towards the
publication of this volume.

Photoset in Palatino by
Kelly Typesetting Limited
Bradford-on-Avon, Wiltshire
Printed in Great Britain by
St Edmundsbury Press, Bury St Edmunds
and bound in Scotland by Hunter & Foulis Limited

Contents

	Acknowledgements	7
	Prefatory Note	8
1	A Glasgow Boyhood	9
2	The Sensing of a Poet	31
3	Tending the Dogs of War	48
4	A Temporary Bureaucrat of the Britannic Mars	63
5	Return to Glasgow	85
6	By Yon Bonnie Banks	105
7	A Temporary Borderer	146
8	Glasgow Once More	186
	Index	219

To Joyce,
who shared so much of it with me,
and to Seona, Kirsteen, Niall and Morven,
who enriched it for both of us.

The party's almost over. Though at times a trifle odd,
I've thoroughly enjoyed it. Thank you for having me, God.

Acknowledgements

I have quoted in the passing from copyright material by a number of authors, but beyond the length generally accepted as critical comment only where a few are concerned. I am therefore extremely grateful to Mr Michael Grieve for permission to quote material by his late father, Dr Christopher Grieve ("Hugh MacDiarmid"); to Mr John Gray for the use of extracts from letters by Sir Alexander Gray; to Lieutenant Commander Dermot Gunn for extracts from letters by his uncle, Dr Neil Gunn; to Dr Magnus Magnusson and the Editor of *The Scotsman* for permission to reprint part of an article on Border Television; to Mrs Hazel Goodsir Smith for permission to quote from her husband's letters and to Mrs Hella Young and her family for permission to use a sonnet by Professor Douglas Young and to quote from his letters to me. Acknowledgements are also due to Messrs David Higham Associates Ltd. for permission to print a hitherto unpublished poem by Ruthven Todd, and to quote from his letters. Thanks are also due to Mr Alexander Scott for allowing me to quote some lines of his verse, and to the Editor of the *Glasgow Herald* for an extract from its piece on Plastic Scots.

For permission to use the drawing on the dustjacket, made originally for the *Scottish Review*, I am most grateful to Miss Morven Cameron. My grateful thanks also go to Dr George Bruce and to my wife, both of whom made many useful suggestions, and to my friend and publisher Mr John Hale, who agreed with their use of the blue pencil! My former secretary, Miss Helen Logan, typed the book through three drafts, and therefore deserves thanks of a special nature. I should also like to thank my daughter, Mrs Seona Barr, who compiled the index, and my friend Mr Douglas McLeman for reading my typescript from a legal standpoint. If I have omitted other acknowledgements anyone may feel due to them, I can only offer my apologies. Any oversight of this sort is entirely unintentional.

M.L.

Prefatory Note

Only two things justify the writing of an autobiography. An author should be able to produce from the ragbag of his recollections portraits-in-the-passing of people likely to be of some continuing general interest; and, while contriving to be as truthful as fallible memory and subconscious myth-making allow, be sufficiently entertaining to hold the attention of his readers. I hope that what follows fulfils both requirements.

"The trouble with you", a grey little man of high Scottish executive rank in the early days of television once declared, "is that you are far too guilty of the sin of enthusiasm". It is probably the only sin which I have absolutely no hesitation in publicly admitting, and one which I have never felt needed any kind of apology.

CHAPTER 1

A GLASGOW BOYHOOD

My birth occurred on July 21st, 1918, in a private nursing home in Lynedoch Terrace, now part of the Park Conservation Area. More than sixty-five years on, I have so far had no cause to regret this, the first Glasgow event at which I was present.

Some weeks before my father, who until then had survived the Great War as an infantry officer and been mentioned in dispatches, was seriously wounded, part of the left side of his jaw shattered by the fragment of a shell. As a result, he spent eighteen months in various hospitals. Much of this time he used to confound the first part of his doctors' prophecy that he would neither speak again nor live beyond the age of fifty. So successfully did he overcome the inconveniences of a clever bone graft that he soon became well known in post-war Glasgow as a public speaker. His favourite subjects were the benefits of insurance, in the profession of which he rose to be Scottish manager of a British company, and, during the twenties and early thirties, the League of Nations Union, of which he was the local secretary, and which he felt to be the only possible moral insurance-policy, however unreliable, against another war.

My father's triumph over his injury was not the first challenge he had met and overcome. Orphaned when he was nineteen and the eldest of a family of five, he found himself faced with the task of ensuring the launching into earning life of a brother and three sisters.

My mother, a gentle creature, had been educated after the fashion of the times in one of those establishments described by W. S. Gilbert as "a ladies' seminary", where balancing a book on the head to cultivate deportment and the inculcation of the domestic womanly virtues took precedence over learning. In later life she was reluctant to talk much about her ancestors, but her mother had died at the time of her birth and her father soon afterwards. My maternal grandmother had been what was vaguely described as "an opera singer" in America, though whether she was a principal, or merely a member of the chorus, family legend never disclosed. It was, however, from this vaguely transatlantic source that I was supposed to have inherited my musical interests.

My parents were married in 1917, during one of my father's brief periods of leave from the Western Front. When he returned to face his last battle, my mother remained in the house of the aunt who had brought her up, Miss Henrietta Brock, a lady as Victorian in temperament as her Christian name suggested. My earliest environmental memories are of the Brock home, 11 Ashton Terrace, on the north side of a private road, since its construction in 1848 kept free of through traffic. The houses on the south side of the street, built half a century later, were occupied by university professors. The whole of the academic side of the road and half the original terrace were demolished in the nineteen-sixties to make way for extensions to the University and the Western Infirmary. The drawing-room, into which I was rarely allowed, had a huge mid-Victorian chandelier, the gas jets of which were only lit on special occasions. Sometimes my mother would play on the upright piano that stood stiffly against the wall, while my great-aunt sat quietly rocking herself in her favourite chair.

My first efforts at speaking could not encompass as formidable a word as Henrietta, so I called my great-aunt "Teta", which thereafter she remained. For the same reason her brother John became Uncle "Doan". "Doan" was for two years a substitute father to me, and for him I formed a deep affection which lasted until his death in 1935.

We remained at 11 Ashton Terrace even after my two sisters and my brother were born, because by now Teta had grown visibly old and Doan was a fiftyish bachelor. From there, aged five, I was taken daily to Miss Bishop's Primary School in Kirklee Circus, another ladies' seminary at which little boys were briefly tolerated.

In these days small boys wore trousers the front of which was fastened at the sides by somewhat inaccessible buttons. Years later, at some glittering social occasion, I was introduced to the wife of the chairman of a well-known company. "We've met before", she said. "I used to take your trousers down", adding, after a careful pause: "at Miss Bishop's, when you wanted to go to the bathroom."

I can still recall a feeling of resentment when my sister was born. Indeed, jealousy so far overcame me that I whacked her on the head with a slipper, a much-deplored fact of which I was regularly reminded whenever some fresh outbreak of childish tantrums suggested I might have inherited my father's temper. Happily, she suffered no ill effect. Another exhibitionist demand for attention was equally primitive. One night when my parents were entertaining their guests with pre-dinner drinks, I heaved myself out of my bed and toddled down to the dining-room, secreting myself under the large Victorian table. I must have fallen asleep, for I awoke to find myself surrounded by a fence of legs and about to succumb to the pressures of nature. In a matter of moments, a powerful aroma from beneath the table led to my discovery, chastisement and banishment.

My introduction to music was conditioned by current educational fashion. I attended a private School of Music, run by two spinster ladies, the Misses Stewart. It was housed in their ground floor flat in Queensborough Gardens. The necessity of learning the basic notation of music was prettily postponed by the pretence that crotchets, quavers and minims were birds flying in an out of stave-like houses. I enjoyed singing in their choir, however, and made my first "appearance" on the air under the auspices of the Misses Stewart. The B.B.C.'s Glasgow studios were then located in the top flat of a building in Blythswood Square. There, I made one of my only two broadcasts as a solo singer, piping "Linden Lee" in a childish treble for a fee of ten shillings. More than forty years later, taking part in a critical discussion programme, "Arts Review", I impulsively sang a phrase to illustrate a point. "Please *never* do that again," said the producer afterwards. "It was a most unpleasant noise."

There is absolutely no way of avoiding learning the basic technique of music, or of anything else for that matter, so soon I had set myself the serious business of learning the piano. My instructress, Sheena Caird—eventually to become a pioneering teacher of Russian on the staff of Glasgow University—told me, years later, that she never understood how a child with musical talent simply dreamt his way through Walter Caroll's *Scenes on a*

Farmyard, specially designed to engage the childish imagination. They certainly did not connect with mine.

My first encounter with death, which took place about this time, most certainly did. Teta, who must have been about seventy towards the end of the Twenties, spent long hours sitting in her rocking-chair staring out of the oriel window in the first-floor drawing-room. Indeed, I can only recall a single summer image of her actually moving about, dressed in what seemed to me a voluminous heliotrope skirt, and wearing a lace choker topped by a heliotrope three-cornered Edwardian hat. She carried a purple parasol, which I never saw her actually open.

My little room led off the master bedroom, for which it had doubtless been designed as a dressing-room when the house was built. One day Teta mysteriously took ill and was moved into the master bedroom usually occupied by my parents. She lay there for several days, white and still, her hands on the top of the quilt like scraps of crinkled paper. One night, my mother roused me from a deep recess of sleep and hastily wrapped me in a shawl. "Something has happened to Teta," she said; "you're not to look." Then she hurried me through the master bedroom. I did of course, look, and what I saw—the scarcely settled washed-up stillness of death—was my first real intimation of mortality.

Although my father had by this time resumed his position as head of the household, there was often an air of tension in the home which a small boy could scarcely fail to sense. The Ashton Terrace house belonged not to him but to Teta. Though she was kind to us children, she had a sharp tongue. Her brother, Doan, had succeeded in rising no higher than the level of travelling salesman in the Brock family grain-merchant's business, managed by his cousin. In my able and ambitious father's view, Doan was therefore "unsuccessful".

Doan kept his samples in carefully labelled thick manilla envelopes, from which he extracted the pulses on broad ivory samplers to show to his customers. I enjoyed watching him check their freshness every weekend. Until his brief marriage late in life, he took me out every Saturday afternoon on what he called our "excursions". We might find ourselves swaying and jolting the length of a tuppenny tram ride to some distant and magically-named Glasgow suburb like Auchenshuggle, or sailing model yachts or tin steamboats, bought by him, across the pond in Victoria Park. Once, there was an illicit journey on a real tanker steam engine from Hyndland depot. My uncle got a row from my mother when we arrived furtively home with tell-tale oil marks on my best jacket.

Sometimes, the "excursion" ended with a two-course high tea in Danny Brown's, an eating establishment in St Vincent Street founded by one of Miss Cranston's contemporaries. Occasionally, there would be a visit to a pantomime, or to a performance by the Scots comedians Will Fyfe or Harry Lauder, both of whom my uncle greatly admired. Now and then we would go to a so-called "celebrity" ballad concert in the City Hall, or to a concert by the Scottish Orchestra in St Andrew's Hall. "I know what I like", Doan would say of the music we heard, "but I don't know why I like it." When Doan did not have to work on Saturday mornings, our "excursions" would last the whole day and carry us outside Glasgow. On the Saturday before the outbreak of the General Strike in 1926 we took a bus-ride into Lanarkshire, buses then being a comparative novelty. Suddenly the bus was surrounded by shouting men who made us all get out. Sweating and swearing, they then pushed the bus over on its side. For months after, the prolonged tinkle of falling glass as the bus crashed over sounded through nightmares in which I fancied myself threateningly leered at by the contorted faces of the protesters, miners, I was told, angered by wage-cuts and unemployment. I was quite unable to understand how pushing over a bus could help anyone get jobs. Doubtless my adult hatred of, and contempt for, violent protest movements and Trade Union bullying were inculcated on that long-ago Saturday afternoon.

By this time my father's household had two servants. There was a cook, who slept in a tiny room, the barred window of which faced the dark underside of the stone stairs that led up to the entrance to the house. There was also a superior domestic, a nanny. As a symbol of her status she enjoyed a bed in the night nursery, the room she shared with the younger children.

One Saturday afternoon, much to my surprise, there was no "excursion". Instead, the Nanny insisted that I come for a walk with her and the younger children. I trailed miserably along, feeling dimly that my world of love and imaginative fulfilment was somehow threatened. At a point in Great Western Road I cried out in protest and refused to go any further. We were outside "Greek" Thomson's Great Western Terrace, where years later I was to acquire a home. There, Nanny told me that Uncle Doan had that morning married. There would be no more "excursions". Resentment at this new unwanted Aunt Janey who had lured away my companion jostled with anger at what seemed my uncle's betrayal.

Of course there was every incentive for him to marry in his late-fifties. With the death of Teta, my father acquired the Ashton Terrace house, and Doan was persuaded to move into nearby lodgings. His marriage lasted scarcely two years. His wife suffered a stroke while sitting on the W.C. I became aware that God, to Whom perforce I had daily to give thanks for breakfast, lunch and high tea (with or without jam and chocolate biscuits) apparently had little respect for the finer points of human decency.

With the family growing up a bigger house was needed. In 1930 we moved to 32 Athole Gardens, an enclosed, hilly U-shaped crescent built in the high Victorian manner of the 1870s round a private fenced common central garden containing a grass tennis court. Early in the summer the pink flambeaux of a horse chestnut tree illuminated the front of our house, its flares of light reflecting on the window-panes. From my high-up back bedroom window, a room I shared with the now widowed Doan, I could see across the roofscape at the back of the house a horizon distantly fretted by shipyard cranes.

The scarcely muted hostility which my father had latterly shown towards Teta in the Ashton Terrace days now manifested itself towards Doan, though perhaps not without cause. Even I noticed that Doan was becoming strangely irritable. He took to absenting himself from meals without warning and would often come to his bed long after I was sound asleep. For a time, my mother did her best to cover up for him by managing his personal affairs. She could not conceal the fact that this meant taking possession of his salary and allowing him only pocket-money. Doan had taken to drink. Almost a year of observing these strange symptoms passed before the day when, in spite of all my mother's protective shielding, I came upon him, flushed and aggressive. It was as if some other creature had taken possession of his body, and my belief that people were constant identities was painfully shattered. I became wary of him and unsure of myself. A few weeks later he was rushed to a nursing home to undergo an emergency prostate gland operation. Afterwards, he lay there white and pale, as if the thing that possessed him had been cut out, leaving him at least a recognisable shadow of his former self. "You and I had good times together," he said, resting his hands on mine. "Yes," I agreed, struggling to hold back tears I had been taught were womanish: "and will have again." He shook his head, shedding a little of his old smile. It faded into sleep. He died that night, and his passing marked my boyhood's end: but he had left me a legacy that was to last a lifetime.

"Glasgow," he had so often said in the days of our excursions, "is a great place. Nowhere else like it." From him, I learned to appreciate what goes to make up a sense of place, which for me has been one of life's deepest pleasures, along with a feeling for the inherent significance of the physicality of things and the savour of words.

Once I had learned to read, words quickly assumed a special dimension. I used to say a particular word over and over again, as one might test the texture of a piece of cloth. The word *Glasgow*, in particular, fascinated me. I would stare at it, separate the syllables and say them aloud. *Glesgie* it was to some; *Glaschu*, "the dear green place," to the Gaels who possessed whatever was there before the Tobacco Lords built up its Georgian elegance. That was torn down by their Victorian successors anxious to reflect in their homes the status conferred by expanding profits from their shipyards and factories; profits expended in the effulgence of public and private building which turned Glasgow into the Second City of the British Empire. Such was still the proud title of this essentially Victorian city at the beginning of the thirties, though by then Birmingham was already doing its best to filch it away.

Glasgow. A place where you were not looked at as if you had some repellent disease when you asked what colour of tramcar you should ride on to take you to wherever unfamiliar district you might want to reach! "Warm heart of Scotland with the generous hand," I called it enthusiastically in schoolboy verses as woefully deficient in knowledge of anatomy as in the function of imagery.

Glasgow. A virile bustle of change, sheer with life: a fricative edge of social difference; ocean-going ships, nosed high in docks or moored to quays almost at the grey heart of the city; cranes towering like flattened question-marks over the Clyde and the depressed streets of the thirties; horse-drawn lorries labouring up hilly West Nile Street; tramcars squealing as they took the corner of Renfield Street and Sauchiehall Street; the stale smell of booze at pub corners; the staler waste of men in dirty white cravats, hanging about the flapping doors of their empty days; the sharp thrust of Glasgow's debased Scots speech, jabbing through elisions and buttressed with sexual oaths. These I can recall from the recesses of boyhood memory. I remember, too, the implied contrast in lucky chance when, coming home from a Sunday afternoon "spin" in my father's car, we had to join a long line of waiting cars to get past a banner-carrying procession of hunger-marchers. These were the sights, sounds and smells of a city already sinking into decline, but somehow mustering enough self-confidence, in what was perhaps by then already non-achievement, still to think of itself as "great"!

Although by the early thirties the City's grey and red sandstone buildings had long since been darkened by coal-fired industrial and domestic smoke and the dense yellow fogs that licked them every winter, the decay and dilapidation of the post-Second-War years had not yet set in. For one thing, the city's wide range of decorated nineteenth-century railings still stood intact. The hasty tearing down of those practical fringes of Victorian fancy on the orders of Lord Beaverbrook during the 1939 war to be recycled for purposes for which they proved totally unsuitable and could not be used, freely admitted blowing street rubbish and a creeping decline the railings had held trimly at bay. There was no awareness of any concept of conservation in those days, though most of the new public buildings put up in the decade before the 1939 war still spoke with a modified version of the Victorian amalgam of earlier styles.

It was not just the buildings in our district that gave it a sense of entity. There was still a sense of community about Hillhead. The Byres Road shopkeepers knew us all by name, and we them. There was Wilkie, the grocer, who sent round a crate of apples at Christmas in appreciation of our custom; the thirties equivalent, I suppose, of such later devices as selling loss-leaders or giving away trading stamps. The three—or was it four?—Misses Horn kept the dairy, with the cows at one time in a byre behind the shop, though I cannot myself recall this. They had hands as blue as the Dutch wall-tiles of their shop, due, I used to think, to so much scrubbing, though their hands were not as raw as those of the daughter of Andrews, the fishmonger, whose fingers were forever lifting moist fillets off chipped block ice. Comfortably

rounded Mr and Mrs Todd, the fruiterers, added their contribution to the Christmas scene with a gift of tangerines to all their
"regulars". Tully, the ironmonger, and Bell of the toyshop
featured less prominently, being on the more occasionally visited
periphery of my childish world of things. Most exotic of all was
Henderson's stable, from which issued forth the musty-smelling
horse-drawn cabs that conveyed us to children's parties. The
cabs had faded yellowish-green seats and were driven by cabbies
wearing greenish bowler hats. They stood slapping their arms
and blowing on their glove-ends to keep warm while they waited
for their winter "fares" to materialise from the streets. In time,
those cabs gave place to cumbersome-looking limousines which
used the same shelter. Cabs and limousines have long since
gone, their base now an Underground station.

My mother devoted much time to the ordering of the household chores. Our cooks and our parlour-maids usually came from
the Highlands, and, like most domestics in these days, spoke
Gaelic. To hear them talk in a language to me incomprehensible
was my first experience of the Scottish dichotomy. That a
dichotomy existed even in the smaller world of the Gael became
apparent when frequently they would argue in English, oblivious
of my presence, about the meaning or correct pronunciation of a
Gaelic word as spoken in Skye, rather than as it was pronounced
in Stornoway. From time to time my mother wrote out a daily
chart of duties for each of the domestics. For the parlour-maid it
went like: Mondays, clean the dining-room silver and polish the
glasses; Tuesday, tidy out the kitchen and pantry cupboards;
Wednesday, brush and dust the dining-room and parlour;
Thursday, brush and dust the drawing-room, the hall stairs and
hall landings—and so on. Cook was supplied with the week's
menus and instructions on the economics of the house-keeping.

There was, of course, in reality a succession of cooks and
parlour-maids who came and went for reasons usually unclear to
us children. Usually they were mysterious temporary allies,
denizens of female warmth in their shining kitchens, where the
fire in the cooking-range made the copper jellypans on the
shelves of the dresser glint and glimmer; allies surreptitiously
chatable-to when the regime of the nursery occasionally slackened. One Lowland cook of exceptional plainness, for whom
Gaelic was simply "a wheen o' blethers", ended unfinished
every promising confabulation by relaxing her bulk and her

perennial problem into the depth of a chair, gasping: "Goad! If only ah could get a man!"

My parents frequently entertained, dinner often being followed by bridge. Their most regular friends for some years were the Thorntons. Joe had retired from a high position with a tobacco concern, well enough off to acquire a magnificent library of leather-bound first editions. I was never able to understand his notion that one should keep books to look at from the outside rather than to read. His premature leisure was said to have been brought about by his hot temper. My father, also hot-tempered, occasionally clashed with him, and loud was their embattled argument. Perhaps they both got something out of these exchanges, for the regularity of the weekly bridge-parties remained unbroken for many years.

The changing year was punctuated by recurring high functions, like the Festive Season and the Dancing Ball. The weekly winter dancing classes were held in the now demolished Hillhead Burgh Hall, conducted at first by a fragile-looking kindly spinster, Miss Brown, and later by the equally dignified but rather less kindly Miss Webster. These ladies, forearms swathed in long kid gloves, were the descendants of the eighteenth century *directrices* who conducted adult dancing assemblies with a propriety that rivalled the discipline of a military operation. While the outside adult world was gyrating to the Charleston and the Black Bottom, we danced lancers, quadrilles, polkas and swirling old-fashioned waltzes, to the chilling tinkle of a distant piano tiny on an empty stage. The culminating moment of this carefully formulated activity was the early summer Ball, held amidst a flurry of lacy dresses and kilts with jabots and ruffles in the Grand Hotel at Charing Cross (where Eugène d'Albert, the composer of the opera *Tiefland*, had been born, his peripatetic pianist mother happening to be there at the time) and graced by a real live orchestra, complete with frock-coated conductor. There, annually I cavorted, along with a future editor of the *Glasgow Herald*, the chairman-to-be of one of Scotland's best-known whisky distilleries and others of equal future local eminence.

Christmas was never such a formal occasion. The collapse of my belief in the legend of Santa Claus, with its startling revelation of the lying potential of parents who constantly preached the virtue of truth-telling, neither shook the melodious glitter from the sound of the carols, nor cooled the glowing feeling that the irresponsibility of happiness could be publicly acknowledged and celebrated for at least a few wintry days each year.

Christmas at Athole Gardens remained a top-floor nursery affair. By the early thirties I had graduated to the then still more traditionally celebrated Scottish adult occasion, New Year's Day dinner, when the relations and family "connections" assembled in the drawing-room, my father passing round before the meal an assorted trayful of glasses filled with whisky or sherry. An agreeable eccentric with a fascinating unfamiliar accent was my Irish "Aunt" Ada, a remote connection by marriage. Every year she announced that she never touched a drop of the stuff, except for her Christmas glass of sherry. On one of her last Christmas appearances I caught her out in another piece of adult double-dealing. After a furtive look round to make sure no one was looking (though I was), she picked up a whisky glass, sniffed it surreptitiously, then downed it at a gulp, glimpsing my watchfulness, so to say, in the tilt. Her recovery was instant and admirable. "Matthew!", she roared; "Oh Matthew! What have you done to me?", quickly helping herself to a sherry "to put away the taste".

By far the most significant of these recurring special experiences was, of course, the summer holiday. Our holidays in the twenties were divided between the Highlands and Ayrshire. My father was a keen fisherman, so for a number of years we went to Nethybridge, near the Spey. It was, and is, a quiet little village on the River Nethy set in a green strath lit up in summer by gorse and broom, an encampment of fertility surrounded by snow-patched mountains. For the month of July we took the house of the Grants, who ran the local store and sub-Post Office. While their home was let to us, they lived, after the Highland fashion, in a hut at the bottom of the garden.

One morning there was uproar in the hen-run. Birds were flying in all directions, beating against the wire netting. Mrs Grant, brandishing a walking-stick, was pursuing a squawking brown hen. Eventually, she cornered it, and to my horrified astonishment, grabbed the triangle of its body, held it on the ground, put the walking-stick across its neck, stood on both ends and gave a sharp pull. Looking as ruffled as her hens she straightened herself and, picking up the still twitching headless corpse, explained: "It's the best way. I can't bear to kill them, but after I've chased one around for ten minutes, I'm that angry, I canna do anything else!"

Another Nethybridge character was Mr Dole, the baker. Covered in flour from hair to shoes, he sold his products warm through the bakery door. Like Mrs Grant he had lost his ancestral Gaelic, but carried its lilt into the speaking of his English.

There was no lilt at all about the droning and roaring of the fearsome Wee Free minister, who left me with a lasting impression of noisy anonymity, hard seats and still harsher nonsense. I was by then beginning to suspect that the humourless creatures in flowing gowns who claimed to represent God on earth, yet regularly fed him trivial information an omnipotent being might be supposed already to know, were merely part of another long-standing adult conspiracy. Man, it seemed, had made God in his own image, not the other way round.

My mother never showed any interest in religion. My father was nominally a member of Glasgow's Trinity Church, in Claremont Street, now the Henry Wood Hall, the home of the Scottish National Orchestra. Although some kind of clarion call to the faithful had evidently blazed from its pulpit in the distant days of the Reverend Dr John Hunter, the incumbent at this time was an actor manqué, the Reverend H. S. Maclelland, whose doctrines appeared to embrace all shades of religious belief and none. Even today, non-churchgoing parents in Scotland still like their children to be inculcated at school with religious beliefs they themselves have consciously rejected. Presumably my agnostical father—who, almost on his death-bed, dismissed Christian belief in an after-life as "absurd damned nonsense"—felt that I would benefit in some way by exposure to Church of Scotland orthodoxy.

So I was sent, first, to Sunday School, of which all I can recollect is another variant of hard-seated boredom, and then to Hillhead Parish Church, a great oval of hanging space built in imitation of the Sainte Chapelle in Paris. There, I listened weekly, first, to the sermons of the Reverend Alfred Warr, who looked rather like a Victorian etching of one of Christ's disciples; then to the thoughts of the Reverend Dr W. D. Maxwell, a scholarly-looking Scoto-Catholic who wore different coloured vestments in accordance with the seasons of the Christian year. Dr Maxwell, who eventually occupied a Chair of Divinity in a South African University, preached ethics to a congregation of elderly relicts of once-wealthy West End business families, professional bachelors who "did" for themselves, and a few middle-aged couples. As a teenager I enjoyed the ethics, but apparently the rest of the congregation did not. Increasingly, they stayed away. So Dr Maxwell turned to dogma.

The bleeding lamb imagery of the butcher's shop revolted me (as also, I discovered later, it had disgusted Shaw). The notion that millions upon millions of dreary, bored Christian people might have to endure each other in some sort of crowded celestial presence for an eternity beyond all conception of time, absolutely horrified me. I felt sorry for God if that was really what He had let Himself in for, though I did not, on the whole, think it likely. Even after I became convinced that the Christian religion, as formalised by the various rival churches, was basically a monk-made structure, I kept on going to church, because the organ, the gift of a famous whisky family, filled the hanging space with the contrapuntal arguments of Bach and Mendelssohn, and the vibrating rhetoric of Widor, Karg-Elert and Rheinberger. These were sounds wholly unfamiliar to the Wee Free congregation at Nethybridge, for within its bare granite walls no hated "kist of whistles" was allowed.

The Augusts of the twenties were spent on the Ayrshire sea-board, mostly at Prestwick. To keep holiday-makers occupied on wet days (not exactly infrequent in a Scottish summer) "The Enter-tainers" performed twice daily in a stucco pavilion at the western end of the esplanade. One wet afternoon, tempted by the prize of a bonbon, I mounted the stage to sing my party piece. "Don't do that to the poor puss cat/Oh no, no, no, no!", I shrilled. The reason urged for such tolerance was that "you might be a pussy-cat yourself some day", an argument I thought somewhat improbable. I won the bonbon nevertheless, thus learning the invaluable lesson that technique could be made to triumph over conviction.

Middle-aged escapees are fond of assuring young people that at school you experience "the happiest days of your life". My decade at Glasgow Academy, from 1926 to 1936, was too full of exciting discoveries to allow the survival of many memories of resentful emotions. Glasgow Academy has produced many distinguished soldiers, statesmen, doctors, businessmen, the playwright "James Bridie" (Dr O. H. Mavor) and his stage-crafting predecessor, Sir James Matthew Barrie. Barrie's brother still taught French at the Academy during my time.

The weakness of the school was that if you were as disinclined to work at uncongenial subjects as I was, nobody made sure you did. Its strength, apart from the breadth of opportunity it offered, was the unobtrusive and, on the whole, humane manner in which it inculcated self-reliance and self-discipline; indispensable qualities often glibly denigrated today. We had to keep our hair short, wear school uniform, and, when in cadet uniform, salute when we passed the War Memorial as a mark of respect to those Academicals who had lost their lives in the 1914 war. It is easy enough to make fun of such a gesture. When I passed the War Memorial the other day I noticed with disgust that it had been daubed with mindless slogans, an act of loose contempt unthinkable half a century ago.

Near the beginning of my time at the Academy I discovered that I was totally unable to comprehend the philosophy of sport. I simply did not enjoy playing games. Like all public schools Glasgow Academy prided itself on its rugby and, to a lesser extent, its cricket. Cricket I found particularly boring, since the intervals of hanging about doing nothing appeared to negate any sense of competition.

My strongest dislike, however, was reserved for rugby. At one of my early appearances on the junior pitch at Anniesland, I somehow managed to be on the underside of a collapsed scrum. Disengaging from it I had my neck stood upon, and as a result, was straddled by a plaster collar for several weeks. Though this was off-putting enough, what seemed the sheer sweaty fatuousness of chasing up and down the field throwing and kicking a ball about proved an insurmountable obstacle to any appreciation of rugby's finer points. Attendance at school rugby matches on Saturday mornings, even when one was not playing, was then more or less compulsory. One such mandatory occasion was greatly enlivened when a nearby boy from the class above me so far forgot himself as to leap from his seat in the grandstand and exhort the side he supported to: "Kick their shins! Gouge their eyes out!" Before the effectiveness of this advice could be put into practice, my favourite teacher, C. A. Wilson—nicknamed "the Crow" because of the sound of her three initials—suddenly stood up and brought down her umbrella with a resounding thwack on the head of the offender calling for such ungentlemanly and unsportsmanlike conduct. Part of the effectiveness of the gesture was deflected, because she broke her umbrella on the back of my seat.

Compulsory hours spent with the Officers' Training Corps were even less imaginatively satisfying, although as things turned out their enforced discipline was to have its practical usefulness. Looking back now, my difficulty appears to have been quite a simple one. The subjects I liked, principally English and Music, generated in me such a compelling interest that they made all but impossible adequate application to the colder attractions of Mathematics, Physics and Chemistry. No amount of parental exhortation on the practical necessity of broadly-based school achievement penetrated my enraptured senses. From time to time politicians declare that the nation needs more engineers and fewer arts graduates; as if human aptitudes could be manipulated like quantities from an industrial line.

True, the teaching of Mathematics at the Academy was not such as to invite much enthusiasm. The former military man who had the task of unravelling its mysteries to me was not over-fond of exposition, and as soon as decently possible used to set us class work to get on with on our own. He would then settle down in his chair and in a matter of moments fall asleep. Tuck-shop bets were laid on how soon it would be before the upper set of false teeth began to creep out from the drooping jaw.

When in due course the School Leaving Certificate examinations had been sat, the final day of reckoning came. The headmaster sent for me. "Lindsay," he said, "I have just had an inquiry from the examination authorities. In view of the marks you secured in your English, History and Music examinations, they want to know if you took ill during the Mathematics examination, in which you secured precisely four per cent. I have told them you did not take ill but are always like that." As a recent devotee of A. E. Housman's poems, I already accepted the fact that probably I was the embodiment of:

> "To think that two and two make four
> And neither five nor three,
> The heart of man has long been sore,
> And long 'tis like to be."

From my earliest schooldays I found myself susceptible to the personalities of my teachers. There remains indelibly etched a fearsome image of the first headmaster I experienced, although he retired during my early months at the school. Dr "Teddy" Temple glowered like a figure out of the Old Testament from beneath a balding shock of white hair as, gown flowing behind him, he swept along the corridor clutching some hapless miscreant on the way to his study and chastisement. He never actually beat me, though on more than one occasion his bald pate bent threateningly in my direction. Temple was succeeded by a gentle though somewhat inarticulate classicist, Roydon Richards. He broadened the class-singing basis on which music had hitherto been taught in the school. Musical history and appreciation were introduced. He founded the first school orchestra of which eventually I became the leader. No double-bass player was available, so Richards taught himself that unwieldy instrument, sticking pieces of stamp edging along the fingerboard to mark the positions of the basic notes.

At Christmas and at the end of the summer term we played before a dutiful audience of parents, brothers and sisters in the school dining-hall amidst the ghostly aroma of long-eaten over-stewed cabbage. My debut as a violinist took place here, playing second fiddle in Purcell's "Golden" Sonata.

The most ambitious of these occasions was a staged perform-ance of *Trial by Jury*. To our astonishment the school managed to persuade the conductor of the Scottish Orchestra, Mr John Barbirolli, and his first wife (the opera singer Marjorie Parry) to be principal guests. Years later, when waiting in the green room of St Andrew's Hall for a television camera to be set up for a film inteview, I reminded Sir John of that visit. "In those days," he reminisced, "the poor old Scottish Orchestra was almost on its last legs, and I had to show my face in public wherever I got the chance."

At about this time my father was president of the Palette Club, an association of professional and business men. It owned handsome premises at 1 Newton Place, Charing Cross. Every Friday evening there was a members' musical "smoker". Barbirolli appeared as a cellist at one of these recitals, and subsequently came to dinner at our house in Athole Gardens. To my delight he brought his cello with him, and I had the terrifying task of accompanying him. With characteristic consideration the pieces he set before me demanded only the most modest of pianistic skills.

The school's first music master, Eric Coningsby, became my teacher of harmony and counterpoint. I was the first boy to take music as a Leaving Certificate subject, and I also studied with him privately. Since my thirst to absorb music of all kinds took me regularly to rehearsals at St Matthew's, Blythswood, the church where he was organist—it stood near Charing Cross, along from the Kings Theatre and more or less on the site of the eastern flank approach road to the motorway—I was often in his company. I soon discovered that he had a reputation among the boys for being what they called "one of *them*". As Coningsby had made no homosexual advances to me and his principal accuser happened to be one of two senior boys known generally as enticers of their juniors to lavatory corners during period-time for the practice of mutual masturbation, rashly I struck him a blow. In the ensuing fight, I regarded myself as doomed from the start. By chance, as we rolled in combat on the gym floor surrounded by a cheering circle, I leant against the inside of my opponent's leg in such a way as to cause him some kind of muscular spasm. He yelled with pain and begged me to desist. Just to make sure, I leant a bit harder, then graciously accepted his apology. I was immediately surrounded by admiring militants anxious to find out where I had learned my ju-jitsu. Since it was a secret with which I was in no position to part, I held my counsel. I was never again bothered by either of the two homosexual bullies.

Poor Coningsby's homosexuality was eventually uncovered, however, and he left the school. During the war he heard me broadcasting in the B.B.C.'s programme "Music Magazine" and wrote asking if I would see him. He came to lunch in London and told me his sorry story. He had lost several jobs, married disastrously, and wondered if I could help him find work with the B.B.C., a quite impossible request. A year or two later, in a station waiting-room, I picked up a sensation-mongering Sunday newspaper that happened to be lying about, glanced idly through it and discovered he had committed suicide.

In these days the Higher Leaving Certificate examination in music had an oral part in which the competitor was required to play a specified piece. At the appointed hour I knocked on the door of the school music-room. While the desks themselves were unoccupied, the whole atmosphere was filled with the fierce-looking white-haired presence of my examiner, on whom I proceeded to inflict the violin test piece, Raff's Cavatina, which he accompanied on the piano. Afterwards, I was astonished to learn that my examiner was Francis George Scott, the composer, one of whose part-songs, a gentle lullaby, I had recently sung with the school choir.

My practical literary beginnings occurred some six or seven years after my Blythswood Square vocalising, and resulted from my falling in puppy love. Pat was a few months younger than me, both of us about thirteen. Tall, skinny, with chuckling eyes and a mop of frizzy hair, she met me every day at the corner of Byres Road and Great George Street. There, we spent many an hour exchanging tender nothings. She "inspired" my first published verses, a stilted declaration of pseudo-Augustan love from Damon to Sylvia. They appeared in the school magazine and attracted the attention of the bachelor Latin master, "Foxy" Clark, a dominie of the old school, who glinted through gold-rimmed spectacles over a peaked starched collar, but whose authoritarian discipline won him respectful affection. "Lindsay's poem", though in English, was given out as the night's home-work. Next day, I was called in front of the class to repeat what I had learned. "You have made three mistakes," gloated "Foxy", lifting his strap from his desk drawer. "Hold out your hand." "But sir," I protested, "I was reciting the revised version." "Your task was to learn the prescribed text. Hold out your hand." There may be some who think that the beating which followed cannot have been hard enough, since it failed to deter me from the making of verses.

A beating of a less acceptably formal kind marked the practical beginnings of my sexual life. Like many Scots, I was physically a slow developer. When I was about fifteen a housemaid, a Lanarkshire miner's daughter, who had been with us for several months but of whose presence as an individual I was not particularly conscious, obtruded herself upon my attention one evening by leaning over me and questioning me about home-work I had just finished. I became aware of the pressured curve of her breasts and her warm female smell, and sensed that she meant me to. Next night she sat on a chair recently vacated by my tutor. One of her hands moved across my trouser leg while the other placed my own hand around the jumpered softness of her breast. The ensuing sensual turmoil and release was a curious mixture of indescribably pleasure and anxious guilt. Saying nothing, she quickly withdrew as stealthily as she had come.

For most of us at public schools, sex education in the early thirties was mainly a matter of lavatorial whisperings. On my fourteenth birthday my father presented me with a curious book called something like *What Every Boy Should Know*. The gist of its message was that if I felt the weakness of the sexual drive overcoming me, I must pray to God for protection and take violent exercise, followed by a cold bath. If I indulged in shameful self-gratification, God would be affronted and the future efficacy of my member permanently impaired. None of these propositions seemed credible, so ignorance persisted. As in most male public schools, there were in the Academy those few bully-boys who from time to time waylaid the weaker brethren and forced them to participate in masturbation sessions. Such furtive enforced experiences strengthened the repulsion I have always felt against homosexuality, though I am not, or course, in favour of the persecution of its unlucky practitioners.

It was against this background of muddled semi-ignorance that the housemaid mounted her wordless assault. Matters reached the point of crisis a few nights later when, as I lay reading in bed, the door opened and, clad only in her dressing-gown, she slipped in. I was ignorant of the gymnastics of sex and the mechanics of birth control, and hardly knew her as a person. Fears of several sorts assailed me. "Out," I hissed at her: "get out. At once." "Do what I want or I'll tell your father you assaulted me," she said, opening her dressing-gown. I jumped out of bed and pushed her roughly through the door. She started to cry. Then I heard angry voices on the lower landing. A few minutes later my father, purple with rage, burst into my bedroom, hauled off the bedclothes and proceeded to belabour me with a walking-stick. A struggle ensued, during which he recovered some of his self-control. Had he not considered how, if I had really assaulted the girl, she came to be leaving my room loudly, hurriedly and naked but for her dressing-gown?, I demanded. He stormed out of the room without comment or apology.

Nothing more was said of the incident. The girl disappeared next day, to be replaced by a bony harridan. The affair, however, did lasting damage to my relationship with my father. I never forgot that unjustified attack, nor forgave him his readiness to accept one side of a story in view of his constantly reiterated belief that every story had three sides to it. Later, when I came to read Freud, another explanation suggested itself; an explanation that gained, so to say, posthumous credence forty years later. When going through his papers after his death, one of my sisters discovered that he had conducted an extra-marital affair over a long period of years with evident enjoyment.

At a critical stage in my school life, I arrived in the class of B. G. Aston, an English teacher known affectionately as "Baggy" because of the cut of his flannel trousers and his rolling nautical gait. "Baggy", who turned out to be a Territorial soldier, not a sailor, made literature live by communicating a quality of enthusiasm pupils rarely associate with schoolmasters. Not that he was in any sense an actor. When he declaimed Shakespeare he fell back upon the intrusive *huh*:

"Is this a dagger—*huh*—that I see before me—
Huh—the handle towards my hand?"
or:

"I know a bank—*huh*—where the wild thyme blows." Yet the *huhing* did not matter. He knew, and brought his pupils to know, that the true end of poetry is delight. Admittedly, he once described Burns as "a minor song-writer you can read in your own time", and led us to believe that poetry died in Greece with Rupert Brooke. Thus ill-armed, I had to flounder through the morass of the New Apocalypse and the linguistic over-assertiveness that animated the Lallans Makars before I learned how to be about what I really wanted to do. All the same, my debt to "Baggy" was, and is, a huge one.

The school was equipped with a well-furnished library, and I read omnivorously. By the time I left the Academy I had devoured all the novels of Fielding and Smollett (both in the beautifully produced Nonesuch Press editions), the Brontës, about half the Waverley novels, much of Thackeray, Stevenson and Conrad, and two or three novels by Meredith, whose style, however, I found heavy going. Among the poets I liked best Shelley and Swinburne; Shelley, because he seemed to confirm on a hugely reassuring scale what I felt to be the absolute importance of poetry—I still think Shelley's "Hymn to Intellectual Beauty" one of the greatest poems ever written—and Swinburne because of the power of his verbal orchestration. By way of an antidote I read Pope with equal avidity.

Wherever I happened to be, when not reading, musical sounds of a more direct sort occupied much of my time. From about the age of twelve, when I abandoned the piano as my first choice of instrument in favour of the violin, it was my ambition to earn my living as a musician, preferably as a composer able to pour out ordered enchantment like Haydn! A broadcast of his "Military" Symphony, heard as I lay on the hearthrug of family friends with the courtesy titles of "uncle" and "aunt" at their home in Courthill, Bearsden, made me shiver physically with inexplicable pleasure. Although I did attempt to follow my ambition to become a composer, I soon realised that words rather than notes were what came more naturally to my pen. Nevertheless, for a long time after that discovery I wanted at the least to be a professional violinist.

My first teacher, Elsie Maclaurin, was a distant descendant of Colin Maclaurin, the great mathematician of Edinburgh's eighteenth-century Enlightenment. An etching of the famous man hung on the wall of her music room in her top-storey flat at 34 Glasgow Street, Hillhead. The similarity of their features, especially the nose, though separated by two hundred years, was uncanny. Apart from my regular lessons, Elsie Maclaurin organised quartet parties and other gatherings, and great was the civilising pleasure these happy informal evenings gave me. She headed a kind of unobtrusive Bloomsbury group in Scotland, her friends including Mackintosh's abandoned first love, Jessie Keppie, and the fey-looking Jessie M. King, whose drawings I detested, though they are now back in fashion.

In due course Elsie Maclaurin decided that I was in need of more advanced teaching, so passed me over to Camillo Ritter, an immigrant Austrian from Graz. Though latterly something of a recluse, he had studied with Joachim and Sevčik, and as a youth had played the Brahms Violin Concerto in the presence of the master himself. Ritter had been the first teacher of the world-famous Glasgow-born viola-player, William Primrose. Though a strict upholder of technical classicism in violin-playing, spiritually Ritter was steeped in the late German Romanticism of his boyhood; with this he powerfully affected me. Slight, untidily white-haired and with a strong jaw that thrust out a further inch at the merest suspicion that a technical difficulty might be thought insuperable, most of his fellow musicians in Glasgow thought him an eccentric failure. Unlike many of them, he refused to play in cafes or tearooms to augment his income. He had certainly failed to amass for himself a fortune, like his many-secretaried cousin, Robert Stoltz, the composer (with Benatzky) of part of that last late example of the Viennese operetta tradition, *The White Horse Inn*.

Meanwhile, down in my basement study overlooking the back garden, when I should have been concentrating on my homework in the "cold" subjects, I was spending two or three hours a day practising the violin, and devoting a further more public hour to piano practice in our first floor drawing-room. Tutors were therefore engaged by my father and briefed to restore me to the paths of academic righteousness.

The first was Wilhelmina Baikie, a well-scrubbed self-satisfied lady smelling perpetually of carbolic, the daughter of a lay preacher who earned his living as a door-to-door traveller selling women's underwear. Her line of attack was incessantly to remind me that while the joys of music were transient and had constantly to be repeated, the joys of worshipping the God of the Plymouth Brethren provided a continuous source of uninterrupted refreshment. She made no progress with me.

Too great a fondness for refreshment distilled from a different spirit was the undoing of her successor, William Nicol, a mysteriously self-supporting sharp-featured pedagogue. For the best part of two years he managed to hoodwink my father over the state of his sobriety by arranging with the cook that he would enter and leave the house through the back door. Drowsy with whisky, he would commend me to the virtues of style, illustrating his conviction with passages from the works of C. E. Montague and Lafcadio Hearn, until he snoozed off, his head sinking gently to the table, leaving me free to pursue robuster authors. As ill luck would have it, one evening, when his face was noticeably redder than usual and his sleep rather deeper, my father came downstairs to inquire about my progress. Poor Nicol made his final exit through the front door, propelled by my father's anger, the backlash of which rebounded on me. In pointed words it was once again made plain to me that the arts could not provide anyone with a reliable livelihood. If, however, against all advice I persisted in neglecting serious study to pursue a musical career, he would continue to maintain me for a limited period, though only against his better judgement. Music, he insisted, was "fine as a hobby", but had nothing to do with the serious business of living, for which I must now prepare myself.

CHAPTER 2

THE SENSING OF A POET

I was, as I have said, a late developer. Puberty did not take full possession of my body until I had passed my fourteenth birthday. Glasgow had nourished my visual senses during boyhood. It was a seaside paradise that awakened my awareness of poetry's power to fix the moment of intensity and articulate the lyric cry.

Throughout the twenties the pattern of our holidays had been July in the heady-scented Highlands and August by the salt-smelling open Ayrshire sea. One spring morning my father announced a change of plan. This year we were going to "The Coast". He and my mother disappeared for a day and came back with the news that they had rented a house for both the holiday months, at Innellan, on the Clyde.

In those days, two months in another place almost amounted to a mini-removal. The advance preparations were thorough. Repeated furtive last-minute checking to make sure that tickets, passport and foreign currency had not been forgotten has become almost a phobia with me in later life. I sometimes wonder if my anxiety to be sure that nothing essential for a journey has been left behind had its origins in the ritualistic preparations gone through annually before the Lindsay family left Athole Gardens for the Broomielaw to board the splendid and venerable Macbrayne paddle-steamer *Columba* for the three-hour sail "doon the watter" to Innellan. Bed linen had to be transported, as well as suitable clothing for all possible variants of Clyde Coast weather.

We usually set out on the first day of July, mother, father, nurse, cook, four children, dog, cat and goldfish. The packing was done systematically during the last days of June. I do not

think I ever slept much on the night before the day of our departure. It began early. We got up at five in the morning and had
breakfast half an hour later. For some reason, that breakfast
always had a special quality of its own. Its ingredients were those
of many a breakfast eaten before and since—porridge, bread and
butter and a boiled egg—but I can still remember the extra flavour
those comestibles seemed to acquire on that particular morning.

After breakfast, we children were expected to keep out of the
way of our elders, for a horse-drawn lorry arrived outside the
house at five o'clock to cart the luggage down to the quay. I was
given the job of guarding the cat while the saratoga trunks were
being grunted and manoeuvred round the bends of the staircase.
The cat, a venerable beast who lived to be eighteen and would
then be about twelve, had the idea that if he managed to escape
while the front door stood open to let the carters move freely in
and out, he would not have to undergo his annual holiday ordeal
of transportation by basket; hence the need for one of the family
to stand guard. At last the luggage had rumbled away, the cat had
been safely basketed, and it was time to prepare ourselves for the
arrival of the taxi.

The new sun shone out from a clean sky this July morning,
glistening the roof-tops of the tenements, and lighting up even
the drabbest side-streets with the promise of a fair day. The
Columba lay on the south side of the river, her two red funnels
topped with black setting off nobly her huge, gilded paddle-
boxes. The moment you climbed up her gangway, your nostrils
were assailed by a peculiar aroma that was all her own: a mixture
of hot engine oil, good galley cooking and well-scrubbed clean-
liness, to which, down the river, the scudding tang of the salt
spray was presently added. But at that time, analysis did not
matter. The smell itself was entrancing.

We were to establish ourselves in the cabin, or "saloon", as it
was grandly called. The saloon consisted of a number of seated
bays lined with dark red-velvet plush, and richly draped with
similar hangings. It gave the impression of well-established
opulence and time-saturated sea-going. All went well at first. I
carried the cat's basket down the companionway, and the cat
remained obligingly silent. But at the entrance to the saloon, a
liveried steward looked at me and my burden with an unmistakable air of hostility.

"What's in that basket?" he demanded.

"Provisions", I answered, with a happier promptitude than I have displayed on many a more important occasion since. He grunted and let us past. We chose an empty bay, and comfortably dispersed our bits and pieces.

Those final moments of waiting seemed the most interminable of all. Above our heads, busy feet tapped out urgent irregular walking patterns on the deck. In the dark orange glow of the engine-room, the great gleaming monsters hissed and sizzled quietly to themselves, as if anticipating the moment when the flicker of a dial and the loosening of a lever would send them plunging backwards and forwards in all their pride of power.

Seven o'clock! Five minutes past! And then the mishanter occurred. A long, thin stream of clear liquid suddenly raced down the floor. Its place of origin was unmistakably the basket at my feet. The steward was instantly at my side.

"Your provisions seem to be leaking, sir", he observed acidly, (that "sir" to one of my tender years an additional humiliation). "You'd better take them on deck."

I was delighted. I certainly had no desire to spend the voyage in the feminine confines of the cabin. Now, someone would *have* to stay on deck to see that the cat was not shipped prematurely ashore.

Up there, too, things were happening. The captain, an impressive and recognisably Highland figure even beneath the disguising weight of his gold braid, was pacing his bridge, which straddled the ship from one paddle-box to the other between the two funnels. (It has always seemed strange to me that until about 1920, it apparently never occurred to the designers of paddle-steamers that the funnel was a fairly major obstacle in the way of the helmsman's vision.) The captain took one last look at his watch, then pulled the clanging brass levers at his side. The paddles began to thresh the water, nosing the ship's bow out towards the centre of the river. With a couple of dirty splashes, the ropes were tossed into the water, to be retrieved fussily by puffing steam capstans at bow and stern. Then the long, lean hull, shuddering a little at first, slid slowly forward.

We steamed past close miles of shipyard, resounding with the racket of the riveters putting together the rusty hulks of the ships that would sail tomorrow's seas; past docks full of towering ocean-going liners and queer-looking tramp ships with foreign characters scrawled across their sterns; past grumphed-up old dredgers, squatting in the middle of the river digging away the mud that forever strives to slip back into its ancient bed; past the chain-drawn car ferries of Renfrew and Erskine; past Bowling, with its pencil monument to Henry Bell; past Greenock and Gourock, and across the broadening Firth to Dunoon and Innellan, names that were to sound music to my senses.

Tucked beneath the Cowal hills and facing across the estuary towards Largs and the seaward arms of the Firth, Innellan was in those days a paradise of childhood. Corraith, the house my parents rented, had been built as a holiday home in the 1870s by a Glasgow tea-merchant, James Pringle. It stood behind a long strip of flower-lined lawn. Looked at from within through ornamental gates, the front garden appeared to reach to the sea, the road between forming a kind of ha-ha, except when traffic passed. Pleasure-steamers crossed and re-crossed the tracery of that gate many times an hour. Creeping along the opposite coast, the Irish packets kept their more distant morning and evening passages. Every now and then, especially at week-ends, liners from Canada and America glided majestically in and out again, to set down and pick up passengers at Greenock's Tail of the Bank. Always, less exalted craft fussed about their smaller occasions. There was scarcely a moment of the day or night when the waters of the Firth were not animated by the movement of some vessel.

The garden was fringed by two herbaceous plots reaching from both sides of the house to the gate. Summer was an untidy riot of colour and scent, a tumbling profusion of roses, tiger-lilies, hydrangeas, phlox, carnations and catmint. Monkey-puzzles and palms stuntedly asserted themselves in the salty but relatively frost-free air. Up the hilly, terraced back garden an overgrown path led through a rusty unused gate to the hill road, on which stood the U.F. church and, a little to the east, the parish church, one of whose incumbents had been the blind Victorian preacher George Matheson, author of the limpingly sentimental but once popular hymn "O love that will not let me go". That high back road ran along the rearward slope of the entire village, gradually narrowing westwards in to a hilly track that led to the grass-covered ruins of an earlier Gaelic clachan.

Like most of the Clyde coast resorts Innellan had developed from a Gaelic-speaking hamlet into a holiday extension of Glasgow when the merchant princes of the nineteenth century took advantage of the coming of steamboat travel to build themselves summer villas in an ornate profusion of borrowed styles. In the face of this determined urban onslaught, the ancient Gaelic culture retreated northwards over those Cowal hills that had once seemed a frontier between Highlands and Lowlands. In the thirties, a few families still owned seaside homes built by their prosperous ancestors. Most of the houses were already in the hands of people supplementing their income in retirement by "letting" to Glasgow families. The villas were well cared for, the row of village shops by the pierhead always freshly-painted and apparently prosperous.

Here, I dreamed on the shore by the side of the burn that fell dankly and steeply from the Cowal hills. Here, I secreted myself whenever possible in a scented corner of the long garden to devour the lastest Faber volume of poems by Auden or MacNeice. Here, I scribbled pages of imitative verses, destroying them in dissatisfaction almost as soon as they were written.

The summer I was sixteen the daughter of an American friend of my father came to visit us. She would then have been, I suppose, about eighteen or nineteen. Though always sweet and courteous, she moved through a strangely distant world of self-possession which the turmoil of my adolescence prevented me from comprehending, let alone entering. The force of her sexuality, particularly the proud assertion of her breasts moulded by her wet bathing-costume as we emerged from swimming together in the chilling waters of the Clyde, for many weeks personalised my dreams, quickened the ardour of my rhyming and left me troubled by longings and desires I lacked the technique to express in words. Thus for me the link between sexuality and creativity was forged; the whetstone on which so much imagery is subconsciously sharpened.

Several of the early pieces in my *Collected Poems* derive directly from these Innellan days, though much more got itself stored away in my subconscious. Indeed, throughout my life the Innellan experience has frequently come to my aid, presenting me with images called forth by some sight or situation with an apparent parallel. So strong was my affection for this place that round it I wove what almost amounted to a personal mythology:

> A wet-nosed morning snuffles around the door,
> fawning upon me not to go away;
> and I, as if I'd never gone before,
> feel half impelled to stay

as I intercept the sun's awakening scrawl
on the village doused beneath a browsing hill;
and I hear the stretch of the waves as they yawn and sprawl,
smiling their aimless fill.

The morning milk-cart jolts its jangling load,
dripping a spitter of stars beside shut gates,
its bored horse pawing sparks from the metalled road
as he trots, and stops and waits.

The red-cheeked postman's out on his cycled rounds,
ferrying news from beyond, through bordered flowers
and, rising from roadside verges, the echoing sounds
of yesterday's sunny hours.

Don't go, the familiar signals whisper, tempt me;
forget what's to do and succumb to the sense of Now,
where time's unhurried turning breathes Forever,
only the heart knows how.

Half of me feels these blood-heard urges are right;
that I'll miss one trailing wheel of a Cowal sun,
burning its layer of coloured change by to-night,
when the news and the milk are done.

Then I think of the way of the world, the buying and selling
that knits it together; how everything's shaped by the mind,
whose insistent inner voice keeps silently calling:
you daren't get left behind.

The fluttering thump of the fussing paddle-steamer
slows as it sizzles and sidles into the pier.
Hurry, the gangway clatters: *for schemer or dreamer*
there's no such place as Here.

There was a poetic link, too, in the connection with Orkney
which I formed at about this time. My school chum, Granville
Ramage, a classical scholar who later became a diplomat, had his
home in Orkney, his father being parish minister on the island of
Stronsay. During the later summer of the thirties, I spent the
month of July with the Ramages in Orkney and Granville spent
August with the Lindsays at Innellan. I felt strongly drawn to the
long clear summer light that lies across the Orkney Islands.

At that time it was an elderly English poet who stirred us both
most deeply. We had fallen under the spell of A. E. Housman.
This late-Victorian master of musical melancholy, who had
published *A Shropshire Lad* in 1896 and *Last Poems* in 1926,
suddenly broke what many took to be a final silence in the

summer of 1936 with *More Poems*. I can recall to this day the excitement with which we tore off Blackwell of Oxford's wrappers from our posted copies, and how eagerly we devoured the contents!

The island of Stronsay was then still a thriving herring port, out of which sailed a sizeable fleet of steam drifters during the summer season. One night we wangled ourselves a trip to the fishing grounds aboard an ancient steam drifter, the *Christmas Morn*. The sail far into the North Sea, on a night near enough the back of mid-summer for darkness to be little more than a few hours of smudged charcoal against a smoulder of deep gold, ended in what seemed to us simply a stretch of edgeless sea, but to the fishermen meant the presence of a possible catch. Distant on the horizon were the faint little silhouettes of other drifters, rolling, no doubt, on the unbroken swell as gently as the *Christmas Morn*. Slowly the nets were tumbled out behind us; then we settled down patiently to wait. Crouched uncomfortably in the wheelhouse we dozed uneasily, the phosphorescent sea glinting around us and softly slapping the vessel's hull.

Suddenly it was uncramping morning, a cold breeze rising, machinery revolving, orders shouting. As the nets were hauled back over the stern the sea gasped out its silver harvest, the herring slithering and twitching over the rim of the hold, or flapping about on the deck, speckled now and then with a crimson splash where the toy-shark teeth of a dog-fish had sunk in and severed. Dog-fish that tangled the net, or lay thumping the deck, were flung unceremoniously back into the sea, their heads first being knocked against the gunnels. On the way home, the smell of oil from the engines and the gritty smoke from the funnel mingled with the aroma of freshly frying herring, a hungry breakfast with a singular edge of appetite.

Years later I went out again, this time from Fraserburgh, aboard a more modern motor drifter, but the thrill of that boyhood trip could not be recaptured. With me on the second occasion was George Alden, the staff photographer of the *Scottish Field* with whom I did a good deal of illustrated journalism during the fifties. George was a fine photographer but a bad sailor. He suffered greatly on the fishing-boat. Next morning, as we walked away up from the harbour after disembarking, George suddenly grabbed my arm and hurried me round a corner. "What's up?" I asked in some alarm, thinking we were about to be attacked.

"There was a bloody great shed with a lifeboat in it back there," said he, "and I thought that if you caught sight of it, you'd suggest to the Editor we go out on that next!"

As it happened, our next and most luxurious trip was aboard the flagship of the Commissioners of the Northern Lights, the *Hesperus*. She was then commanded by the brother of the skipper of the Clyde turbine steamer *King George V*, which for many years did the daily summer excursion run from Gourock to Inveraray. We sailed out from Oban aboard the *Hesperus*, and I landed calmly on Skerryvore. But, rolling and pitching off Dubh Hiortach, the change of keepers had to be accomplished by a cat's-cradle swinging perilously along its cables above the reaching waves. Much to my disappointment I was not allowed to try the contraption. When I protested, I was told bluntly that if they actually managed to set me down on the rock safely, I might very well find myself stuck there for three months until the ship called again.

From one of the lighthouses on our itinerary we picked up a young keeper for whom the loneliness of the life had proved too much. He came aboard with a huge Newfoundland dog. Man and dog sat together on the deck, he staring out over the expanse of empty water as if expecting distance to divide into revelation.

On one of the Orkney holidays, we spent some time on Shapinsay. Granville's aunt was married to Captain Bill Dennison, who operated the regular service between Shapinsay and Kirkwall with an ancient wooden-hulled steamship, the *Iona*. One of his sons, Billy, was about our age, and had a yacht. Once or twice that summer we swooped about the headlands and inlets on her, her white sail teased erect into a life of its own by the sunny breeze. But not often; for even in summer, what most frequently blows over Orkney is a grey, flattening wind. Orkney's charm is not to be found in its climate, but in the vigour of its Nordic traditions and legends that still slant perceptibly across the lives of those who dwell there.

George Mackay Brown's poems and stories have nowadays made the "speak" of Orkney familiar to all who read English. In the thirties, the Orkneys had produced Edwin Muir, whose subtle but sometimes over-bookish poetry drew little enough from his native islands, and the picaresquely-gifted Eric Linklater, whose early novel *White Man's Saga* reflected the custom, once common in many peasant communities, of ensuring a prospective bride's fertility before marriage. It was his next novel, *Poet's Pub*, that convulsed us with innocent merriment in days when the expectations of novel-readers ran rather less to salacity than they do now.

In 1936 a great pageant was held in Kirkwall to celebrate the coming of the Norsemen to Orkney. Eric Linklater, attired in a dark bardic cloak, boomed the narration most impressively. Open air pageants in northern climes nearly always end in coldness and wetness for participants and spectators alike. Whatever the weather, mishaps easily occur. In Kirkwall, on the day I was there, a horse ran away with a Norse chieftain of bygone days, bringing him an ignoble cropper into the limping present. At least it was a reminder of how dangerous, brutal and brief life must have been during Orkney's Nordic heyday, a conclusion reinforced for me by my reading of the *Orkneyinga Saga*, where someone begat someone, who begot someone else, who then either burned somebody else's wife and family alive in their home, or was himself cleft by an unhygienic axe in battle. The English version of the book circulating at that time was by Dr. A. B. Taylor, known to Granville's parents, and who, at the end of the pageant, briefly introduced us to a cold Linklater, bardic robe clutched closely about him as he hurried off to his changing room.

It was on one such Orkney holiday that an incident of a different kind occurred. In these days the yellow-funnelled steamers of the North of Scotland Steam Packet Company sailed from Leith, stopped over at Aberdeen for a few hours, then steamed across the wide estuary of the Moray Firth to brave the Pentland Firth *en route* for Kirkwall. There are, I suppose, certain occasions in every man's life he never forgets; the first kiss with a sexually available woman; the startling bitterness of the first sip of beer; the choking unexpectedness of the first draw of a cigarette.

On this particular northward trip, Granville and I had made a bet as to whether he could eat a larger number of meals of sausage and egg than I could consume dishes of bacon and egg during the voyage from Leith to Kirkwall. The outcome of the contest escapes my memory, but not the consequences of buying my first packet of "Craven A" cigarettes and determinedly smoking them.

We were aboard the S.S. *St Rognvald*, a doughty old tub that took North Sea buffetings in her stride, if at times a trifle unsteadily. In those days passengers were not packaged in airless layers of saloon, as they are now. A sail on a coastal steamer meant easy access to open decks and the salty spray-laden winds that swept them. It also meant a thin partition between the cheapest passenger accommodation and the holds where the cattle travelled. As the *St Rognvald* crossed the bar of Aberdeen harbour and pointed her bow due north, I lit my first cigarette; then my second; and my third. Towards evening the Scottish mainland fell away from us, and the sea grew rougher and rougher until, as we reached the Pentland Firth, the ship was heeling and pitching like a fairground roller-coaster. It was then the practice of mariners negotiating that treacherous interwining of two seas at a certain state of tide and current suddenly to swing the ship to port, so that she changed course dramatically, at an angle of forty-five degrees. When this manoeuvre occurred I was on my sixth or seventh cigarette. A few moments later the ship suddenly heeled round back on her original course, carried this time by the current-twisted force of the sea. From the hold beneath a strangely nauseating smell was filtering up to the deck. With the yawing motions of the ship the smell suddenly thickened inescapably. It attached itself to the nostrils, clung to one's clothes, and finally fastened itself on to the taste of the cigarette. I suddenly felt very ill and made for the nearest rail.

The smell, a sailor later explained from the practised centre of his thick-black pipe fumes, was that of cattle being seasick. I was never able to light up another cigarette, though for many a pleasant year I succumbed to the delights of pipe and cigar until the predatory greed of successive Chancellors of the Exchequer convinced me I was wasting both my money and my health.

Holidays apart, my leisure moments were comparatively few and far between. I was practising the violin for many hours a day wherever I went, my ambition still being to follow the career of a musician.

My father had always hoped that I would get myself to Oxford. When it became obvious that I was not cut out to be an academic, he still hoped that I might take the recently established degree of Bachelor of Music at Glasgow University. But that was not to be either. Roydon Richards' truthful reply to the Scottish Education Department's examiners in due course confirmed the deserved result of a Leaving Certificate minus the mathematical ingredient then essential to enter a university. In the autumn of 1936 I was therefore enrolled as a student at the Scottish National Academy of Music, now the Royal Scottish Academy of Music and Drama. Its towering, authoritative, untidy-looking but charismatic Northumbrian Principal was W. Gillies Whittaker, a minor composer but a leading authority on Bach's Cantatas.

Immediately a difficulty arose. It was common knowledge in musical circles that, however excellent the institution in other ways, it did not at that time possess a violin teacher remotely as able as Camillo Ritter. A compromise was eventually reached whereby I continued to study the violin with Camillo Ritter, but attended the Academy for lessons in piano and theoretical subjects, also taking part in the Academy's communal music-making.

In those days the Scottish National Academy of Music aspired to much lower attainment than the highly professional standards achieved by the restructured Royal Scottish Academy of Music that succeeded it. Very few of my fellow students had the drive or talent to become practical professional musicians, most of them intending simply to teach music in schools. One violinist, Peter Alexander, was the acknowledged front man among those thought more or less to be in the solo class. Indeed, he later became the leader of the violas in a major British orchestra.

From the autumn of 1936 until the end of 1938 I spent an average of six hours a day practising the violin. My only exercise in musical creativity, if such it could be called, was to prove to myself, and to my teacher, Percy Gordon, then music critic of the *Glasgow Herald*, that as a composer I had nothing remotely original to say.

Apart from the satisfaction of getting to grips with the violinist-composers who wrote first and foremost for their own instru-ment—to this day I retain a profound respect for the studies and concertos of Rode and Kreutzer, and a positive affection for the music of Spohr and Viotti, happily now more frequently heard in the concert hall and on records—music, whether participated in or just listened to, was constantly yielding up fresh imaginative riches, and in such profusion that my feet were scarcely ever, metaphorically speaking, on the day-to-day ground. I had no time for anybody, or anything else, and must have appeared an insufferable prig to those not suffering from a similar delicious madness. It was a madness that encompassed experiences as

diverse as Tallis's forty-part Motet "Spem in Alium", Bach's B
Minor Mass, the elegancies of the Symphonies and Sinfonias
Concertanti of J. C. Bach (which Whittaker was especially fond of
conducting), an unending supply of diverse miracles by Mozart,
the ardour of Schumann and the voluptuousness of Wagner.
There was even the jagged excitement of the first two movements
of Walton's First Symphony, performed on their own by the
Scottish Orchestra before the work was completed.

Nevertheless, inescapable day-to-day reality was steadily
eroding the base of my musical ivory tower. During a school
holiday, whilst walking a friend's dog, it and I scrambled up a
disused coal bing. A run of scree loosened and the dog began to
slip down the far side. In an effort to pull him back to safety, I lost
my own footing and took the fall while the dog, recovering its
balance, looked curiously down at me. Soon after, my supposedly sprained wrist started to swell and stiffen under the
strain of a long day's practising. I began to suspect that I was not
going to be able to rely on it to maintain, let alone increase,
bowing expertise. By the end of 1938 I felt that I had no alternative
but to go to my father and admit that this by now confirmed
physical disability—an impounded fracture of the scaefoid
bone—must force me to abandon all ideas of a career as a
violinist. He took my decision in surprisingly good part, though
he could not resist pointing out that by previously ignoring his
advice I had cut myself off from any possibility of falling back on
an academic musical career.

Within weeks, through the good offices of one of his Rotarian
friends, he had found me a position as a managerial trainee with a
firm of colour printers and Christmas card manufacturers.
Hoping against hope, I still kept up my musical studies, although
my father refused to pay for further violin lessons. Camillo Ritter,
however, insisted on continuing to teach me without a fee.

I now joined the grey trek of early morning factory workers
traversing the city by tram or underground in the half-light of
early morning. The eight months I spent in the factory at
Hillington taught me sympathy for those whose tasks are
boringly routine.

Being a managerial trainee turned out to mean running er-
rands, doing odd jobs about the factory—including guillotining
paper on an ancient machine without a safety-guard, which trade
unionists refused to operate—and generally, in accordance with

traditional Union practice, being shown the tricks of the trade at about a tenth of the pace necessary to master them.

During Spring and Summer the office filled up with paintings and drawings of all sorts submitted by commercial artists for possible use in the following year's output of calendars and Christmas cards. Usually, these were accompanied by a similar postal stream of rhyming greetings. In that ominous early summer of 1939, however, the poetasters' inspiration must have dried up, for the supply was insufficient. "Any fool could write these things", said I to the more jovial of the two elderly brothers who ran the place. "Well, one fool can just go and have a try", he snapped back. I was shut up in a small office with pencil, paper and the feeling of having been sent to stand disgraced in the schoolroom corner. Within an hour I presented my boss with some fifty or sixty rhymes as variedly corny as any of those submitted by the regular freelances. "But these are good," he protested: "very good indeed," marking his satisfaction by giving me a miniscule pay rise and the promise that henceforth the Christmas card side of the business would become my special care, since, clearly, I "showed an aptitude for it".

For some years thereafter I occasionally encountered those frightful rhymes in cards sent me by less discriminating friends. Fortunately, the fashion for sentimental rhymed greetings soon receded before the rise of the trendy jokey card, and the small substance of my glib contribution to the artificial bonhomie of Christmas has in all probability long since been mulched into oblivion.

I was destined never to become a king of the anonymous Christmas trade jingle. The outbreak of war put an end to my putative future as an industrial tycoon as well as to my still lingering desire to devote my life to practical music-making. More than most, perhaps, I had good reason to feel sure that war was coming. Because of his idealistic belief in the League of Nations, my father was unfashionably indignant at Hitler's illegal reoccupation of the Rhineland territories, and from then on a voluble opponent of appeasement who repeatedly rehearsed his public unease on his family.

A few weeks after enrolling as a music student, I fell seriously in love for the first time. I brought to this experience the same intensity of commitment I had previously given only to music and poetry. I encountered her at a students' party. She had lost a round of some guessing game, and her forfeit was to be "crucified" and kissed by all the men. I refused to take part in this indignity, and thus accidentally attracted her attention. She was a pianist, a little older than me. For a while she responded to my impractical ardour, and the mad, sweet illness overwhelmed us both, though the conventions of the times kept our lovemaking within bounds less likely to be observed today. The nettle danger of the Czechoslovakian débâcle—that autumn I joined a newly-formed Territorial battalion of my father's old regiment, The Cameronians, and after being six months in the ranks was duly commissioned in it—and an obvious absence of any apparent direction to my future career, made her think again. She began to recover from love-sickness, catching for a time an even less promising dose of illusion by falling in love with a Catholic priest. Then one day she announced that she now found watching an operation on a sheep's stomach every bit as enjoyable as listening to a piano concerto by Mozart. I did not believe her, but felt grateful for her understanding in thus softening the severing blow. She had chosen to marry a vet, a decision that turned out happily for her.

Poems are rarely simply direct autobiographical reportage, but my ensuing period of heart-ache was eventually sublimated into "London, 1940", which stands at the beginning of my *Collected Poems* and accurately reflects that long ago me.

> Helplessly the wavering searchlights probe
>   where stuttering bombers fly:
> each thud and flash their faceless pilots lob,
>   anonymous numbers die,
> shaking a length of protest from the ground:
>   ack-ack guns chatter,
> More distant heavies boom, and make resound
>   the emptiness they batter.
>
> Watching these beams meet in the cloudy blue
>   of this unsummered night's
> bewildered terror, foolishly, it's you
>   who lingers in my sights,
> eyes wide upon *Les Sylphides*. I remember
>   you sitting at my side
> through the uneasiness of that September
>   when thought of peace died,
> the sway of whiteness as the music dreamed
>   what only music knows;

joy, more intense since it already seemed
   lost in our long-agos:
applause; the broken spell; cheer upon cheer
   for delicate civilisation,
as if the audience sensed that they'd been near
   some final consummation:
the heavy curtain tumbling from the ceiling;
   the glow of the house lights;
lifting a fur around your shoulders, feeling
   love must set all to rights:
helping you rise; the popping-back of your seat;
   a statue's marble stare;
your clinging little shudder as we met
   a coldly threatening air;
the newsboy hoarsely calling—*Hitler speaks;*
   the separating fear
of distance, blanched like powder on your cheeks
   at the mere thought of war . . .

Now it has happened. Searchlights take the sky,
and naked in another's arms you lie.

This intense love affair annoyed my father, and brought about
another of those confrontations which soured our pre-war
relationship. On the night of the coronation of King George the
Sixth and Queen Elizabeth, my girl and I joined the crowd in the
Queens Park to watch a display of fireworks. When we had
separated on her doorstep, I made the disturbing discovery that I
had missed both the last bus and the last tramcar from the South
Side to the West End, no later service having been laid on for the
occasion. There was therefore nothing for it but a walk home
through the centre of the city, a distance of six or seven miles. As I
let myself in with my latch key at half past two in the morning, my
father appeared from his study quivering with suppressed rage.

"Where have you been?" he demanded. I explained what had
happened. He accused me of lying and suggested that I had really
been "in bed" with my girl. (How I wished I had!) I, too, lost my
temper, and a violent shouting match ensued, rousing my gentle
mother, who, greatly distressed, appeared on the scene in her
dressing gown. As in the case of the incident with the housemaid, his lack of trust and the related overt dislike of acknow-
ledging the realities of sex were the impressions that remained. I
resolved to examine my own reactions and speedily dismantle
any traces of this Paulian heritage I might find in myself.

There are those today who worry themselves to distraction

about the possibility of nuclear war. But war, especially the nuclear variety (which, once unleashed, would probably destroy all human life anyway) has for the first time become hopelessly unprofitable. Dangerous as the decades of the late twentieth century undoubtedly are, they do not carry the burden of inevitable disaster that weighed down the thirties.

No doubt it is difficult for those who were not then out of childhood to understand the desperate game of make-believe we played with ourselves. Neville Chamberlain's "peace in our time" speech was merely the public reflection of our deepest private wishes. From the successful accomplishment of Hitler's march into the Rhineland to his rape of Czechoslovakia, the certainty that a militantly re-arming Germany was bent on conquest by war was plain enough for all to see. We chose, quite deliberately, not to see. It is easy enough to explain through hindsight our wilful blindness. Those who were middle-aged at the beginning of Auden's "low, dishonest decade" had scarcely had time to get over the numbing losses of the First World War. Those of us who were newly adolescent felt the sweets of youth threatened with meaningless blighting. Watching the self-deception of our elders and betters, we turned to the pressing urgencies of the flesh, pretending not to hear the promptings of our consciences. We knew in our hearts that we were living on time borrowed from reality.

In the warm and brilliant summer of 1939 it was especially difficult to believe that the scent of the old-fashioned roses in the garden, the soft peach-down on the arms of the girls with whom we played idle tennis or gently dallied, and the cheerful phut-phut-phut-phut of the busy paddle-steamers fussing over the glinting, sunny Clyde, was but a surface cover over the menacing march of distant soldiers bearing death and destruction on a scale we could not visualise but found it impossible not to fear. Yet so it was. Soon, reality demanded repayment.

More than a single summer's pride vanished with the Fall of 1939. It was a different peace-time world, and a much changed Innellan, that eventually I came back to in 1946; a faded, discarded film-set paradise entered relentlessly upon decline.

Since 1946, most of the Victorian villas have been divided into flats. The once-quiet roadway at the foot of the long garden of *Corraith*, now itself an hotel annexe, has been widened to carry traffic for an oil-rig construction yard at the mouth of the Ardyne.

That yard, an environmentally destructive project welcomed by short-sighted politicians for the sake of one or two transient orders and a little brief employment, has despoiled forever, the beautiful approaches to the Kyles of Bute. For all his technological skill, man cannot emulate to order the patterns carved by the retreating Ice Age!

Other estuarial environmental blightings have included the construction of an economically unnecessary, though no doubt politically expedient, ore terminal on the Hunterston peninsula and—worst of all—the building of an electricity power station at Inverkip, its chimney thickly prodding the sky above the ridge of the Renfrewshire hills; a station, given a mere modicum of co-ordinated planning foresight, that could properly have been sited westwards near the bleak Dundonald coastline, where its bulky shape might even have proved a visual asset.

It is no longer possible to look over the Clyde from the garden of *Corraith* and see the ceaseless motion of ships of every shape and size criss-cross its waters. The Irish boats and the great Atlantic passenger liners have alike long since disappeared, victims of the development of air travel. The fleet of almost forty Clyde steamers—turbines and paddlers named after characters in the Waverley novels, planets and Scottish duchesses—has given place to practical but ugly-looking short-link car ferries. But on the eve of the Second World War, the loveliness of the Firth of Clyde still seemed secure.

On an ominously close late-August afternoon in 1939, the last year of my youth, I had enjoyed a swim and was drying myself in a deck chair in the garden when I was roused by the shrilling of the telephone. It summoned me, as a Territorial officer, four days before hostilities actually commenced, to the long-expected misadventure of war. I crossed the estuary on the paddle-steamer *Duchess of Fife* and travelled to Glasgow in a darkened train from which the carriage light-bulbs had been hurriedly unscrewed.

CHAPTER 3

TENDING THE DOGS OF WAR

After it was all over, drinking Eric Linklater's champagne in the company of Neil Gunn and James Bridie at 11 o'clock in the morning—"the only civilised time to drink champagne", our host resonated from beneath his shell-scarred dome—in Edinburgh's Caledonian Hotel, I was foolish enough to bewail the lost war years that deprived me of the experience of being freely young. "Don't be ridiculous," Linklater barked; "You've had plenty of experience, even if not of the kind you might have chosen. To a poet, of all people, no experience should be unimportant."

He was, of course, right. Temperamentally, I could never have been anything other than a bad soldier. I hated the whole business but, like most people, was kept going by the thought of what might very well happen, not to a hypothetically raped grandmother but to me, were the Nazis to win.

My early war months were spent with the 9th Cameronians at Hawick. The heavy weekend drinking habits of the soldiers from Glasgow sometimes upset Border susceptibilities. Soon after our arrival I had to act as "prisoner's friend" in the local court on behalf of one of my soldiers. At the end of an injudicious Saturday-night celebration he had painted bright red the testicles of the life-size horse that formed part of Hawick's famous statue of the Flodden standard-bearer, an adornment not appreciated by the locals. After hearing my plea for leniency, the bench delivered a lecture equating Glasgow hooliganism with the brutality of the Nazis, and implying that by defending this man I was as guilty as he was.

The troops were billeted in old woollen mills, one at least so ramshackle that it was possible to see those beneath through gaps between the floor-boards. The fire-risk was horrifying. Smoking was forbidden, though doubtless indulged in. Fortunately, no one ever set the place alight.

The Officers' Mess was in the Crown Hotel. During the winter of 1939/40, the so-called "phoney" war period, Sir Harry Lauder—whom I had first seen with Doan on the Glasgow stage and, years later, sat next to on a bus near his Dunoon home—paid a visit to Hawick to entertain the troops. Memories of the 1914 war in which his own son, a captain in the Argyll and Sutherland Highlanders, had been killed—some say, shot by his own men—proved too much for the old man, and he followed his first song with lengthy and lugubrious reminiscing. The troops, much more ready to be amused by hanging out "the washing on the Siegfried line", rolling out the barrel, or roaring "Run, rabbit, run", had no interest in the dated stage-Scotchery of Lauder's humour, and resented the sentimental patronage of his patter. Through the polite applause led by the officers, the sound of booing was unmistakable.

Afterwards, in the mess, Sir Harry revived, sinking what seemed to me an astonishing quantity of whisky, my share of the cost of which startled my second lieutenant's mess bill at the end of the month. Lauder was aware that something had gone wrong with his show, though he was not sure what. After supper he began reminiscing again, couthily boring; a pathetic old man who had somehow outlived his success. It was a success that had brought laughter to many, though there are still some who think he made his fortune by caricaturing his own countrymen.

A few months after this encounter with a ghost from Scotland's past, the battalion was rushed down to the Essex coast. There was no more talk of running rabbits, or hanging out the washing on the Siegfried Line. The smell of defeat was suddenly in the air. The sight of exhausted soldiers evacuated from the Dunkirk beaches, dropping asleep wherever they landed, seemed to make a victorious German invasion a matter of weeks away. None of us talked about the immediate future, though I fancy most of my companions were as thickly dulled in private despair as I was. Then over the radio came the mannered resonance of Churchill's voice, rallying us out of our anxieties with the fierce alchemy of a kind of rude poetry:

We shall fight in France, we shall fight on the seas and oceans, we shall fight with growing confidence and growing strength in the air, we shall defend our island, whatever the cost may be, we shall fight them on the beaches, we shall fight them on the landing grounds, we shall fight in the fields and in the streets, we shall fight in the hills; we shall never surrender.

Nowadays, youthful critics who did not hear the defiant growl of Churchill's words in the dreadful context of their occasion, are apt to sneer at his "outmoded Augustan rhetoric". Those of us who heard the phrases roll out, newly turned, felt our ebbed courage stir again and a faint hope arise.

There were to be other blacker moments in the weeks and months that followed; in particular, the experience of helplessly looking skywards from an Essex marsh beneath a gathering drone as wave after wave of German bombers flew heavy with death for London; and the hot September night of Operation Sealion, when the platoon I commanded scanned the misty early-morning sea with one fully operative bren gun, a box or two of ammunition and a few dozen explosive beer-bottles known as "Molotov Cocktails" to meet an anticipated fully-armed assault force that, fortunately, never left the coastal waters of France.

As things turned out, my wartime role was not destined to be that of a combatant soldier. My gammy wrist, first injured in the incident of the dog, suffered a second, military accident. Jumping in full fighting gear from the top of a broad wall during a battle-training course, I misjudged the distance, struck the wall with my shins and crashed down on the other side, landing on my damaged limb. As a result of the further injury thus sustained, I was in due course medically down-graded.

Although at first I felt mildly ashamed that I had been found physically wanting, I cannot pretend that I regretted my relegation. Had I continued as a fighting soldier, I fancied that I should probably have been killed in my first engagement. I worried dreadfully over the possibility that my natural ineptitude in the practicalities of military business might be responsible for the death of some of those I was leading. A relatively secure privilege not of my own seeking had thus unexpectedly been conferred upon me, and I was duly grateful.

I then spent several bored and aimless months engaged in various administrative jobs that were nobody else's duty. I was always a handy "body" who could be despatched without being much missed on courses regarded by the adjutant as a waste of time. One of those excursions into irrelevancy took me to Perth, where I spent three days having explained to me the mysteries of the working of the Army Pay Corps. I called at the home of the bed-ridden poet William Soutar, with whom I had corresponded briefly. His father explained that I had come at a bad moment because the doctor was with him. In any case, his son was now too ill to see "new people". I was not to find myself in Perth again until after the war, by which time Soutar had been dead three years.

In spite of bouts of deep depression induced by the feeling that the war would never end, my Cameronian days were not without their lighter side. There were those who, coming from a different background to my own, seemed "characters". Most of the regular army officers I encountered at the beginning of the war were cast in the peace-time colonial polo-playing mould. Some were difficult to live with, none more so than Captain Jim MacLeod, a man who knew no fear and was the most accomplished beer-drinker I have ever met. Years of beer-drinking had taken their toll on his bladder. When he went to bed he lined up on the floor within handy reach ten cocoa tins numbered consecutively with red paint, each of which he filled during the night in strict rotation. He suddenly disappeared from the battalion after he had tossed a grenade into the vulgarly ornate fireplace of a Victorian mansion in which we were billeted, "just to find out what would happen."

There was the suave Welsh officer whose sexual appetites were so urgent that he rarely considered the risks involved in gratifying them. One of his conquests was the glamorous but bored wife of a merchant seaman who, in an impulsive moment, had married "beneath her station". Her husband, perhaps aware of her too-ready availability during his frequent absences, saw to it that neighbourly vigilance made it imprudent for lovers to approach her through the front door. Our Welsh brother therefore arranged to climb by ladder direct to her bedroom under cover of darkness. His escapades were joked about in the mess, and were obviously much less discreet than he supposed.

One Sunday morning, while the Adjutant was away on leave and I was temporarily filling his place, there was, in the language of the stage direction, a "commotion heard without". A moment later the door was thrown open and a huge ugly man stood in the frame, swayingly taking his bearings; a kind of human King Kong whose head seemed almost to touch the upper lintel.

"Good morning," I said politely. "What can I do for you?"

"I'm goen to bleeding well break your neck," he answered. "My wife. I know all about it."

I assured him I hadn't actually the pleasure of knowing his wife, a choice of words in the circumstances perhaps a little unfortunate.

"Pleasure!" he roared. "You must be the only bloody Jock round here who hasn't had the fuckin' pleasure. Your neck's as good as any other."

Naturally, this was not a view I shared. Retreating before his simian advance, I kept talking reassuringly in an attempt to distract his attention until I could ring the bell at the far side of the desk and summon help from the Orderly Room. He was over-powered and duly ejected, protesting that he would have the law on me. In spite of his threats neither I, nor the regiment at large, was cited in his divorce, an honour that eventually fell to a local coal merchant.

The story of my alarm greatly amused the Commanding Officer, Lieutenant-Colonel H. H. Story. He was a strange character, the possessor of the Military Cross and enough literary talent to enable him to write a readable volume in the history of The Cameronians. He also had musical pretensions. At that time I carried a violin around with me. As mess evenings wore on, Harry Story would order me to produce my violin. We would then embark on a series of salon pieces. Since the repertoire was limited and not one that benefited from too much repetition, this quickly had the effect of clearing the mess. After an hour or so Story would summon the yawning mess waiter and order three drinks; one for himself, one for me and one for the piano, which he administered by opening the lid of the battered old upright and anointing the strings, a procedure that did nothing to improve its tone. Nevertheless, I became quite fond of Story and when he suggested that I might write a march for the pipe band of the battalion I named it after him. It was published in the regimental magazine and played on ceremonial occasions while he remained in command.

Although I was never a very practical soldier, I got on well with all the Commanding Officers with whom I served. During another period of temporary adjutancy, this time under Lieu-tenant-Colonel H. D. K. Money, D. S. O. (who later commanded a Brigade at Arnhem) I had to introduce a new padre to the C.O.

This padre, like many ministers of religion, was a naïve character, and unfortunately looked so. As he stepped through the door, peppery old Money raked him up and down with a searching glance, then snorted: "I want you to understand two things, Padre. I've no time for sparrowfart; and I can't stand fellows who fart and fly forward." The padre blenched and said: "Quite sir," Though the sentiments might have been expressed with greater literary subtlety, the idea behind them was fundamentally sound.

Money's hobby was bird-watching. On one occasion he "suggested" that I might accompany him on an early morning expedition. Lying at first light on my stomach in a drizzling East Anglian marsh convinced me that bird-watching was an over-rated pastime.

Another Commanding Officer turned out to be something of a fitness fanatic, and one day ordered that the entire battalion would undertake a seventeen-mile cross-country run. For those unaccustomed to covering long distances on foot seventeen miles is a considerable walk, let alone run. There were to be no exceptions, however, except on medical grounds, and no officers were to be excused.

So off we set. After the initial lung-bursting agony, I settled into a bearable trot. Unfortunately, most people adopted a much faster trot, and I was constantly being regaled by the wisecracks of those overtaking me. It takes a long time for a complete battalion to pass one in such circumstances, but eventually all eight hundred or so did. I would then have been quite alone over the final three or four miles had not a Scots terrier, thinking me in pursuit of some doggy interest, decided to accompany me. He was still trotting hopefully beside me as I staggered past the finishing line—a distinguished last, creating a new slow record— when he abandoned me as suddenly as he had joined me.

In 1943 I finally left the battalion to become a trainee Staff Officer at the Headquarters of 15th Scottish Division, then located near the village of Diss, on the landward boundary between Suffolk and Norfolk. My mentor was a civilised and affable tobacco executive, Alick Money-Coutts. He had been a senior executive with the Glasgow firm of Stephen Mitchell, whose "Prize Crop" cigarettes were popular in the thirties.

Others on the staff were much less affable. One day, on a divisional exercise, I came upon a crashed Signals truck. Its driver appeared to have been badly injured. As I was about to organise help, the Divisional Signals Commander, Colonel Victor Warren, arrived on the scene. He berated me roundly for halting the convoy and holding up the exercise merely because of an injured driver. "You are training for war," he roared, "not playing games."

Some weeks later, strolling across the estate grounds after dark to dine in the Officers' Mess, I encountered a bedraggled figure in mess dress covered from head to foot in slimy mud. Victor Warren had been ambushed by four masked men and thrown into a stagnant lily-pond. His assailants were never traced. This time I was threatened with nameless disciplinary terrors if I dared as much as breathe a word of the fact that I had thus encountered him. Content to observe that not only poets can administer poetic justice, I held my peace. Warren survived the war to become one of Glasgow's many less distinguished lord provosts.

On my arrival at Divisional headquarters, I was billeted in Eye, a village just across the Suffolk border. Mrs Swanky, my land-lady, a member of some obscure religious sect, would not allow men wearing army boots to cross her threshold. My batman and I therefore had to take off our footwear as soon as we entered the front door. I was never entirely clear about the theological significance of this manoeuvre. Another of her conditions was that the front door must be locked by ten p.m. Personal keys were not issued. One celebratory night I arrived outside the front door at five minutes to midnight. No amount of knocking or bell-ringing produced any response. Scouting about at the back of the house I found a ladder. I brought it round to the main street, laid it against my first-storey bedroom window and began shakily to ascend.

"What exactly are you doing?" a voice inquired when I was half way up.

"Going to bed," I said, nearly falling off when I saw that I was answering a policeman.

"I think you had better come down and explain why you aren't using the inside stairs."

The ensuing denouncement involved Mrs Swanky, the police-man and a passing Afghan hound, who casually nosed the good lady's behind just when she was reaching the peroration of her denunciation of the British Army, young men in general, me in particular, and the unsatisfactory nature of the protection afforded by the local constabulary to householders who felt themselves threatened by godlessness. Her sudden angry shriek gave the policeman the opportunity discreetly to withdraw, the dog to disappear, and me to scuttle up to my bedroom for what was destined to be my last night under the Swanky roof. Next day I moved into army quarters at Diss.

From Diss, I organised a weekend Recorded Music Club. Its purpose was to give gramophone concerts of serious music in rotation at each of the three Brigade centres, making use of the library resources of Eastern Command. Reproduction equipment was hired from a local electrical firm. I provided programme notes run off on an army duplicating machine. Unfortunately, the firm supplying the equipment went out of business, so I wrote to the presenter of the B.B.C. Sunday morning radio programme, *Forces Music Magazine*, asking if our Club could either hire equipment from the B.B.C., or buy some that had been discarded. Alec Robertson replied, telling me that the B.B.C. neither hired equipment, nor disposed of it under any circumstances to the public. He seemed greatly interested in the Record Club, however, and announced that he would like to see me.

The outcome of his visit was an invitation to go up to London one weekend and tell the story of the Club in *Forces Music Magazine*. This I did. To my astonishment, a few weeks later I was invited back again, this time as a member of a panel answering listeners' questions. One question ran: "I cannot easily distinguish between the music of Haydn and Mozart. Can the panel assist me?" It was not an easy question to deal with.

In battalion days, to help me keep sane, I had formed an interest in the music of the eighteenth-century cellist-composer Luigi Boccherini. I inflicted my enthusiasm on a brother officer, Bill Legatt Smith, later to become, among other things, Dean of the Faculty of Procurators in Glasgow, a governor of my old school, the Glasgow Academy, and Chairman of the Glasgow School of Art. With the assistance of his wife, Yvonne, who translated the floridly vague French of Boccherini's first biographer, Louis Picquot, Bill and I produced an article about Boccherini for Eric Blom's elegant quarterly *Music and Letters*.

To illustrate for the benefit of my questing radio listener the manner in which individual variants of late-eighteenth century style differed from the common period currency I quoted some music by Boccherini who, though an Italian from Lucca, had spent the greater part of his creative life in Spain and had composed music with a "nationalist" flavour long before the upsurge of the Nationalist musical schools. At that time he was known solely, though widely, for the Minuet from his String Quintet in E, opus 13, No. 5, and for a "composite" cello concerto heavily edited in the nineteenth century by Grützmacher. Boccherini, however, was a distinctive melancholy minor genius, an early romantic in the high noon of classicism, through whose music bands of soldiers march, the skirts of dancers twirl, clacking feet and castanets sound, guitars strum and gently melodious night-scented intrigues unfold for our delight. Cartier, the compiler of a French anthology of 1798, *L'Art du Violon*, opined: "If God wanted to speak to Man through music, He would do so through the works of Haydn; if He wished to listen to music Himself, He would choose Boccherini," while in 1805 the aesthete Chenedollé, in even more flowery terms described the composer's music as being "like a poem, like a dream, like a fragrance". In other words, the hauntingly elusive personal quality of the music is difficult to define.

Whether or not I really answered the listener's question about the stylistic differences between the music of Haydn and Mozart, I most certainly established my enthusiasm for Boccherini, for a few months later I was invited to prepare a feature programme to celebrate the bi-centenary of his birth, and a well-known string quartet was put at my disposal to provide the musical illustrations.

Needless to say, I enjoyed this experience hugely. The recording safely "canned", Alec Robertson took me to dine at his club. There, he introdued me to the Honourable Edward Sackville-West, brother of Harold Nicolson's wife, the poetess Vita. "Eddie", as everyone called him, hid the talents of a perceptive producer behind an effete and rather stagey aristocratic drawl. He had asked Alec to bring me along because he wanted to invite me to prepare a programme on contemporary Scottish poetry.

Once again I thoroughly enjoyed the business of communicating my pleasure to the microphone, already, in my eyes, simply a willing listener, a silently appreciative friend. The reader turned out to be the Scots character-actor John Laurie, and this occasion marked the beginning of a life-long friendship. In the middle of the rehearsal an air-raid warning sounded. We retreated to a tiny airless basement studio, from which the programme was in due course transmitted.

Sackville-West achieved a personal *succès d'estime* with his classical verse play for broadcasting, *The Hero*. Sometime later I happened to be in his company when Alec Robertson remarked that a book of essays was being prepared to celebrate Benjamin Britten's birthday. "I should be *most* embarrassed," drawled Sackville-West, "if anyone ever did that to me." "I shouldn't worry, Eddie," said Alec. "Nobody will."

Thus, entirely by accident, I began broadcasting, an activity I was to practise regularly, and with great enjoyment, for more than forty years.

After the first taste of broadcasting, I put in a further stint with my regiment. The battalion had by now given up its defensive role and moved to Keighley, in Yorkshire, to begin training seriously for the invasion of Europe. It was an event that could not directly concern me, since I was still awaiting a posting to the Junior Staff College at Camberley. My duties were therefore once again frustratingly peripheral. I was billeted in the home of a musically-minded industrialist, and found myself singing bass in a characteristically sonorous, if rough-edged, North Country performance of Handel's "Messiah".

Because of my injured wrist, my practical interest had shifted by this time from music to poetry. In the prevailing wartime climate of English-dominated Britishness, it irked me that much of the fine Scottish poetry produced in the twenties and thirties had attracted little attention in England; and the same was true of good new work then being written. Especially unworthy of such neglect, it seemed to me, were the breathtaking early lyrics of "Hugh MacDiarmid" (C. M. Grieve), whose work had recently temporarily ousted that of A. E. Housman from my affections.

During one of my time-wasting training courses, I met in London the editor of the then influential magazine *Poetry London*, a lavish publication modelled on the pre-war literary periodical *Poetry Chicago*. *Poetry London*'s typography was clean and imaginative, and it had richly-coloured lithograph covers designed by some of the most highly-regarded artists of the day. It was run by a charming Sinhalese, Meary J. Tambimuttu.

At our first meeting "Tambi", as his friends called him, told me of his ambition to inspire similar publications in other countries to proclaim the "new poetry": "an honest poetry about anything and everything, and not afraid of emotion."

"Why not *Poetry Scotland*?", I suggested.

Encouraged by Tambi's immediate enthusiasm and with the backing of the resources and ambitions of the young Glasgow publisher and printer, William Maclellan, the first number of *Poetry Scotland* appeared in the autumn of 1943, from premises appropriately located in Glasgow's Hope Street.

Maclellan had a genuine feeling for Scottish literature, and behind him a family printing business that appeared to be held securely together by his mother and brother. Unfortunately, Maclellan's pale blue eyes and disarmingly mild smile, in these days set off by a lemon-coloured waistcoat, were not topped by much of a business head. He suffered from a convenient vagueness where the current state of accepted manuscripts was concerned. Yet I entered enthusiastically into many of his projects, and worked closely with him for about three years. By then, the chorus of complaints from dissatisfied authors had become too loud to be ignored or parried. The parting of our ways came over a projected anthology, *Poets On Poets*, for which T. S. Eliot agreed to write on Byron, MacDiarmid on Burns, Sydney Goodsir Smith on Gavin Douglas, Edwin Muir on Henryson and Douglas Young on Hogg. A few of the typescripts were delivered, but never heard of again.

Maclellan's brother moved to Canada, and, later, his mother died. Eventually, the business went bankrupt. Maclellan made some sort of a come-back, but in 1978 was the subject of exposure over some characteristically unexplained publishing delays on Esther Rantzen's B.B.C. television consumer-interest programme, *That's Life*.

In his muddled way Maclellan achieved a great deal, helping many young writers to establish themselves. His enthusiasm was boundless and infectious, and although perhaps he never quite came to terms with the maxim that an idea is only as good as its execution, his contribution to the Scottish Renaissance movements was a considerable one. As Sydney Goodsir Smith, who quarrelled furiously with him, later put it: "Maclellan, for all his faults, has at least produced a creditable amount of stuff of permanent value, and now that my personal rancour has subsided I feel that we should be grateful to him."

To attract as wide as possible a circulation, and counter any possible charge of chauvinism, *Poetry Scotland One* contained sections devoted to work by English, Welsh and Irish poets as well as the main Scottish section. For this precautionary internationalism I was roundly taken to task by Sir Compton Mackenzie, who provided a welcoming though by no means uncritical Introduction. Mackenzie declared it to be "no use writing Scottish poetry unless the poet writing today sustains his imagination with his own willingness to sacrifice himself to and if necessary for Scotland, that Scotland may be recreated. If the country cannot produce vivifying, fertilising poets, the country will die."

That issue of *Poetry Scotland* included the first publication of MacDiarmid's "Two Memories" and "A Glass of Pure Water", Sydney Goodsir Smith's "Largo", George Bruce's "Inheritance" and Edwin Muir's "A Birthday", all poems that have since become well-known through inclusion in later anthologies.

It was my original intention that *Poetry Scotland* should appear annually. Maclellan, however, was never able to adhere to his promised production schedules. *Poetry Scotland Two* did not appear until 1945. It carried a Foreword by Neil Gunn. At about this time he attacked me for being too deeply involved with the militant MacDiarmid camp. I got a ticking off (quite properly) for calling those who despised literature "yahoos," an offence I had committed in an article published in an English magazine. Wrote Neil to me: "I had recently read my old friend Hugh MacDiarmid's autobiography, wherein all Scots are yahoos (occasionally reduced to a mere 95%). Fine, for him. Then someone asked me to read something . . . and it opened at a page where you called 'em yahoos also. Not so fine for you! The simple point being that if I were to look down my nose and call a fellow a yahoo he would thereupon be shamed into being one. If he had any spirit in him, he would be more likely to land me one . . .

"Having read your poetry, I had got the notion that you considered the love principle as *the* creative one. I don't know myself of any more powerful. I felt somehow that you were talking out of character . . . Of course the vast bulk don't care for literature. Not, anyway, as you would like them to care. Same when it comes to getting fishermen in their own interests to form a Cooperative or Union. Always the struggle to provide light. Wearisome pretty often. But the fishermen do know how to fish."

Neil Gunn was certainly very good for me.

Like *Poetry Scotland Three*, which came out about a year later with a Preface by Eric Linklater, the second issue was devoted

entirely to Scottish verse. Between the three of them apart from
the poems already mentioned, they also introduced to the public
George Bruce's "Kinnaird Head", Adam Drinan's "Three
Measures", William Jeffrey's "Native Element", Sydney Goodsir
Smith's "Loch Leven" and MacDiarmid's "Talking with Five
Thousand People in Edinburgh". ("You've got a nought too
many", quipped the poet's friend, the composer Francis George
Scott, when I presented him with a copy of the anthology: "Chris
never talked to that number of people at once in his life
anywhere.")

In due course, the long-awaited vacancy at the Staff College
materialised. The only notable incident during my four months'
stay at Camberley occurred during an instructional debate.
The motion was: "That regimental tradition is a vital part
of British Army morale." I was detailed off to oppose it.
Regimental tradition was a subject upon which I held no views
of any kind. I had, of course, some experience as a debater
during schooldays and later, in swaying army opinion when
acting as Defending Officer at Courts Martial. Everything said
at a Court Martial had to be taken down in writing. Witnesses
and Defending Officers were therefore forced to speak at a
writing pace. I soon discovered that the trick of putting across
a convincing defence was to arrive with a typed speech already
duplicated for distribution to each member of the Court.
Its members then had no reasonable grounds for hobbling one's
eloquence. My most surprising success with this technique was
my defence of a walnut-faced Glasgow toughie who was
the possessor of a passable tenor voice and frequently sang
Scots songs at battalion concerts. "If you get that fellow off,"
warned my Commanding Officer, "I'll . . . I'll . . ." "He sings
like an angel," said I. The man got off. As we left the court room,
two police officers from Glasgow loomed out of the waiting
shadows to arrest the newly-acquitted angel on a charge of triple
bigamy. The C.O.'s comments in the Mess that night were unrepeatable.

In the Camberley debate I therefore found no great difficulty in
presenting a convincing, though impersonal, case for the aboli-
tion of those outward symbols of regimental tradition, by some
held dear. Before the seconder of the motion could rise to his feet,
the Commandant of the College, craggy Major-General Douglas
Wimberley, a former commander of the 51st Highland Division,

bounded from the back of the hall, where, unnoticed by me, he had been listening.

"I'll answer that man", he roared, and thereupon set about a passionate defence of the value of regimental tradition, with particular reference to its Scottish significance. Needless to say, my side lost the debate. Indeed, I was somewhat surprised eventually to discover that I had even passed the course!

Years later, when Douglas Wimberley was President of *An Comunn Gaidhealach* and I was about to film a television interview with him, I reminded him of the incident. "You made me mad at the time", he laughed. "Some of those fellows might actually have believed you!"

While on leave in Glasgow, just before going to the Staff College, I paid my first call on C. M. Grieve, better known, and hereafter referred to by me, as the poet "Hugh MacDiarmid". He was then engaged on war work—heavy engineering, to which, somewhat surprisingly, he had been directed—and was living in lodgings in Havelock Street, Partick, not far from Athole Gardens. He received me with a curious, almost exaggerated courtesy that contrasted strongly with the public image created by his vituperative prose articles and verbal duels in correspondence columns of newspapers. He was dressed in a pair of shabby grey-flannel trousers and an old kilt jacket. He puffed continuously at a pipeful of "thick black" that frequently went out and had constantly to be relit. I came to associate him with the pungent scent of this tobacco to such a degree that for years a whiff of it experienced on the top of a bus or tram instantly conjured up the image of his stocky, assertive frame.

Being "received" by MacDiarmid seemed at that time rather like presenting oneself at some sort of Court in exile. He spoke of Scotland as if its liberated reawakening was politically imminent, the prelude to a splendid new democratic dawn. Forty years on, when practical experience has shown that for Scotland, there is only likely to be a continuation of weakening self-identity and increasing English absorption, it is perhaps difficult to convey the quality of intensely optimistic nationalist enthusiasm inspired by MacDiarmid's sing-song Border voice, or the finality implied by its regularly flattened cadences.

Round him he had gathered a group of young writers romantically dedicated to the restitution of the Scots language through poetry. William Soutar had been MacDiarmid's only significant

follower during the thirties. Now, there was tall, bearded
Douglas Young, whose considerable intellect fizzed and bubbled
infectiously over whatever happened to engage it, but who
mildly enjoyed mischief-making and did not much like to be
disagreed with; New Zealand born Sydney Goodsir Smith, the
kindliest, most talented rakehelly poet I ever did meet; the Gaelic
poet George Campbell Hay; droll and witty Robert Garioch and
fringe characters like Maurice Blytheman (who called himself
"Thurso Berwick") and John Kincaid, both more notable for their
expression of left-wing beliefs than for their poetic abilities. To
this motley group, led by MacDiarmid, I gave my temporary
allegiance, though never quite my full conviction. The security
provided by group membership can be helpful to a young writer
finding his feet. The difficulty arises when, having found them,
he sets off to walk his own way hoping to leave the company
unscathed!

Although I did not then know it, by 1943 MacDiarmid's
greatest poetry had long since been written. It was still virtually
unread, even in Scotland, although in England T. S. Eliot knew of
Sangschaw and *Pennywheep*, and spoke of their author as his
equal. During another home leave I went into the once-elegant
Lyons' store—it stood on the corner of Sauchiehall Street and
Elmbank Street, until a runaway lorry crashed down the opposite
hill, virtually demolishing it—where Valda, the poet's wife, was
then working in the book department. For two shillings and
sixpence (twelve and a half pence) I bought copies of the first
editions of *Sangschaw*, *Pennywheep* and *A Drunk Man Looks at the
Thistle*. A mere five hundred copies of these, his three finest
books, had been published a quarter of a century before, but so
poor were the sales that they were still available. Such copies now
would easily fetch a sum running into three figures.

On leaving the Staff College I was appointed to the operations
room of that section of the War Office which dealt with the Far
East, thus becoming, in Douglas Young's words, "a temporary
bureaucrat of the Britannic Mars."

CHAPTER 4

A TEMPORARY BUREAUCRAT OF THE BRITANNIC MARS

My first London digs were in number eleven Ebury Street. The boy Mozart had moved from Frith Street, Soho, to one hundred and eighty-two Ebury Street in 1766, when it was part of the fresh-air village of Chelsea and his father was convalescing from an illness. My room was in the letting house of Miss Bamborough, a vague but kindly spinster who lived in the basement with her short-legged, over-fed terrier, Rover. During bombing attacks the lodgers congregated in the kitchen, more for the comfort of companionship than greater physical safety. At the first sound of gunfire Rover staggered to his feet and made for the gas oven, the door of which Miss Bamborough opened for him. He sat inside it quite calmly until the "all clear" sounded, often an hour or two later, when at once he emerged.

After a few months I moved to Hamilton Terrace, Maida Vale, the home of John and Christine Wills, where I stayed for two years. John Wills was senior accompanist with the B.B.C. A fine musician and a gentle little man, he had married as his second wife a seaside landlady who exhibited most of the music hall characteristics traditionally attributed to her kind. Her groundless jealousies and outbursts of temper must have caused the gentle John as much pain as it brought embarrassment to their lodgers.

It was very much an establishment for musicians. The Scottish soprano Noel Eadie, then nearing the end of her active career, lived in the house with her invalid husband. The cellist John Swan and his young wife also had a room there, he destined to become the leader of the cellos in Sir Thomas Beecham's last orchestra, the Royal Philharmonic.

The most important fellow-guest, as far as I was concerned,

was Alec Robertson, in whose top flat suite I had a room looking out over the leafy gardens behind Hamilton Terrace. From him I learned the craft of broadcasting, and, more importantly, a fuller apprehension of music's significance in relation to the other arts and to the changing nature of the society which it reflects. Alec had a large collection of books about music and an extensive collection of scores. These he was always willing to let me borrow. Under his guidance I did more broadcasting. In his company I met many of the leading musicians and critics of the day. Some of these pleasant acquaintanceships, like those with Clifford Curzon and his wife, the American-born harpsichordist Lucille Wallace, Delius's amanuensis Eric Fenby and the composer Edmund Rubbra (whose music I still much enjoy) inevitably did not survive my London sojourn. Others matured into lasting friendship; short-lived, unfortunately, in the case of the First War Georgian poet Robert Nicols, an oddly over-introspective man whose sensitive account of Delius at Grez-sur-Loing was, however, the most magically evocative piece of broadcasting I had then heard, its word-texture positively Delian; lifelong with Anna and Julian Herbage, who took over the running of *Music Magazine*, the successor to *Forces Music Magazine*, after the war, and to whose programme I contributed for many a year. There was, too, Scott Goddard, the fastidious and elegant critic of the *News Chronicle*, who was later greatly to enjoy his visits to festive Edinburgh, when my wife and I showed him round many of the capital's attractions.

When I arrived at Hamilton Terrace Alec Robertson had begun work on his study of Dvorak for Dent's Master Musicians series. It was to become the first systematic biographical and critical work on his study of Dvořák for Dent's Master Musicians series. It was to become the first systematic biographical and critical work on Dvořák written originally in English. The series was advice on the techniques and responsibilities of music criticism was of great value to me. He laid emphasis on the importance of the integrity of a defenceless dead composer's indications and intentions, a principle to which I have held firm throughout my own career, and which accounts for the intensity of my dislike for that late twentieth-century phenomenon, the tasteless opera producer who takes a self-indulged visual ego-trip at the expense of the composer.

Alec Robertson was a complex character. He hated his late

father, an industrialist of Scottish descent, and never forgave his mother for deifying the memory of his elder brother, killed in the 1914 war. The first time I stayed at his beautiful home, Apsley Cottage, near Pulborough—the elderly Belloc was then still his next door neighbour a field or two away—I met the old lady, and had to be surreptitiously shown the brother's room, "frozen" for more than a quarter of a century, down to the stub of a forgotten shaving stick casually dropped on the washstand before its user set out for France. Although Alec had been brought up an Anglican, he had become a Catholic convert, attending the Scots College in Rome. His story to me was that the religious demands of unaesthetic priestly isolation had proved too much for him. He therefore sought, and received from the Pope, dispensation to return to his career as a musician. Once, when he came upon me in mildly amorous dalliance with a sloe-eyed Welsh piano student who was staying in the house at the time and for whom I nourished a passing fancy, I was astonished at the petulance and irrelevance of his anger, and at the protraction of his sulkiness over several days. When I became engaged to the girl I later married, I brought her along to meet him. While he received her with the utmost courtesy, he thereafter steadily withdrew his friendship from me. For whatever reason, he burned inwardly. In spite of his outward sense of fun he was clearly a deeply unhappy man.

Long before a younger generation decided that Mahler's *angst* expressed its own feelings of worldly unease, Alec Robertson had convinced me that Mahler was a very great composer indeed, with an enduring message for our times, a view then regarded in British musical circles as absurd. Nor was Alec afraid to stand up for his own musical convictions. As is now, of course, well known, Wagner's music was officially banned from the air by the B.B.C. in 1939, Hitler having misappropriated it to support his racial ideology. Because Richard Strauss (whose daughter-in-law was of Jewish extraction) lived throughout most of the war in Germany, and was alleged by some to have Nazi sympathies—an untruth shamefully exploited, years later, in a vulgar and dishonest film by Ken Russell—Strauss's music was also effectively banned. I happened to be contributing to the edition of *Music Magazine* nearest Strauss's eightieth birthday when Alec Robertson improvised a birthday greeting to "a great composer who has given so many people much pleasure". A furious row followed, and Alec had to endure abusive letters and phone calls from people who insisted he had insulted the memory of their dead sons.

In later years I saw Alec occasionally, usually in a London BBC studio, or over an hotel breakfast on one of his brief visits north to lecture to Scottish music clubs. While I could easily enough accept his enlightened and sincere Catholicism, he found it more difficult to tolerate my settled agnosticism, and we ceased to meet, although we exchanged cards at Christmas almost to the end of his life.

He died in his eighties, during his years of retirement once again dressing in the habit of a priest, reconciled, apparently to his mother church. Through his broadcasts he opened up the gates to the world of music for many who might otherwise have remained ignorant of its wonderful existence, and so gave more than most to his fellow men.

What worried my parents about my wartime friendship with Alec Robertson was not that he was an unmarried ex-priest, but that very possibly he might convert me to Roman Catholicism. A curious verbal intolerance of Catholics lingered in the middle classes of Scotland during the thirties, even among people of no obvious religious conviction. With it went dislike and distrust of the Jews, although I always assumed this simply to be national-istic jealousy, so many Glasgow Jews being conspicuously successful in business. My mother was aware that in my final year at school I had had one or two furtive exploratory sessions with a Jesuit at St Aloysius in Glasgow, before my final disen-gagement with Christianity. One day she warned me that if ever I became a Catholic she would cut me out of her will. With youthfully unctuous smugness I replied that if I became a Catholic, it would be with my Maker's will rather than my mother's that I would be concerned. Now, I assured her that although I craved for the comfort of certainties as much as the next fellow, man-made fairy tales, religious or secular, could not provide it, quoting at her Meredith's:

> "Oh what a dusty answer gets the soul
> When hot for certainties in this our life!"

One thing, however, I did become certain about at this time; the enduring value of the best of the songs of the Scottish composer Francis George Scott. By chance, I found on a shop counter two of the five volumes of his *Scottish Lyrics*, all but one published by the Glasgow firm of Bayley and Fergusson at Scott's own expense. I was at once struck by the harmonic adventurousness of some of the settings of poems by MacDiarmid, and in his setting of lyrics by Burns and others the recreation of a kind of folk idiom that gave the impression of emerging out of a secure tradition. Scotland, of course, has had no such continuing tradition, the flow of her art and music having been forced underground, and subsequently dissipated and dispersed, as a result of the Reformation, which allowed music no serious place in the grim Presbyterian bare-board system of worship devised by Knox and further "refined" by Melville. What Scott had therefore apparently done was to "invent" a continuity that did not, in fact, exist, basing it on his extensive understanding of the fertile Scottish literary tradition. One of the dangers which obviously he had not wholly managed to avoid was that of lapsing, now and then, into over-simplified banality. That he achieved as much as he did remains, in the circumstances, matter enough for wonder.

I bought the other volumes of *Scottish Lyrics*, read them through and showed them to Alec Robertson, who reacted positively to my enthusiasm. On Alec's recommendation Eric Blom invited me to write an article with music illustrations for *Music and Letters*. With this in view, and with the eventual intention of promoting a broadcast featuring the songs, I wrote to the composer asking if I might call upon him when next I was in Glasgow. As it turned out he was then depressed, suffering acutely from a feeling of neglect. My approach, as a representative of the younger generation, greatly cheered him. His reply turned out to be a long autobiographical letter, which features extensively in my biographical and critical study *Francis George Scott and the Scottish Renaissance* (1980)

Scott had been an English teacher at Langholm Academy, in the Borders, when the poet MacDiarmid, then the twelve-year-old C. M. Grieve, had been one of his pupils. From the correspondence between them extending over many years, it is clear that Scott's encouragement was of the greatest value to the young MacDiarmid, although the poet's increasing capitulation to Communism and to political versifying resulted in the erection, first, of an intellectual, and eventually of a personal barrier between them in later years.

From a letter written by Scott to me in 1946, and now in the

National Library of Scotland, it is quite clear that Scott not only suggested to MacDiarmid the idea of *A Drunk Man Looks at the Thistle* in the first place, but played a considerable part in its construction. Scott recalled:

"I outlined the plan and supplied the title of the poem during a rainy hike on a night in Glen Clovis Hotel. Christopher usually wrote his poetry in snatches: he never had any sense of form and after some months of scribbling on the back of envelopes and odd bits of paper, he sent to Glasgow an urgent call for me to come for a weekend and see the litter (and mess!) he'd been making of my bright idea, as Blackwood's were asking for the MS and there *was* no MS. It was late at night when I reached Montrose and after his wife and youngsters went off to bed, we sat down to a table, a great heap of scribbled bits of paper and a bottle of whisky. I can still see Christopher's face when I was indicating the shape the poem, or for that matter a musical composition, ought to take— he was literally flabbergasted either by the extent of my know-ledge or by the whisky—it's anybody's guess! We spent until day-break sorting out the items worth keeping, Christopher arranging them on the table like a pack of cards in the order that I indicated as likely to give the best sequences, climaxes, etc. My plans necessitated a pianissimo close, after so much bustle ('The Stars like Thistle's Roses flower') to be followed by ('Yet hae I Silence left, the croon o' a') and I'm pretty certain I supplied the last two lines to bring the thing to some kind of conclusion."

The painter William Johnstone, in his autobiography, *Points in Time* (1980), a friend of both men, confirms the story, though adds some variation. Mrs Scott could not, as Johnstone claimed, have supplied cups of tea throughout the night, since she was in Glasgow, eighty miles away. Johnstone, however, part-writing, part-dictating in extreme old age, cannot be blamed for setting the scene in the wrong town, since unlike Scott, he was not a participant in that momentous literary evening.

Latter-day MacDiarmid hagiographers have questioned Scott's honesty. One wonders why. The genius which lights up the poem is MacDiarmid's alone. To seek to discredit facts about its origin and construction—facts, indeed, so well attested—can neither increase the proportion of the poet's work that is of the highest quality, nor affect his poetic stature.

The *Music and Letters* article duly appeared. Later, the script was accepted by the B.B.C. Before it went on the air, however, I was to have a foretaste of that littleness of spirit which was increasingly to characterise the Scotland to which I had determined I must eventually return. The Director of the newly-formed Scottish Home Service tried to have the programme stopped, on the grounds that it was the sort of material he would in due course want to broadcast from Scotland. He failed.

But that is slightly to anticipate. Two years were to elapse between my initial discovery of Scott's songs and the broadcast.

In the interval, I had found a friend and patron in Robert Herring, a civilised character of Welsh extraction who edited the lively *Life and Letters Today*, a well-produced "little" monthly review that had succeeded Sir John Squire's pre-war *London Mercury*. Its offices were in a handsome triangular-shaped turreted building (recently internally reconstructed within its elegant façade) opposite Charing Cross Station, and it regularly published issues devoted to the literature of individual countries, for which service in the cause of international understanding Herring was believed to receive some sort of official subsidy. I in due course undertook the task of editing a Scottish issue.

Herring published a number of my early poems, and gave me much encouragement and a regular trickle of books to review. He also took me at frequent intervals to lunch at Rule's in Maiden Lane, then a fashionable howff for theatre people. He owned a home near Sheffield, where he was a neighbour of the Sitwells at Rennishaw, and had a beautifully furnished house in Cheyne Row, Chelsea, where I was several times his dinner guest.

It was on one of those evening occasions that a bizarre encounter took place. The Italian campaign was in progress. The Germans had fortified Monte Casino, and were successfully holding up the advance of the liberating Allies. In the end, the Allies subjected the monastery to bombing. Just after this attack I was dining at Cheyne Row. Over coffee, the door of the drawing-room opened and a large depressed-looking baggily-dressed aristocrat shuffled in. "You know Maurice," Herring stated rather than enquired. The newcomer did not, and I was fixed with a vaguely preoccupied stare. Then the drooping fingers of the right hand moved languidly towards me. "Isn't living *hell*, dear boy?" said Sir Osbert Sitwell, leaving me short of an answer and puzzled about what to do with the downturned fingers.

The destruction of this famous monastery along with, as was then wrongly supposed, all its pre-war artistic treasures, distressed him so deeply that he was moved to condemn outright "this dreadful war". I shared his distress, but not the rationale he used to relieve his feelings. For one thing, I did not believe that the bombing of a major religious building would have been sanctioned had it not been operationally essential for the saving of soldiers' lives. In any case I was never able to accept the pacifist beliefs of some of my literary friends, whose personal safety and continuing liberty to hold their views depended entirely upon the success of the actions of those who disagreed with them.

Herring left London soon after the war ended. I never heard of him again. One night, after a Cheyne Row dinner when he had drunk more than usual, he told me that his South African mother had left him "a fortune" on condition he never married. Sometimes I wondered.

Among poets whose work I admired, I particularly enjoyed the company of chain-smoking, heavily bespectacled Ruthven Todd, the diffident, nervously over-charged Edinburgh poet who was working in Zwemmer's Charing Cross Road bookshop when I first met him. His poems in a lopingly rhythmic colloquial manner often contrasted the brittle intensity of human love with the huge impersonality of war's destructiveness, and moved me to emulation. I also enjoyed the East Coast clarity of light and colouring that washed through some of his early poems:

> "My face presents my history, and its sallow skin
> Is parchment for the Edinburgh lawyer's deed:
> To have and hold in trust, as feofee therin
> Until such date as the owner shall have need
> Thereof. My brown eyes are jewels I cannot pawn,
> And my long lip once curled beside an Irish bog,
> My son's whorled ear was once my father's, then mine . . ."

Todd's marriage had recently failed in embarrassing circumstances well-known to the Edinburgh literati. By the time I met him he had developed a duodenal ulcer, because of which he had been removed from his work in Civil Defence. After downing his second double whisky he would explain that although he received a special milk ration, he had no intention of being dictated to by his ulcer, which would just have to learn to "make do" with Scotch. I became very fond of him, finding especially delightful an insouciant gaiety that had nothing to do with material circumstances. I have never encountered it in any other poet, although it was a quality the novelist Neil Gunn also possessed.

Ruthven helped me to free myself from the apocalyptic morass into which I had strayed at the beginning of the war. "Never put down in verse what you don't actually feel or think. You're homesick for Glasgow, you're in love, and it's Christmas next week," he said. "Go and write a poem about all these things." The resulting "Poem at Christmas", to be found now near the beginning of my *Collected Poems,* was the outcome of that counsel. Not surprisingly, it carries Todd overtones, though the voice is, I hope, clearly enough my own.

Neither my physical stamina nor my purse, however, could keep up with his astonishing drinking propensities, so we saw less and less of each other; imperceptibly, in the war-time manner. We continued to correspond for a time even after he settled in America. There, alas! his drinking was, in the end, to blight the extent of his achievement.

Like so many other poets, Todd quarrelled with Maclellan. Writing on 3rd December, 1945, from Tilty Mill House, Great Easton—his Essex home that was all but totally vandalised by two homosexual Scottish painters to whom the generous poet had been unwise enough to lend it—Todd reported:

"For once in my life I am comparatively well off (I spend an occasional fortnight writing hack thrillers under a false name at £200 a piece—I don't treat 'em seriously but they keep me alive) and having just knocked one off to make certain I didn't have a lean Christmas, I have been devoting some time to arranging my affairs. McL [sic] published my poems a year ago and since then I have no word from him about them: he was to give me a nominal advance of £5—at a time when I very much needed money and was collecting all I could raise. I telegraphed McL and received £2 . . . McL's principal trouble seems to be that he is too unbusiness-like. His books are badly distributed and booksellers find difficulty in getting hold of them. So I do not expect much from the sale of the A[creage] of the H[eart], but I would like to have a properly prepared account of the position . . . Yours affectionately"

Almost a year later, on 26th March, 1946, in the last letter I received from him before he left for America, his not unreasonable request still remained unsatisfied:

"I don't seem to hear anything from MacLellan [sic] about the sale of The Acreage of the Heart, but I've rather given up worrying about that as I've got a new book on the way, and have already got about twenty-thirty poems for a book after that . . .

I'm writing the devil of a lot of things at the moment . . . and I'm
gradually managing to get on top of my debts and my depres-
sions. I hope to sell my poems to the U.S. while I'm there."

With the letter he enclosed a delicate elegy for the recently
killed Keith Douglas who, though brought up and educated in
England, was of Scottish extraction, according to what his
mother later told me. I met Douglas once briefly, in Ruthven's
company. So far as I am aware the elegy has never been
published and since it sums up just about all there was to be said
about the deaths of fellow-writers in the war, it seems worth
quoting here:

> "It is a pity that one whose careful words
> Were always so gently and delicately poised,
> Should somehow have turned up the unlucky cards
> And known his end before it was disclosed.
>
> It is a pity—yes, and of so much
> We can say that—it is a pity that he
> Who was just learning what images to catch
> Should so soon have blended with the sulky clay,
>
> And that all his living dreams should be dead,
> So that only his chosen words are left, a city
> Where the sad traveller slowly nods his head
> And murmurs quietly that indeed it is a pity."

Through Ruthven, I met two American poets temporarily serving
in London with the U.S. armed forces; the friendly and amusing
Harry Brown, who was to find fame with his powerful war book,
and the subsequent film of it, *A Walk in the Sun*; and Karl Shapiro,
the realistic up-to-date "feel" of whose poetry—far ahead of
Brown's in energy—matched the sophistication of his conversation.

I also got to know Fred Urquhart. In many of his short stories,
and in his early novel *Time Will Knit*, he had developed an urban-
ised version of the Grassic Gibbon tradition, notably enriching
mid-century Scottish fiction. Fred was then acting in a secretarial
capacity to the Duke of Bedford at Woburn, but visiting London
frequently. Together, we edited for Maclellan an anthology of
new short stories, the purpose of which was proclaimed by its
title, *No Scottish Twilight*. Later, I tried to organise a new volume
of Urquhart stories to be published from Hope Street, but that,
too, led to trouble over Maclellan, Urquhart writing on 19th May,
1944: "I don't think he has very much idea of publishing . . . I do

not like the style of Maclellan's books at all. They're attractive enough to look at, but the *type of printing* is really bad. For instance the advertising on the back pages. Such and such a book, price 7/6, post 6d. This business of putting post is so *provincial*, so terribly Scottish."

Another Scottish friendship was with W. S. Graham, whose *The Seven Journeys* (1944) was published in the *Poetry Scotland* series. His style of imagery and sonorous manner of personal delivery were both reminiscent of Dylan Thomas.

Though I never greatly admired so-called "pure" poetry, such as Thomas's and Graham's, the essence of which is the warp and woof of its own vocables, I very much liked the serious-looking Sydney Graham himself. He and I took part together in several war-time poetry readings. At one of these, during a Glasgow leave, a rather boisterous Sydney mingled with the audience and found himself alongside my delightful but now elderly former violin teacher, Elsie Maclaurin. "And what are you doing for the war effort, Mr Graham?" she inquired. "I've just taken the glass roof off St Enoch Station," he replied. "Oh dear!" she said: "I do wish you'd put it back on again. One gets so wet without it." Moving over to my brother, Stanley, he announced: "I'm the poet W. S. Graham. I'm picking violets in Cornwall just now." My startled brother observed amicably: "I don't think we've met before?" "That's all right," Sydney assured him. "I'm talking to anybody tonight."

I invited Sydney to appear with me at a poetry reading in the beautiful London home of the Poetry Society, 33, Portman Square, an institution then presided over by the Chevalier Calloway Kyle, an aged dignitary whose prejudices and mannerisms were of the minor Victorian variety. I arrived in my uniform of a captain in The Cameronians, having no civilian clothes in London that could match such surroundings. A tieless Sydney turned up in stained flannel bags and accompanied by an unannounced girl attired even more loosely. With frigid politeness the Chevalier introduced us to the audience, a collection of upper middle-class ladies in fluttering hats and chintzy summer frocks quite unprepared for the dose of Scottish Renaissance naturalism that engulfed them. I enjoyed that reading. The other two put up quite outstanding performances, Sydney interspersing the sonorously rolling declamation of his poetry with wickedly provocative comment. We retired to applause like the slow breaking of china tea-cups.

There was another memorable poetry reading of the late war years. Edwin Muir, working for the British Council, was running Czech House in Edinburgh. He had given an Apocalyptic collection of mine, *No Crown for Laughter*—put out by the enterprising Fortune Press, which made its money from literary erotica but was not very good at selling much else—a guardedly encouraging radio review, and wrote to ask if I would debate with Sydney Goodsir Smith the viability of Lallans as a language for contemporary poetry. Smith's then much admired early lyrics struck me as being too often rhythmically defective, lacking in visual imagery and often simply banal. The magnificent *Under the Eildon Tree* was, of course, still half a decade away.

The debate at Czech House was lively. Muir was a charming host and a fair chairman. During question time Sir Alexander Gray, a distinguished academic whose main poetic successes were several vivid re-creations in Scots of German and other folk-songs and ballads, challenged Smith, quite justifiably, about the artificiality of his Scots; "a Scots," claimed Sir Alexander, "no one ever spoke." Smith observed that no one ever spoke the kind of English Keats wrote, and proceeded to defend the archaic idea of an unspoken language reserved solely for poetry. "Mr Smith," Sir Alexander roundly declared, "if that is your reasoning, I wouldn't have you in a class of mine for five minutes." "Professor Gray," Sydney replied: "let me assure you that I wouldn't stay in a class of yours for five minutes." It was good-humoured banter but Muir, who appeared to dislike open controversy of any kind, grew decidedly flustered.

Sir Alexander was later to become a much-valued friend to both my wife and myself. My first visit to his home, 8 Abbotsford Park, Edinburgh, was postponed when he found he had to address a gathering of dentists. When I arrived on a re-arranged date, my reception was unconventional and my stay all too brief, since I had a broadcasting deadline to meet. I wrote apologising for my hasty departure. He replied:

"Do not say that the dentists had a greater claim upon me! Indeed, I did not greatly enjoy the dentists. About 300 had been asked and about 500 turned up, so there was rather a squash . . . It was just one of those many things which one does because it is supposed to be part of the job. This perverted, Presbyterian, covenanting Conscience! . . . And also do not say that you ran away in an 'unmannerly fashion': Say rather that I received you in a most reprehensible fashion, lying asleep like a shepherd's dog on the rug before the fire, and no one to call me."

There were several subsequent visits to Abbotsford Park, as well as a succession of witty letters dropping through my letter-box, because I edited for Maclellan a volume of Sir Alexander's *Selected Poems* (1948). A small white-haired ripe nut of a man, merrily large in spirit, who spoke with a pronounced Angus burr, my life was the richer for knowing him.

A poetry reading in Glasgow's Stevenson Hall during a 1944 leave—a photograph of those taking part was published in Kulgin Duval's *Festschrift for Hugh MacDiarmid* (1962)—was notable in that two members of the audience, the sculptor Benno Schotz and the composer Francis George Scott, met each other there for the first time. An eventual outcome was Schotz's two magnificently sculpted heads of Scott. When it came to MacDiarmid's turn to perform he moved to the platform, opened his book, but remained silent. There was an embarrassed ripple among the audience. Douglas Young rose, looked over MacDiarmid's shoulder, removed the book from his hand, turned it the other way round and sat down again. As if nothing odd had happened MacDiarmid then began reading; like a needle being placed on the edge of a 78 r.p.m. gramophone record. For all his praises of "the golden wine of the ghaidhealtachd", MacDiarmid had a poor head for drink. A couple of double whiskies was enough to blur the clarity of his speech. Someone had been detailed to make sure that there was no "strong drink taken" before MacDiarmid's turn to read came, but the poet had given his watchdog the slip.

My closer acquaintance with Tambimuttu also developed about this time. He was always hard up. One day he invited me to lunch at London's Café Royal. Although the cost of war-time meals was held to a legal maximum of five shillings (25 pence), drinks and house charges could add quite a bit to a bill. I felt touched that Tambi should want to entertain me so grandly.

I was the first to arrive at the restaurant. When Tambi turned up, he had with him two floppy-breasted young women. Almost before the first soup was spooned, it became clear that it could not be their literary acumen that had brought them to Tambi's notice. After coffee had been ordered, Tambi politely excused himself "to go to the loo", as he put it. He evaporated like an oriental spirit, leaving me to pay the entire bill and dispose of the two tarts. My jocular excuse for declining their parting offer—that regrettably, I did not possess the equipment for dealing with two women at once—was not well received.

On another occasion Tambi rang me up while I was on duty in the War Office. When was my day off? Would I come with him to Heal's to choose cushions for his new flat? Two afternoons later we were inspecting a range of second-hand cushions in that famous store and "choosing". "Now come to my flat", he insisted, "and see how they go with my things."

We turned off St Martin's Lane, and stopped outside a weary-looking blue-painted wooden door for which he eventually found the key. After fumbling up a sloping dark staircase, he flung open the door of his room. The only furniture was a broken-down settee on which a heap of bedclothes lay crumpled. On the bare floorboards several dozen empty beer-bottles had been ranged in platoons, each with a leader at its head. "Mendelssohn once stayed here", Tambi declared.

Tambi accepted some of my early verses for *Poetry London*. By then, however, he had got caught up in the prolificacy of his own enthusiasms, as well as in changing publishing economics. The war-time mood of hectic endurance and the constant public highlighting of strong emotions had led to an increase in the sales of poetry; an increase that did not survive the return of peace. Tambi's accepted unpublished poets, good, bad and indifferent, had therefore to be lumped together in a final bumper round-up *Poetry London* volume.

The prevailing tone of much British war-time verse had been set by the writers of the New Apocalypse movement. Deriving its artistic credo from James Joyce and Dylan Thomas, it reacted violently against the socially aware verse of the group of the thirties, the so-called Pylonites. The New Apocalypse was led by a Welshman, Henry Treece, later to produce a series of exciting novels based on ancient mythology and pre-history. Treece was a warm-hearted man troubled at that time by eye strain. It was to him that I confided my increasing frustration at the difficulty I experienced in finding time or energy to work out my poetic ideas. "I'm sorry to hear you are so fed up," he wrote: "There'll be years and years for us later, and we may even look back on this time as a necessary factor in our development . . . In the meantime, keep as happy as you can."

A year or so later I edited the Scottish section for the third

Apocalypse anthology put together by the movement's theoretician, Stefan Schimanski, a critic of middle European ancestry who was to be drowned when his transport plane crashed early in the Korean campaign.

The other leading New Apocalyptics were J. F. Hendry, a withdrawn and taciturn Scot with whom I found it difficult to make contact, and Nicholas Moore, the amiable son of the Cambridge philosopher G. E. Moore, whose poetic stripping of his lady, Priscilla, flexed the eyebrows of some readers considerably more than would be the case now. Peripheral to the movement were two other Scots. One of them, G. S. Fraser, whose father had been Town Clerk of Aberdeen, was able to etch with freshness and clarity the "feel" of being a pre-war eighteen-year-old. After the war he appeared largely to have deserted poetry for literary journalism and criticism and latterly an academic career at Leicester University, although his *Collected Poems*, published in 1980, the year after his death, show that he went on cultivating his skill in commemorating through poetry life's lost moments. There was also Norman MacCaig, later a fine poet but at that time sorely muscle-bound from his struggles with metaphysical imagery. As things turned out, the best Second World War poetry came, not from the New Apocalyptics but from the Englishman Sidney Keyes, the Welshman Alun Lewis and the Anglo-Scot, Keith Douglas, none of whom survived the fighting.

What perhaps lent the New Apocalypse its brief relevance was its insistence on the value of the individual against the contrasting impersonalism of the war and of the state. It took its motto from D. H. Lawrence's *Apocalypse*: "The rider on the white horse! Who is he, then? . . . He is the royal me, he is my very self and his horse is the whole Mana of a man. He is my very me, my sacred ego . . . And he rides forth, like the sun, with arrows, to conquest, but not with the sword, for the sword implies judgment, and this is my *dynamic* or potent self."

The rejection of "judgment" meant that no comparative standards could really be applied to Apocalyptic work. According to Fraser, writing in *The White Horseman*, one of the movement's banner-carrying anthologies, the New Apocalypse derived from "surrealism . . . one might even call it a dialectical development of it: the next stage forward", in so far as, Fraser claimed, it was meant to allow that "the intellect and its activity in willed action" was "part of the living completeness of man." But "willed action" without "judgment" produced an excess of confusion, as Robert Conquest later pointed out: "In the 1940s the mistake was made of giving the Id, a sound player in the percussion side under a strict conductor, too much of a say in the doings of the orchestra as a whole. As it turned out, it could only manage the simpler parts of melody and rhythm, and was completely out of its depth with harmony and orchestration."

For a time I threw in my 'prentice lot with the group, and appeared in the second, third and fourth of the Apocalyptic anthologies. Fortified privately by a reading of David Daiches's *The Place of Meaning in Poetry*, I eventually decided that romantic obscurity was not for me.

The hold the movement had for a time on the little magazines was considerable. I submitted some verses over my own name to one such magazine—*Pivot, Hinge, Fulcrum*, or some such title—and had them promptly returned. Two debunking Australian airmen had set down whatever came into their heads and published an obscure paperback collection of verse under the pseudonym "Ern Malley". The supposed virtues of their work, even after the two men had confessed their fraud, were extolled by a celebrated critic of the day as the "subconscious imaginative work-outs of natural poets, in spite of their conscious manipulations". I sat down deliberately to write whatever floated into my mind, chopping the resulting outpouring into lines and numbered sections. I then sent them to the same magazine that had refused my work, this time using a pseudonym. My nonsense was immediately accepted and in due course published.

It now began to seem likely that, barring such ill luck as happening to be in the precise spot where a V1 flying bomb or a V2 rocket landed, I might be lucky enough to survive the war. The urgency of getting into print therefore slackened, and I decided to shift direction. I wanted to try my hand at expressing my Scottishness through Scots (or Lallans, to use Burns's word, fashionably resurrected in the Forties). I was also anxious to bring together and widen the appreciation of the work of those whom Eric Linklater, in his Preface to *Poetry Scotland Three*, had dubbed the "Second Wind" writers of the Scottish Renaissance.

The unreliability of Maclellan's publication dates made it seem unlikely that *Poetry Scotland* by itself would be an adequate vehicle through which to achieve this end. Few copies went on sale south of the Border; yet if the quality of the new Scottish

poetry was to become generally accepted, English acknowledge-
ment would have to be secured. I therefore wrote to T. S. Eliot in
his capacity as a director of Faber and Faber, proposing that I
should edit for his firm a collection to be entitled *Modern Scottish
Poetry: An Anthology of the Scottish Renaissance*. I was invited by
return to call at the firm's office in Russell Square.

He appeared not to have quite outgrown the look of a confiden-
tial bank manager doing his best to be pleasant about refusing an
overdraft; yet his kindness and courtesy were reassuring. We had
China tea and triangular brown bread cucumber sandwiches. I
was delighted at his ready agreement to my proposal, and astonished by his accurate and up-to-date knowledge of Scottish
affairs. He had read, for instance, a recently issued pamphlet in
which the scholar and patriot Douglas Young wittily recounted
the events of his Edinburgh trial. On grounds of conscience
Young had objected to being called up, not for pacifist reasons
but because he maintained that under the Act of Union of 1707 a
London Government had no power to conscript Scots for British
military service. For this legally mistaken stance he was found
guilty and sent to Edinburgh's Saughton jail, an unpleasant
ordeal he could have escaped on the grounds of weak eyesight
merely by submitting to a routine medical examination.

During the course of the preparation of *Modern Scottish Poetry*
there were to be other similar tea parties with Eliot. One was
occasioned by the printers Maclehose of Glasgow, who objected
to propagating the word "schitten" in Douglas Young's Scots
version of a section from Sorley McLean's Gaelic sequence *Dain
Do Eimhir*. Eliot overruled Maclehose, but himself raised objec-
tions at the page-proof stage to a line in a now discarded early
poem of my own about John Knox, in which the Reformer was
said to have "ground grace beneath his staff." Over the now
expected tea and sandwiches I received a precise lecture on the
theological meaning of "grace". As a settled agnostic, I could no
more appreciate the great poet's soft-voiced conversational
theology than in later years I was able to draw comfort from the
mellifluous cadence of one of the last sections of his *Four Quartets*:
in which he reassures us "All shall be well, all manner of things
shall be well."

When *Modern Scottish Poetry: An Anthology of the Scottish
Renaissance (1920–45)* eventually appeared in the summer of 1946,
John Betjeman wrote to say that he had reviewed it "shortly, as I

am bound to do in the *Daily Herald*", but wrote again from his
Wantage home to add: "How grateful I am for your anthology of
Modern Scottish Poetry." Treece enthused from his home at
Barton-on-Humber: "What a lovely book! . . . The whole thing is
splendid—from your careful and illuminating Introduction and
selection—the fine pieces by Young, Hendry, MacCaig, Todd,
never forgetting yourself, and the great idea of printing the
Gaelic of Donald Sinclair together with its translation, right down
to the glossary . . . I am delighted with it and for it, and happy
that you have done it. Thank you for it again and again—a lovely
book means much to us now." The elderly playwright Gordon
Bottomley wrote to say that "it made a splendid acquisition for
Christmas."

It was well received, too, inside Scotland. Almost forty years
later, though under another imprint and twice updated, it
survives in a third edition with the New Apocalypse section
somewhat thinned.

Another session with Eliot related to my enthusiasm for the
work of the Greenock-born poet John Davidson, whom Eliot also
admired. I had proposed that I should edit a collected edition, or
at least a selection of his work, for Faber. Eliot was personally in
favour of the idea, and duly wrote: "I have finally been able to
discuss the Davidson project with my Board. I found, to my
surprise, that Davidson was not unknown to anyone present.
The Board proved more favourable to the suggestion of a volume
of selections than to such a large volume as you say the complete
works would make. It has occurred to us, however, that if the five
verse plays were omitted, the complete poetical works otherwise
might not be too extensive."

Davidson's literary trustee, Grant Richards, thereupon put a
stop to further negotiations on the grounds that in his Will,
Davidson expressly forbade the re-publication of his work other
than in the manner it first appeared. As Mrs Davidson and her
two sons were then still alive, living in America, a selected edition
was out of the question. Later, a Glasgow bookseller, R. J.
Macleod, published a somewhat prettified selection. In 1961,
Hutchinson put out a more representative selection edited by me,
and carrying introductory material by both Eliot and
MacDiarmid. It had always amused me to think that Davidson
managed to influence two such diverse poetic followers! Now, of
course, there is a collected edition of the poems—though still

lacking the verse plays—and a valuable biography. Adversity soured Davidson, and he committed suicide in the erroneous belief that he was suffering from cancer. A poet of his own volition puts himself as well as his wares in the market-place of posterity, and in my view does not really have the right to define posthumous terms of "No Sale".

In spite of the intensity of my pre-occupation with music and literature, most of my time was naturally being spent on my War Office duties. Although I had to work long and concentrated hours, and there were obvious inconveniences, London was an exciting place in which to be living. The engine noise of approaching flying bombs promoted a remarkable degree of agility in people, evidenced by the speed with which they took the useless precaution of scrambling under the nearest table when the stuttering sound of a V.1 engine cut out overhead. I was a member of the audience at one of Dame Myra Hess's National Gallery lunch-time concerts when the noise of a flying bomb roaring over our heads suddenly ceased. Immediately there was a frantic scramble as everyone fell to the floor, shoving their craniums under flimsy folding wooden chairs. In a few seconds there followed a shuddering explosion, nearer and louder than usual. The bomb had come down somewhere behind the Regent Palace Hotel, only a few hundred yards away. Shamefacedly, the audience picked itself up and sat down again. Throughout this pantomime the Belgian Piano Quartet—caught, so to say, in the middle of the first movement of Mozart's E flat Quartet—went on calmly playing without so much as the tremor of a bow-arm.

The V.1 first announced itself by falling on the Guards Chapel, causing much loss of life, during a Sunday morning service when I happened to be on duty in Whitehall. The V.2 that succeeded it gave no warning at all. Rumours of major gas explosions soon spread round London. Eventually, these had to be officially discounted, since it seemed hardly credible that gas mains throughout the metropolis should suddenly have taken to blowing up with increasing frequency. Fortunately, both Vs had only to be endured for a few weeks before the allied armies overran the launching sites. They provided a battering test of civilian morale, and I have always felt that had Hitler been able to deploy the weapons several months earlier, Londoners might have found such an assault impossibly hard to bear.

One of my close colleagues at the War Office was the author

James Pope-Hennessey, by then already the winner of the 1934 Hawthornden Prize with his book *London Pride*. James, an Intelligence expert, possessed a kind of Byronesque beauty. He was a sophisticated and entertaining companion on the long regular stints of duty when together we formed one of several teams that took it in turn to prepare overnight situation reports on the Far Eastern theatre of the war. Our reports had a distinguished readership, which included the King, the Chief of the Imperial General Staff, Sir Alan Brooke—always testy over hesitant morning explanations—and, the most exacting reader of them all, the Prime Minister, Winston Churchill.

Once, in a thoughtless midnight moment, I referred to the Burmese town of Myitkyina as "a city". Returning from breakfast I found myself summoned to the august presence to defend my choice of word. "Are you the officer who described Myitkyina as a city?" he inquired through a cloud of cigar smoke. I confessed that I was. "Justify yourself," he commanded.

Naturally, I was not so foolish as to appear before the most important person in Britain without having thought out some kind of riposte. I therefore proceeded to reel off an impressive list of statistics; population figures, the number of pagodas and temples the place possessed; even the name of Myitkyina's cinema. None of this frantic attempt to secure major urban status for Myitkyina was of the slightest avail. "But has it a *cathedral*?" the famous voice thundered, characteristically emphasising the middle syllable. I admitted that it had not. "Then in future call it a township", he pronounced, dismissing me with a wave of his cigar.

As I left the presence, General Sir Ian Jacob, then in charge of Churchill's military officers, said, "Don't worry. He does this every day to a Junior and a Senior staff officer, just to keep them on their toes. You should hear how he treats the seniors!"

Homosexuality being socially less acceptable in those days than it has since become, James did his best to conceal this aspect of his nature from those of us whose heterosexuality might perhaps have made them uncomprehending. One evening, however, we were both invited to some pseudo-artistic socialite's party, along with our "wives or girl friends". I arrived alone. James turned up with a dumb-looking twentyish blond lorry driver painfully aware that he did not know an aria from Ariosto, and who at once proceeded to get self-revealingly drunk. James's petulant arrogance and embarrassed attempts at a cover-up struck a strange and chilling note in the kind of very English society to which, as the son of a major-general and a Dame of the British Empire, he naturally belonged; though not, of course, the lorry driver; nor, for that matter, Scottish me.

After the war James and I kept in occasional touch. He persuaded me that from the point of view of an Englishman, there was a need for a popular study of Robert Burns; a study that would separate fact from myth and incorporate the discoveries of modern scholarship and modern critical methods in a style that would appeal to the non-specialist reader. He volunteered to recommend the commissioning of such a book to the director of one of the leading British publishers. Typically, he became so enthusiastic about the idea that he let out what he had in mind at a party at which he happened to meet the head of one of the smaller publishers who had set up in business just after the war. As a result, that publisher immediately got in touch with me. A bird in the hand being better than whatever may be concealed in the proverbial bush, I accepted this commission. *Robert Burns: The Man, his Work, the Legend*, much revised and improved, survives in a third edition, though under a different imprint, thirty years later.

James and I shared two other unusual experiences, one of them unforgettable. There was the luck of our evening location on V.E. Day, May, 1945, when the war in Europe ended. The whole population of London seemed to have surged into Whitehall; a tightly-packed happy mêlée of jostling, shouting, singing, cheering people, the human noise punctuated by the ceaseless honking of vehicle horns. Communal relief had at last burst through six years of weary constraint. Gazing down from an open War Office window on this spectacle of unbuttoned happiness-in-action, it felt as if we were right at the bubbling epicentre of an historic moment. The future seemed euphorically optimistic, the age-old casual confusion that is history forgotten in rejoicings that appeared to promise some sort of lasting order.

Almost half a century on, these V.E. Day reflections sound like phoney film rhetoric. Yet for those of us who so warmly experienced them for a few escapist hours, they were deeply and movingly real. The world *was* going to get better; get better; get better . . . We had certainly earned a little escapism, however short-lived.

It was not to last long. Those of us in the Far Eastern section of the War Office were constantly reminded that V.E. Day only represented a partial peace, whatever the public might think. There was still the Japanese problem.

Far Eastern war or not, the Trade Unions lost no time in flexing their muscle against the community. Scarcely had peace in Europe been declared than a nasty attack on the war-weary public was launched by London Transport employees over the number of passengers allowed to stand in the inadequate fleet of buses left in service on the city's streets.

The other unforgettable experience shared with James was our first news of the atom bomb. Early in August some of us on duty were summoned to the War Office map room and in matter-of-fact military terms given an official explanation of what had newly happened at Hiroshima. The most astonishing wash of relief it is possible to imagine all but carried the feet, so to say, from beneath my senses. For the only time in my life I came near to fainting from sheer intensity of emotion: not, I fear, out of pity for the unfortunate people of Hiroshima, whose national leaders had brought disaster upon themselves: but in thankfulness that the children of tomorrow's world would be the first generation in the long march of Everyman to grow up under conditions that should make a future world war profitless and therefore impossible; or, at the least, unlikely. I held to this belief throughout the Berlin siege, Korea, Cuba, the Israeli wars and even Vietnam. To this day I find it difficult to imagine what calculated motivation or lunacy of chance could lead to that deliberate self-destruction of the human race which nuclear war must inevitably bring about.

As a result of Hiroshima and Nagasaki, my stay at the War Office suddenly seemed likely to be of much shorter duration than had appeared probable a few hours before. Throughout the long years of war service I had rarely allowed myself the luxury of visualising myself as a comfortable money-earning civilian again. Without warning, the return to civilian life had become a matter of months away. A career in music was out of the question, and the thought of devoting my life to producing Christmas cards filled me with horror. There was also a delectably compelling reason why I should quickly find something gainful to do. But what?

CHAPTER 5

RETURN TO GLASGOW

During my final months at the War Office I had fallen in love, proposed and been accepted. It was therefore crucial that I should find some sort of career offering reasonable financial prospects. There was the possibility of remaining additional months in the army under special contract, but apart from my dislike of military life, this would simply have postponed the issue, and was therefore unacceptable. The prospect of a Music Talks producer's job with the B.B.C. in London also presented itself. I was totally obsessed, however, by a desire to return to Scotland and play some part in reshaping it along, as I thought, the brave lines of MacDiarmid's vision of independence. Although I had published several short stories, I felt fairly certain that I did not have the kind of sustained narrative inventive talent necessary to become a successful novelist. I therefore decided to thole the colour-printing business once again, until I could establish myself as a freelance writer and broadcaster, with time to devote to poetry.

On 26th March, 1946, I took the train to York. At a demobilising centre I was given a brown suit, two shirts, a pair of brown shoes, and despatched back to civilian life. Having a few spare hours, I wandered delightedly round the old town, then caught my train for Glasgow, wondering what lay before me.

It was a shabby down-at-heel Glasgow to which I returned. Doors and window-frames thirsted for paint; the grey sandstone seemed dirtier and flakier than before; and the spaces left open by the dismantled Victorian ornamental railings were already allowing decay to blow freely around.

Little, however, had changed in the colour-printing business. I soon found its limitations intolerable, so set about establishing broadcasting contacts. For Robert Kemp I introduced a weekly series of ten-minute *Poetry Notebook* readings, and contributed regularly to his monthly "Chapbook" features. For Robin Russell, I became a regular contributor to his critical programme "Arts Review", appearing on the second issue, and regularly thereafter during its long "life" of twenty-one years.

Kemp, Orcadian born but educated in the North East, was a former *Guardian* journalist and a skilful writer and producer for radio, first coming to general notice with his vivid war-time features. He was a good trainer of young writers, and a charming and lovable man. As a student, he manifested an effortless cleverness, though one easily undermined. Perhaps because of this, he appeared always to speak from the sidelines, avoiding confrontation with major crises. In his play *A Nest of Singing Birds*, for instance, based on a true seventeenth-century episode, two sisters quarrel about an issue of church worship. The real matter of consequence was the ferocious division of opinion in Scotland over the method of approach to God represented by the Presbyterian and Episcopalian styles of worship. Kemp turned it into an argument over whether God meant singers to be trained or remain untrained. His plays are thus usually more noticeable for the fluency of the Scots dialogue of the characters than for what they actually say. His play about Burns and Clarinda, *The Other Dear Charmer*, is still regularly revived, as is his very skilful adaptation into Scots of Molière's *L'Ecole des Femmes, Let Wives Tak Tent*. His greatest success was his adaptation of Sir David Lyndsay's four-hundred-year-old morality play *Ane Satyre of the Thrie Estatis*, which scored what has remained the most outstanding dramatic success of the Edinburgh Festival's first thirty-five or so years.

In later years, after he had resigned from the B.B.C. to devote himself entirely to writing, he published a series of amusing light-weight Scottish novels, though he was reputed to earn the major part of his living producing under a pseudonym episodes of detective fiction for television. His last few years were embittered by a belief that he had not received the recognition due to him. He was obviously deeply distressed over the outrageous proposals to drive a ring road through the New Town of Edinburgh—proposals made before the concept of Conservation Areas was created by the Civic Amenities Act passed the same year, 1967—and sadly, died in that year, still in his fifties.

The intensity of feeling from which clearly he suffered neither transmitted itself to his plays nor affected his outward manner. Indeed, one of his most endearing characteristics was an apparent cool vagueness. Once, during a rehearsal, he put a point to me that required the rewriting of a sentence or two. Time was short. When I returned to show him how I had made the adjustment, he had vanished. From a neighbouring studio came the sound of Robert happily tinkling a piano. It was, I suppose, a coolness disguised to generate self-confidence in others.

As soon as possible after Joyce and I became engaged, I introduced her to Francis George Scott, calling with her on him at his home, 44, Munro Road, Jordanhill. I also organised a similar introduction to MacDiarmid.

We were invited to tea one Sunday afternoon at the poet's rented flat in Langside. MacDiarmid was at his most gallantly affable. The afternoon wore on, but neither his wife nor the promised tea appeared. Just as we were making shift to leave, MacDiarmid excused himself. His wife, he explained, had been friendly with a Norwegian sea captain. This was the mariner's last weekend in Scotland, so naturally, Valda wanted to be with him. He himself would put on the kettle for the tea.

Joyce and I were married in Westbourne Church on 3rd August, 1946. She arrived twenty minutes late, her father having miscalculated how long it would take to travel from Scotstounhill to Kelvinside. My brother, Stanley, was my best man. At that time he was in love with a Sunday-school teacher, and had "got" religion. During what seemed an interminable wait, he and the minister engaged in earnest discussion on the organisation of Sunday schools while I paced the floor, fancying that I could hear the wondering of the guests through the organist's increasingly desperate improvisation.

After a night in Stirling we spent our honeymoon in Onich, on Loch Linnhe, visiting, among other places, Iona, a difficult journey in those post-war days of poor communications and still poorer tourist hospitality. But we laughed at everything; even at the discovery of how lamentably ill-informed we were about the physical business of establishing the married relationship, my wife having been armed by her mother with a work by Aristotle, my own more recent manual on sexual matters being only a little less evasive. Alex Comfort, whom I met during the war years when he was anxious to be known as a poet and novelist, was still a long way from writing his illustrated guide, *The Joy of Sex*. We had to discover that for ourselves.

Back in Glasgow, we settled into a tiny rented flat in Jedburgh Gardens, by Kelvinbridge. Still being something of a romantic, I picked up my bride to carry her over the threshold and almost dropped her. The thing is not as simple as it seems on the stage. Indeed, unless you happen to be a ballet-dancer or an athlete, carrying women about is really quite impractical!

Our flat stood in a cul-de-sac at right-angles to a Catholic school. By day, the noise of the children singing in class, or romping around in the playground, was a distraction that made concentration impossible. In the evening, the gymnasium was used for adult recreation, when the hoots and hoyas of netball players proved even more disturbing. Serious writing had therefore to be done late at night.

A desk and a bed were the two essential items given to us as wedding presents. Much of the rest of our furniture came from second-hand dealers and salerooms. Our first bookcases were up-ended orange-boxes. Our bath was a high-canopied cast-iron affair that immediately chilled the hot water filling it. We tried to create an illusion of warmth by painting it bright red. Unfortunately, those who emerged from it for some time after carried patches of scarlet on their persons.

One sale in particular stands out in my recollection. It was held in a West End house, and we went to it to buy fire-irons. The room was hot with a press of people and that heightened atmosphere which affects even well-ventilated salerooms. When the lot-number we were after was announced, we found to our astonishment that as well as the firearms, it contained an assortment of worn-out kitchen utensils and two large family portraits. When the bidding started we were opposed by a sweaty-looking man we took to be a dealer, and by another voice whose corporeal attachment could not be established because of the size of the crowd. In the end it was Voice versus Lindsay, and Lindsay won. "Knocked down to the gentleman with the beard", the auctioneer said—in those days I sported briefly a thin beard, hastily removed after Eric Linklater likened it to such as might have been attempted by an indecisive Viking.

When we handed over our modest cheque and went to collect our purchases, the man wanted us to take away the kitchen junk and the two life-size Victorian portraits. Slanted against a wall, they stared at us from heavily-chipped gilt frames; he, a portly, bushily-bearded gentleman of decisive mien, his right hand resting magisterially up on a polished table-top; she, a delicate beauty concealed in voluminous frills and looking as if she was not quite sure what life was all about.

"We don't want these," I said politely to the cheque-collecting man. "You've bought them, whether you like it or not," he snapped, "and you'll have to take them away. They're your responsibility."

To be responsible for one's own ancestors can be trying enough, but to have to assume responsibility for someone else's was altogether too much. After a whispered conspiracy with a man who owned a barrow and the passing from hand to hand of a pound note, worn-out utensils and discarded relatives set out for an unknown destination.

Regular visitors to Jedburgh Gardens included Douglas Young, then working for the Scottish National Party and still being denied an academic position because of his war-time views. His bearded, slender height—he looked like one who had suddenly outgrown his strength in youth, and remained that way—and the glint of his searching eyes behind thick glasses, made him seem an awesomely formidable figure. Yet he was a delightful companion, witty, compassionate, restlessly curious, and with an irrepressible, almost child-like enthusiasm for everything he took up. He had been granted so many talents that probably he was never able to exploit any of them to the full. As a poet, certainly, he scarcely penetrated beneath the surface of intellectual wit-writing, the neatest example being his much-anthologised epigram, "Last Laugh".

It was his usual practice to arrive at Jedburgh Gardens early in the afternoon and demand the use of a bed, his theory being that a sleep after lunch gave him the refreshing advantage of making one day do the work of two. After one such visit, by way of a thank-you he sent me an amusing acrostic sonnet, subsequently published in *The Voice of Scotland*:

M   Maurice, musician, makar, monifauld
A   Anthologies you plan and execute,
U   Urbane, warmhertit, catholic, astute,
R   Radiant o hope, wi sweirties unappalled,
I   In spite o kiaughs an comitees untauld
C   Castan your nets for renascential loot,
E   Editor, critic, eident to recruit

L   Leal Scots for our Kulturkampf, slee and bauld,
I   I scryve this thrawn acrostich raw on raw
N   No cataloguan aa the credit due,
D   Dear Maurice, to your zest for tune and rhyme.
S   Scotland's Renaissance awes a feck to you,
A   Anither Allan Ramsay come in time.
Y   Your wark's weel ruitit, as its fruct sall shaw.

Another visitor was Hamish Henderson, the skilful and tireless folk-song collector and author of *Elegies For The Dead In Cyrenaica*, certainly among the finest sequences of Second War poems to come out of Scotland, if not indeed, Britain. On one occasion he arrived unannounced when my wife and I happened to be out of town. Undismayed, he rang the door bell of the couple across the landing, with whom we had left our house-keys. So successfully did he convince them of the strength of his friendship with us that they themselves provided him with a bed for the night. They later reported that once he had eaten his supper, Hamish embarked on his favourite pursuit of singing long Gaelic ballads. Twenty minutes after he had begun, his host and hostess politely indicated that they wanted to go to bed. Hamish, it seems, ignored them and sang on. Eventually, leaving him in vocal mid-flight, they slipped out of the room and retired, half expecting to find him still singing to himself next morning.

The Welsh poet R. S. Thomas, who resembled in appearance a grimly determined Scots lad o' pairts come to town to study on a bag of oatmeal, also came to Jedburgh Gardens. He stayed a day or two during what must have been his first Scottish lecture tour, leaving us a signed copy of his newly-published first collection, *Stones of the Field*. The quality of his personal intensity and the vivid spareness of his verse made him seem to us in these days a kind of non-conformist Gerald Manley Hopkins.

It soon became clear that freelance broadcasting was likely to be erratic work, hectic during the winter months but falling away in summer. I therefore wrote to the editors of several Glasgow newspapers seeking additional employment. Most of them replied. Sir Patrick Dollan, Glasgow's wartime Lord Provost and the Scottish Editor of an English Labour-orientated paper, the *Daily Herald*, explained that he had invited me to see him because recently he had read some of my poetry. The Editor of the *Glasgow Herald* felt he was doing me a good turn by refusing his help in person rather than by letter, since he knew my father. The only one of them to respond positively was James Macarthur Reid, the kindly and learned editor of the Scottish pictorial daily, *The Bulletin*. What, he asked, could I do? Features, leaders, music criticism, I suggested. As it happened, his music critic, the widely-read but elderly H. K. Wood, whose father had entertained Chopin in Glasgow, was ill. How about a critique of a concert that night? I agreed, and quickly found myself assisting the ailing Wood on a regular basis. A few months later, Wood had a stroke and was forced to retire. I was appointed his successor, and for fourteen years remained music critic of *The Bulletin*.

In the early winter of 1946, on the strength of these new but unproven activities and on promises of editorial and writing work from the publisher Maclellan—none of which, in the event, materialised—I threw up my dull but "safe" job in colour printing and embarked upon the unpredictable career of a freelance author, journalist, music critic and broadcaster. My wife approved, my own parents were anxious, hers absolutely horrified. Writing for newspapers and broadcasting in their eyes was not real "work". For my own part, I felt relief. Outwardly at least I should now be my own man. I was soon to find out, however, that freelancing is an all-or-nothing career. As nature abhors a vacuum, so do editors and producers the freelance who is not readily and reliably available. I made it my business to be both.

The next producer to employ me was to become not only one of my closest friends, but an invaluable literary mentor throughout my life. George Bruce was a North-Easterner from Fraserburgh with the traditions of the sea and the herring-fishing industry in his blood. He began his career as a school teacher in Dundee, but in 1946 he became a radio producer with the B.B.C. in Aberdeen.

I knew him as a poet some years before I actually met him, because among the many fine things of his published in *Poetry Scotland* had been not only the much anthologised "Kinnaird Head", but my own favourite among his early poems, "Inheritance":

> This which I write now
> Was written years ago
> Before my birth
> In the features of my father.
>
> It was stamped
> In the rock formations

West of my hometown.
Not I write,

But, perhaps, William Bruce,
Cooper.
Perhaps here his hand
Well articled in his trade.

Then though my words
Hit out
An ebullition from
City or flower,

There not my faith,
These the paint
Smeared upon
The inarticulate,

The salt crusted sea-boot,
The red-eyed mackerel,
The plate shining with herring,
And many men,

Seamen and craftsmen and curers,
And behind them
The protest of hundreds of years,
The sea obstinate against the land.

My future wife in fact met him before I did. Whilst a student at St Andrews University she attended a lecture on contemporary Scottish poetry which George happened to be giving there. Afterwards she introduced herself. George knew me as "the Army Captain who always uses green ink". (For a time the green ink gave place to brown, until Sydney Goodsir Smith asked me if I was really so hard up that I had to resort to watering down *that!*) Very soon after George took up his B.B.C. appointment I suggested to Andrew Stewart, then Director of the Scottish Home Service, that I might edit and introduce a poetry magazine. He put the idea to George, who felt we ought to broaden it out and produce a more general literary broadcast magazine. Thus in 1949 *Scottish Life and Letters* took the air. Although my direct association with it ceased in 1961, I remained an occasional contributor, and indeed, took part in its final issue, broadcast on the fifteenth of March 1970.

Extraordinarily widely read, the spare and wiry George preserved his well-spring of enthusiasm into his seventies, perhaps because originally he trained to become a professional footballer.

From the fifties until this day, I have shown him the final draft of virtually everything I have written in verse. His detailed criticism has been of the utmost value. He had never let himself be influenced by prejudices of any kind, and although his own style differs fundamentally from my own, he has always been able to put his finger unerringly upon a weakness or a fault. Nor was he ever short of praise when he felt it to due.

Poets—indeed, artists of every kind—need praise and applause as reassurance of contact with some sort of an audience there outside. The creative cycle is incomplete until the reader or listener can be known to be responding. During the late forties I recall the late James Bridie delivering a speech to a gaggle of pressmen in the foyer of Glasgow's Citizens' Theatre, then still surrounded by the as yet undemolished Gorbals. He was arguing for more publicity and more understanding criticism for his struggling company. "Mr Bridie," said one reporter, "it seems to me that what you really want is praise, not criticism." "That's right," Bridie snapped back. "It's praise we want. Praise, damn you, praise!" He was echoing, doubtless unconsciously, Rachmaninov's definition of the three essential requirements a creative artist needs to keep him going: praise, praise and praise!

It was largely due to the regular broadcasting work which I undertook for George Bruce that I found my feet in the precarious world of the freelance writer. When I took our joint future in my hands and resigned from the Hillington colour-printing business, my salary was four hundred pounds a year. I reckoned that I could earn half of that sum through my music criticism at ten shillings a notice, and the rest from broadcasting. Luckily, I made nearly eight hundred pounds during my first year as a freelance. During the next fourteen years I always managed to increase my earnings, thus keeping ahead of inflation, then by no means the menacing threat to thrifty security and social justice it was eventually to become. In those days it actually paid to work hard.

The noises from our neighbours of the school, however, made it essential that we moved to quieter surroundings. Eighteen months after our marriage we were once again lucky in securing another rented flat, this time at 13 Southwark Avenue, just off Great Western Road, in an area already beginning to be "colonised" by Glasgow University. This roomier flat had more accommodation than we needed immediately, so for six months a recently married sister and her husband, then still without a home of their own, stayed with us. She was interested in bulldogs, and soon we had two of them plodding about the house. A near neighbour was Marion Harvey, at that time well-known as a sketcher in crayon of dogs. Bambi, one of the bulldogs, "sat" for her. The finished likeness in pastel crayon seemed uncannily lifelike, until at a show of Miss Harvey's collected work we discovered that whatever the breed, all her dogs wore a similar benignly intelligent expression.

Although Joyce and I briefly succumbed to the bulldog lure, we had reservations about the attractiveness of their constant slavering. Our own bulldog, while still a puppy, overindulged its omnivorous appetite, consuming two-thirds of a bound copy of the poems of Ossian, several pairs of slippers and an ounce of foil-wrapped Player's Navy Cut pipe tobacco. Not surprisingly it became ill, developing a skin disease that eventually left it pink and completely hairless. In spite of the costly attentions of two vets, it had in the end to be put down.

I decided that if we really were going to be dog-owners, there was no point in doing things by half measures. So I wrote away for the particulars of a St Bernard pup. When the details arrived, I was so horrified at the enormous quantity of food St Bernards apparently eat every day that I immediately bought a dachshund, thus beginning our association with soulful-looking long-bodied dogs certain to make their owners laugh frequently. Since a well-known Scottish strain of dachshund was named after varieties of the better champagnes, a drink I could not then afford, we decided to call our animal "Blotto".

When my sister and her husband did find a house and move away, their place at Southpark Avenue was taken by Alex and Cath Scott. I had first met the Aberdonian Alexander Scott a year or so before when, under his aegis, a group of mature students at Aberdeen University invited me up to take part in a poetry reading. On Young's recommendation, Scott had sent me poems for *Poetry Scotland Four* which, with MacDiarmid as co-editor, appeared belatedly in 1949 from an Edinburgh publisher. In Glasgow, Alex and his wife spent six months with us while flat-hunting. After a short spell in Edinburgh as an Assistant Lecturer, he had become a Lecturer in Scottish Literature at Glasgow University, a Department of which he became the first Head in 1971.

A gallant soldier who won the Military Cross in 1945, Alex had the self-confident energy of the North East; the kind of energy that, years later, was to enable the North East to cash in on the development of North Sea oil and its related industries with spectacular success while the rest of Scotland was sinking into decline. In Alex's case, it was an energy which sometimes seemed to make him pronounce value judgments in terms of black and white where others might have determined subtler shadings. His enthusiasm for the cause of the Scots language, however, led not only to the building up of the only separate Department of Scottish Literature in any Scottish university, but also to the training over the years of most of the teachers who have with moderate success reintroduced Scottish literature into Scotland's schools, from which for more than a century it had been totally banished in favour of the more "proper" literature of England, the larger absorbing partner-nation.

As a poet, Alex writes best in Scots, his natural speech when he was young. The pithy vernacular energy of his verse is indeed "centred on a stubborn, passionate and sardonic realism", as our common friend, the poet Norman MacCaig, has so neatly put it. Alex has thus been quite unsentimental about Scotland's short-comings, as his devastatingly accurate series "Scotched" demonstrates. Among these gems of concentration I particularly admire—

> *Scotch Religion*
> Damn
> Aa.
>
> *Scotch Equality*
> Kaa the feet frae
> Thon big bastard.
>
> *Scotch Passion*
> Forgot
> Mysel.

and
> *Scotch Education*
> I telt ye
> I telt ye

a nation's hang-ups unerringly hit on the head with deft poetic hammer blows. Not the least of his kindnesses to me was his skilful editing of my *Collected Poems* (1979), for which he provided a perceptive introductory appraisement. For all his satirical force, his personal warmth and generosity over almost forty years of friendship have greatly enriched my life.

Throughout that time we have shared many literary interests and ploys, including the editing of *The Scottish Review*, founded in 1975 and still flourishing. We had already collaborated over its less durable predecessor. In 1949, we took over the editorship of an ailing monthly journal, *The Scots Review*, reviving its fortunes and keeping it going until, some months later, circumstances outside our control forced its closure.

The Scots Review had been founded by a group of four men, three of whom took an active interest in it: Edinburgh solicitor A. D. MacEwan, a son of the Scottish Nationalist Sir Alexander MacEwan, whose political exposition *The Thistle and the Rose* made a stir in the thirties; George Scott-Moncrieff, an ardent Roman Catholic and distant relation of the famous English translator of Proust; J. M. Reid, the Scottish Nationalist Editor of *The Bulletin*, and of course by now one of my employers; and a mysterious sleeping partner, said to own land in Galloway, but who never appeared at any of our Board meetings.

The first Editor had been the columnist of *The Scotsman*, Wilfred Taylor, who entered journalism from St Andrews University trailing a reputation of undergraduate brilliance which never quite transcended the wit-level of the daily column, that most debilitating of journalistic undertakings. The *Review* then had a readership of just over two thousand. In these days there was no such thing as a Scottish Arts Council subsidy, and the wealthy Galloway partner frequently had to make good a hefty deficit.

Alex and I enjoyed putting the paper together, filling the missing gaps with our own overnight scrieving, and paying monthly visits to Galashiels to correct the proofs and do the paste-ups. But as I have said, several unalterable factors operated against us. One was the insistence of the proprietors that each should have the unquestionable right to contribute whenever he wished. Reid, a knowledgeable historian and a lifelong patriot, believed that the Church of Scotland still had some practical influence on daily affairs, a view not shared by many of our readers. Worse still, he had already begun to drum out his insistence that the discovery of how to split the atom was inherently evil, should not have been attempted, and should now be abjured, an aberration the reiteration of which played some part in bringing about the demise of his newspaper, *The*

Bulletin, thirteen years later. I was never able to understand why so able a man failed to appreciate that a discovery cannot be undiscovered, its issues made to disappear simply by pretending they should not be there.

Another difficulty was Trade Union success in forcing up the wages of provincial printers to a level nearer that of city printers. There was no way in which the resulting inevitable price increase could be absorbed by our readership. Since the owners were unwilling to provide an additional subsidy, the venture came to that trailing end that sooner or later drags down all "little reviews".

The Scots Review was one of the many publications involved in the great Lallans row of 1946/47. Burns had written in the late eighteenth century:

> "They spake their thochts in guid braid lallans,
> Like you and me."

Using as justification this reference by Burns to the Lowland Scots tongue, Douglas Young extended the word to cover not only the so-called synthetic, plastic or dictionary-propped Scots that Hugh MacDiarmid had dredged up and deployed with much imagination in his early lyrics and in *A Drunk Man Looks at the Thistle*, but also to include the Scots being fashioned and employed for literary purposes by the second generation of Scottish Renaissance writers, the group that included Goodsir Smith and himself.

By 1946 I, too, had become deeply involved in this movement of Young's to restitute Scots. For my own part, it was a reaction against my association with the New Apocalypse movement, though I always felt some unease at the dichotomy which yawned between our literary Scots lingo and the broken-down dialects still spoken in various parts of Scotland. Young confidently prophesied that the day would come when the *Glasgow Herald* leader would be couched in Scots, a proposition clearly ridiculous. At that time, however, the feeling of a Lallans resurgence of some sort was compellingly in the air.

It was a *Glasgow Herald* leader-writer, Mr (later Sir James) Fergusson of Kilkerran, who brought the whole thing to a head during the late summer of 1946. He instituted what was to be dubbed "the great Lallans row" with some remarks in an otherwise favourable review of my then recently published Faber anthology, *Modern Scottish Poetry: An Anthology of the Scottish Renaissance 1920–1945*, a work designed to demonstrate the dimensions of the Scottish Renaissance, in the sense of Ezra Pound's belief that some anthologies can "sometimes be significant criticism." Fergusson's criticism was directed primarily against the synthetic and unspoken quality of the Scots used by MacDiarmid, Goodsir Smith and Young as opposed to the more folk-orientated rural Scots employed by Sir Alexander Gray, Violet Jacob and Marion Angus.

Fired by the intemperance of youth (of which I then had a plentiful supply), a feeling that I must stand up for my first serious publication, thin-skinned touchiness (that endemic disease of poets,) and perhaps a little uncertainty as to the defendable nature of my ground, I launched a vigorous attack on Fergusson through the correspondence columns of the *Herald*. More or less simultaneously, Young and MacDiarmid (for some reason uncharacteristically using his own name, C. M. Grieve), did likewise. For several months the correspondence columns of the *Herald*, and the pages of other papers and journals, resounded with highly-coloured arguments for and against Lallans. The *Herald* Editorial Diary added to the fun by promising a series of lessons on how to write "plastic Scots". The first "lesson" began:

"It is, of course, much easier to write plastic Scots than to read it, and the art can easily be mastered with the help of a few simple rules.

"Manner is your concern rather than matter. Your subjects need be few—Hugh MacDiarmid, Glasgow, the Highlands, the English, love, drink and Hugh MacDiarmid: this is *de rigueur*. After all, he invented synthetic Scots, from which the plastic form is derived . . . It is not necessary for what you write to have meaning, but it is vital to conceal your meaning, if any, as much as possible."

"A draft in English," readers were told, was permissible, "this being your natural language." But thereafter, "you must work over your draft and find synonyms for as many words as you can, such as *forfochen* for *wearied* and *whummelt* for *overturned* . . . Next, there are the dialectic words . . . It doesn't matter if they belong to Peebles or Paisley, to the eighteenth century or to the twentieth. After all, you're not writing a language that anyone ever spoke . . . Begin an occasional stanza with the ejaculation *Cwa'*."

With what now seems to me absurd disingenuousness, I retorted:

"As one of those poets who use the language, let me tell you—the verse does *not* begin as an English draft. To those well read in Scottish literature, and familiar with the Scots spoken by country folk today, the phrases and words used by Scots-writing poets are common currency. Words must always be handled by poets in a new way, and your suggestion that they should be employed only in company with other words of the same period is belied by every poet's work from Chaucer onwards. Poetry often starts from words, but because the words set something going in the heart. Otherwise, the subject comes by impulse or instinct . . . Once the draft is finished *in Scots*, you chisel it, as a sculptor chisels his stone, until you feel you cannot improve upon it. During this process you adjust your words to gain the greatest effect in sound values from the arrangement of vocables. You use a dictionary only as an English poet uses his—very, very occasionally."

While that still seems to me, in outline, a reasonable description of some (though not all) of the ways in which a poem can come into being, there were few other points in that letter which I would now uphold without qualification. The correspondence volumed on, and overflowed into street conversation and pantomime jokes. At the Citizens' Theatre, in Glasgow's Gorbals, during one of their pantomimes the titles of which always had thirteen letters, three weird Celtic sisters satirised the Lallans makars in rhymed couplets, the problem of my rhymeless name being glossed over with:

> "Here's the latest piece of whimsy
> From the pen of Maurice Lindsay."

In the *Glasgow Herald*, Edwin Morgan advocated the use of whatever language, or amalgam, came naturally to a poet; MacDiarmid thundered against Scots users of English, more or less irrelevantly; Young's voluble responses enshrined one remarkable reproving comparison, directed against a certain classically learned Mr A. Montgomerie, who had rashly propounded a not quite accurate Greek comparison.

"Corinna's advice to Pindar related to his juvenile plethora of saga material and of bold abrupt metaphors, not to his choice of words and forms," Montgomerie was told. "She, good lady, wrote a relatively pure Boeotian, as Sappho wrote more or less her spoken Lesbian with Homeric elements, but Pindar wrote a highly synthetic Panhellenic literary amalgam, which no one ever spoke or employed for common writing. The term 'synthetic' applied to Hugh MacDiarmid's neo-Lallans was originally meant in a philosophic sense, but has since been misunderstood through the association of 'ersatz' chemistry. MacDiarmid synthesised elements rightly belonging together, the 'disjecta membra' of the early Renaissance Scots 'Koine'. He did not synthesise rightly separated Ionic and Aeolic, as Violet Jacob synthesised Scots and English."

Fergusson, with whom in later years I was to become friendly, answered devastatingly a suggestion by MacDiarmid that no Scots poets writing in English ever did well enough for their work to be included in English anthologies or enjoyed by English readers:

"The pretence that Scottish poets cannot fully express themselves in English if they wish to is pure nonsense. Messrs. Grieve, Young, Saunders* and Lindsay have themselves proved the contrary; and Mr Lindsay's latest book is in English throughout.† As for Mr Grieve's extraordinary contention that neglect by English anthologists proves the inferiority of Scottish poets' work in English, since when have the English been recognised as the best judges of any Scottish product?"

Against MacDiarmid himself, Fergusson, in another letter, thrust even more tellingly:

". . . Burns was read with understanding and delight in his own time, as Robert Heron recorded, by 'ploughboys and maid servants'. Plastic Scots, on the other hand, on Mr Grieve's own admission, is 'not intelligible to the man in the street'—though, he says, much appreciated by English and other foreign scholars. This sheds a revealing light on the views of some modern Scottish poets on the proper relationship between them and their public."

It did indeed; and it was a light that troubled me like a migraine dazzle throughout the meetings of the Lallans Club in the back room of the Abbotsford pub in Edinburgh's Rose Street. There, the Scots poets met on three occasions to agree upon a set of unifying principles for the future use and spelling of Scots.

At one meeting Douglas Young, anxious to demonstrate the

* R. Crombie Saunders, the editor of the war-time journal *Scottish Art and Letters*.
† *The Enemies of Love* (1946)

living quality of Scots, held up his empty beer glass and called to the barman "Some mair." To everyone's astonishment the barman presently came across carrying a long pole and pulled open an upper window.

After much argument, a style-sheet was eventually drawn up and published. Few writers stuck to it for long. Reaching even this limited theoretical agreement disclosed such a divergence of irrelevant political views—the moderate centre against the extreme left—that I became increasingly dissatisfied with the realities of the situation. Most of those who argued the loudest in the backroom of the Abbotsford all those years ago subsequently produced nothing of noticeable significance in Lallans, or in any other language.

The most obvious practical difficulty facing a poet bent on using Lallans was finding a publisher. Naturally, no London publisher found poetry in Scots much of an attraction. Long delays and increasing unreliability made Maclellan's war-time publishing venture seem unlikely to survive for very long in the competitive years of peace. It was therefore to Serif Books, in Edinburgh, a short-lived venture that put out work by John R. Allan, Fred Urquhart and the first edition of Goodsir Smith's *Under the Eildon Tree*, to whom I turned for my next collection, *Hurlygush*, which was entirely in Lallans.

London publishers like to discover their own poets and nurture them through their careers. I had been unwise enough to try to get Eliot to publish, through Faber, a composite volume of Lallans verse by Goodsir Smith, Young and myself. On 6th October, 1946, Eliot wrote: "For books exclusively in Lallands"— he always added that 'd'—"the public in England would presumably be very small . . . Furthermore, I think that whatever the obvious material advantages, it might be injudicious from your point of view to have such a book brought out in London. It would imply to many of the public the suggestion that Scotland was unable to publish its own poets and that recognition, like everything else, had to be centred on London. It seems to me better in the long run to stick to Edinburgh or Glasgow for such books, and I hope you realise that I speak as a firm and sympathetic supporter."

Glasgow and Edinburgh, however, in these days simply could not deliver the goods. The lack of a major publisher to market my later poetry was for long to prove a serious handicap, many of the smaller firms with which I became involved, both in Scotland and in England, being poorly organised on the selling side, and sometimes lacking even the basic ability to survive in business.

Hurlygush carried attractive black-and-white drawings by Susan Yorke and a preface by MacDiarmid, who generously prophesied of me:

"Accomplished as his earlier writings were, he has undoubtedly found far fuller and finer utterance in Scots. The rapidity with which he has attained his remarkable mastery of it is in itself an unmistakable pointer . . . Great and varied as his accomplishment already is his promise is still greater, and, having youth too on his side, he should go very far."

Few poets could have launched a volume with a more favourable encomium from an established writer. The fact of the matter was that with the exception of about half-a-dozen poems and a series of bairn-rhymes I wrote for my two eldest children, my Scots verse was very much contrived under the stimulus of nationalism, a quality commented upon adversely and vigorously—indeed, almost offensively—by Douglas Young when my second Lallans volume, *At the Wood's Edge*, appeared, also over the Serif imprint. Wrote Young: "I have now had leisure to consider your At The Wood's Edge, and am sorry to say I find it decidedly disappointing . . . A great many of the themes have little urgency about them . . . The personality and aspiration behind the book cannot make up for these defects . . . What was all the hurry to publish? Horace recommended poems being kept for 9 years. Why run a Heurigerausschenk?" Fair comment and thoroughly sound advice; but at the time I resented it.

Perhaps the most balanced verdict on my work in Scots as a whole came, years later, from Christopher Rush in a long review of my *Collected Poems*.* Wrote Rush: "The involvement with Lallans in the later forties produced a number of knacky little items. But significantly, few of these have that sense of the living which characterises his best work . . . The majority of the Scots pieces have the vibrancy of clock-work toys—we admire briefly then leave them to the children . . . The use of Lallans divorces Lindsay from the human scene where he is so much at home . . . Yet these pieces have many good points: the total identification

* *Scottish Literary Journal*: Supplement No. 12, Summer 1980.

with the child's innocence and wonder, the charming music, the strong appeal to the senses."

Only a few of the poems in these two Scots volumes, (some heavily revised since their first appearance) found their way into my *Collected Poems*. Others provided themes for subsequent poems in English.

I have always thought that the most successful of my Scots pieces was the title poem of my first book, *Hurlygush*. Neil Gunn once remarked that it "got to the heart of the matter." In its revised form it has been much anthologised, and, indeed, is one of the two early poems by which I have been represented for many years in the *Oxford Book of Scottish Verse*. The burn whose varied music it onomatopoeically describes tumbles from the hill behind Innellan to merge with the Firth of Clyde a few yards along the shore from the garden of our one-time summer house, Corraith.

Corraith, our house at Innellan, remained in the family until my mother's death in 1953. Since the beginning of the war my father had made himself financially responsible for its upkeep, the widow of its owner, a retired railwayman, having found the cost of maintaining it long since beyond her means. On my mother's death my father was faced with the choice of buying the house and living alone in it in his retirement; or keeping on the Glasgow house at Athole Gardens, where at least he was within easy reach of his family and friends. He settled for Glasgow. The house at Innellan was therefore sold, to be incorporated in a neighbouring hotel.

My mother, with whom I had enjoyed so close a bond of supportive sympathy since adolescence, suffered some sort of retarding shock during the ferocious Nazi blitz on Clydebank on 13th and 14th March 1941, when some bombs descended on Glasgow. Just before the first bombs fell my father had gone up on to the roof of the house at Athole Gardens with a water pump to guard against the possibility of falling incendiaries. What actually came out of those skies was a stick of high explosive bombs, some of which fell across Kelvinside and Hillhead. My father was shaken but unharmed, but my mother became hysterically convinced that he had been killed, suffering some kind of shock from which she seemed never wholly to recover. Although she entered enthusiastically into war work, taking a leading part in the running of canteens in Glasgow for the men of

Europe's free forces serving in Britain, a progressive deterioration had set in. My father kept a private diary recording his hopes and disappointments, and also details of my mother's intense private sufferings during her final years; sufferings both he, and she, completely concealed from the family. Retrospectively, it seems obvious, though never admitted, that the underlying cause was probably cancer.

By the time I was demobilised in 1946 she had already begun to suffer from what was called "a glandular deprivation." Over the next few years she underwent a slow but steady personality change, causing her to recede out of her recognisable self. In the end her illness reduced her to distraught skin and bone, mentally distancing her from relatives and friends. This led to such unpredictable behaviour that she had to be hospitalised. A few months later, confused and unhappy, she died of what was officially described as "a heart attack." The dreadful experience of watching the receding of a warm and generous loved one into the childishness of near insanity meant that her physical end was not much more than a sad tidying-up. Death had already done its subtracting work.

After three years in Glasgow, my wife and I decided that we wanted to live in the country. My sister had acquired a cottage on the road from Balloch to Gartocharn. The southern end of Dunbartonshire had been the ancestral home ground of our branch of the Lindsays. A cousin of my father's had once owned a jeweller's shop in Dumbarton, and another Lindsay manufactured those early granolithic pavement slabs which carried the maker's name engraved inside a brass oval, some of which were still doing service underfoot in Helensburgh when I was a boy. To Dunbartonshire, therefore, we turned our house-hunting attentions.

CHAPTER 6

BY YON BONNIE BANKS

My Dunbartonshire ancestors succumbed to the wily entice-ments of Sir William Alexander of Menstrie, who had won from his employer, King James VI, the right to colonise Northern Ireland with Scots, the dire effects of which have not yet ceased to trouble the rest of us. The seventeenth-century emigrating Lindsays settled on the western shores of Loch Swilly, near the beautiful but sleepy little village of Rathmelton. For more than a century and a half the Lindsays apparently lived full and useful lives in this Scoto-Irish community. Like Scots settlers every-where, they probably worked harder than the natives. The Lindsay achievement may be read in the tombstones in the village kirkyard, where schoolmasters, ministers and farmers take their rest. Late in the eighteen-forties, (so far as I have been able to gather) the most substantial land-owning Lindsay got entangled in a dispute with a Stewart, went rashly to law, lost his case, and was, in consequence, financially ruined. His grandson, my grandfather, came to London, where he practised as a doctor, but suffered ill-health, retiring early to Rathmelton. There he died, leaving my father the eldest of five children. My father came to Glasgow, finished his education at North Kelvinside School, went into Insurance, served in the 1914–18 war with the Glasgow Highlanders and as a Cameronian officer, and returned in due course to Glasgow to become the Scottish manager of a major British insurance company.

As I have remarked, not all the seventeenth-century Lindsays left Dunbartonshire, but their descendants have now either died out or become so far "removed" in relationship as to be untraceable. My wife and I found our first footing in my ancestral stamping ground as week-end "travelling folk", having bought a half share in a caravan with my sister and brother-in-law.

To the eye of the layman one caravan looks more or less like another: a box on wheels with windows and a door. No doubt most of the caravans on sale today are all that a good caravan ought to be. The half which we bought in 1948 was not.

We read about it in a newspaper. Full of that first time enthusiasm which is so often the undoing of the otherwise canny purchaser, we tracked the caravan to a back-yard in an obscure suburb of Glasgow. As soon as I had introduced myself, the man who owned it assumed that off-hand of-course-I-don't-care-if-you-buy-it-or-not-for-another-man-is-coming-round-to-close-the-deal-at-half-past-six attitude usual on such occasions, and kept reiterating that it was an unrepeatable bargain.

It probably was. Of its three cross-bars beneath the floor, only one was intact, one had been broken and faked with flimsy metal plates, while the third had been broken and not fixed at all. Furthermore, the caravan was not lined. This meant that it warmed up in summer until it became a hot-box, and cooled to the condition of a refrigerator under the lightest fingering of October frost. Nevertheless, enthusiasm prevailed over common sense. We bought our half-share in the contraption without having found anywhere to put it.

The first thing the freshman caravan-owner discovers is that he cannot park his caravan even with the difficulty he may park his car. The moment of truth is the discovery that farmers are no more partial to itinerate vanners than the city police are to static ones.

Up and down the countryside around Glasgow the other half-owner and I towed our liability. One laird assured us he would have been delighted to have had us on his land, but he feared we might catch a contagion from the pollution which affected his river. Another would not have us because our coming and going might disturb his beasts. After listening to about a dozen such pseudo-sympathetic refusals we began to feel like lesser Flying Dutchmen, doomed to travel the roads for ever. Then someone suggested Gartocharn, a tiny village at the middle of the base of the mountain-folded triangle of water which is Loch Lomond. There, we found a smallholder willing to allow us rest our caravan on his land.

Our arrival was unpropitious. We were granted permission to

put our caravan in a field near the lochside. On the evening of our hesitant approach and eventual arrival the rain came down with an intensity it rarely musters, even in Scotland. Our caravan was being towed by a venerable Rolls-Royce; a proud, stiff-backed vehicle, which, in its hey-day during the twenties, had conveyed some patrician dowager once a week round two or three of the better shops.

In its elderly state of social decline it was certainly not at all the sort of vehicle to pull a caravan down a country lane rutted with grass-topped troughs of mud. The old car slid and juddered in protest, until finally it won its way. The caravan had to be unhitched and squelched into position by four pairs of wearily inexpert hands.

It was, however, something to have secured half a caravan-hold in the lands of Lennox. At least we now enjoyed a position of some advantage in bidding for a more permanent home. During the next eighteen months my wife and I inspected, hopefully, something like twenty properties. These ranged from vast deserted mansions—"desirable, easily run family homes", for which only a "modest" price was being asked in return for a quick sale—to tumble-down cottages harbouring various combinations of wood-worm, dry-rot and common or garden wet-rot.

The most unusual house in this collection of might-have-beens was a villa at Fintry, a hilly village in the foothills of the Campsie range, put up for sale by one of the best-known property agents in the West of Scotland. One Saturday afternoon we de-bussed in the main street of Fintry, a bleak linear village. Angry little mutterings of people clustered round the bus stop waiting for a bus back to Glasgow.

We soon discovered the reason for their discontent. Tempted by the enticing description of the villa, their natural suspicion of property agents lulled by the high reputation of the firm concerned, between thirty and forty would-be country dwellers had come out to Fintry to look at a hovel that had been lived in by a hermit for half a century. Since the hermit's demise the roof had collapsed, a beam had crashed through the first floor and the outer walls had started to crumble. In the middle of this dripping wreckage stood a new bath, unconnected and forlorn, which a relative of the deceased had ordered, apparently with the idea of modernising the ruin.

Eventually, after long months of unrewarding search, a cottage fell, metaphorically speaking, into our laps. We were sitting round a local fireside when a contractor called to discuss the felling of some trees. "I don't suppose you know anyone who wants to buy a cottage in Gartocharn, by any chance?" asked the contractor. "I want rid of one, quickly."

Fate does not do that sort of thing twice, so the man got an answer with an alacrity that surprised him. A few days later we had a home in the land of my ancestors.

For twelve hundred pounds we acquired Fir Tree Cottage. It had a tiny living-room, a bedroom, a boxroom, a stone-floored kitchen and a rudimentary stone-floored bathroom. The water was heated by an old-fashioned back-fired boiler. Cooking and lighting were fuelled by paraffin. We moved to Gartocharn in September 1950 with a young baby in my wife's arms, and another on the way.

The North of Scotland Hydro Electric Board already had plans to bring electricity to our village, so these primitive conditions had to be endured only for about a year. Four years later we moved round the corner to the larger Rose Cottage, which we promptly re-christened "Corraith", after the Innellan holiday home of the thirties. Perhaps because our two youngest children were born there, it has remained my favourite among our many homes.

During the war the cottage had been let to the violinist David MacCallum, leader of the pre-war Scottish Orchestra and later of Sir Thomas Beecham's Royal Philharmonic. There, the musician's actor son, also David, had been brought up. The cottage possessed one large room, converted from what had formerly been an adjacent joiner's workshop. This became my study, and I lined it from floor to ceiling with books. It also housed my first long-playing gramophone, and in it, in my double reviewing capacity as Gavin Brock of the *Scottish Field* and M. L. of *The Bulletin*, I listened to the first ten L.P.s to be issued in this country. Two of them are still in my large record collection, the building of which has been my main hobby over the years.

Dogs continued to play an important part in our lives. Blotto, the first dachshund, was joined by a companion, Bunkum. Dachshunds are unfortunately subject to a disease which in old age ossifies their spines, causing paralysis. Both Blotto and Bunkum eventually succumbed to this, so we decided to change to a more hardy variety. We settled for basset hounds, also long and comically mournful, but stronger in the spine. Hector, our first basset, came from Beverley, in Yorkshire. Soon he was joined by Peter, who arrived by rail in a crate from Bournemouth. I drove with the children to the cavernous depths of the parcels department of Glasgow's Central Station. There, his crate was duly identified and prised apart. The railwayman who did the opening gazed in astonishment at the small white wriggling length that walked out, and exclaimed: "Goad! A white dachshund! A've nivver seen yin o'thae before!"

The "white dachshund" grew up, but developed an awkward taste for the sport of tossing hens into the air. To enable him to evade certain execution, we gave him away to an innocent-looking new owner in a henless area. She turned out to be a dog breeder, he a champion. His life thereafter was profitably spent in what is doubtless the happiest of dog circumstances.

George Bruce came to stay at "Corraith", and like most of our friends thought well of Hector; so well, in fact, that he described Hector, his manner of acquisition and his habitat to his friend (later also mine) the poet Edwin Morgan. So accurate and vivid was George's description that Morgan then "immortalised" the animal in his much anthologised poem "An Addition to the Family".

Another visitor to "Corraith" was the English poet George Barker, who arrived unannounced with Dom Mores. Barker, a man rich in poetic ideas but weak in the organisation of his invention, had done the round of the Scottish poets. He repaid their hospitality with some light-hearted versified mockery in "Scottish Bards and an English Reviewer", setting the piece in Edinburgh, where he claimed to have seen:

> ". . . strutting up and
> Down the Mile
> The uncrowned Laird
> Of Scottish style
> —Is it a Scott
> He's walking with?-
> The only kilted
> Kiwi—Smith
> There's a Lindsay this
> And a Lindsay that
> There's a Craig tit
> And a Craig tat

There's a Robert Tweedle
And a Robert Tum
And a Campell looking
A bit glum
—They are all there
Chests stuck out
Pouring down gallons
Of Irish stout
And with the whiskey
Flowing free
Damning the Sassanach
Lickpenny.
'Why dinna ye
Lairn frae us?
Canna ye see
We're marvellous?"

Gartocharn was a wonderful place for children to grow up in. We were able to keep ponies—indeed, I became co-founder of the Loch Lomond branch of the Pony Club—and to swim in summer among the sand-fringed bays of the Loch and in the pools of the River Endrick.

Some of the local farmers were none too particular about the efficacy of their fencing. On more than one occasion we were roused by the village policeman in the middle of the night to retrieve the horses from a narrow back-road; or, worse still, the garden of someone else's property. This was an imposition my wife found particularly galling when I was away from home, since she regarded horses as dangerous at both ends and uncomfortable in the middle.

On one particularly dark winter's night the friend and neighbour who had first introduced me to horse-riding—I nicknamed him "The Expert"—called me on the telephone about one o'clock in the morning. In the cold darkness we set together out to recover our straying mounts. We searched several fields in vain; then saw green eyes staring at us from the middle of a more distant field. Carefully we stalked towards those hidden watchers, halters in hand; as we got near, with a noiseless flurry the green eyes suddenly switched off. We had been stalking, not the missing horses but a herd of startled roe deer.

We bought and sold our ponies at the spring and autumn Kelso horse shows, where our visits were not without adventures. Buying a pony or a horse is, of course, an event of some significance in a man's life: of much greater significance, for instance, than buying a motor car. While it is important to be sure that both are working properly in the purely mechanical sense there the comparison ends. However affectionately a man may come to regard his car, he does not expect it to respond: nor does he have to stroke it under the nearside front wing, whispering gently into its bonnet, in order to ensure that it does not buck or sidle in evasive circles as he tries to establish himself in a position of control. Horse-buying is therefore a business which creates considerable anticipatory excitement.

We set out early in the morning from Loch Lomondside and arrived at Kelso about half-past nine. Already, so many cars had filed through the gate into the field which was doing duty as a parking-place that the single-tracked, wooden-posted pass was a phutter of mud, through which wheels whirred and squelched unsteadily. But, miraculously, no car stuck in the mud-churn, and we soon joined the long lines of tightly-packed vehicles inside. Horses and ponies stood tethered round the perimeter of the show-ground. Here, a hunter was being put through his paces; there, a prospective buyer was venturing a timid canter. In the centre of the field stood a wooden grandstand overlooking the main ring, in which finely-groomed horses of blood and breeding were being shown. A little to the right there was roped off a smaller ring, without a grandstand. Here, less fashionably overlooked, sturdy little ponies were proving their points, many of them ridden by children. Both these performances had their clusters of admirers, but the biggest crowd—the kind of crowd that drifts from one focal-point of interest to another—had newly knotted itself around the long racks containing second-hand saddlery and equipment, which an auctioneer was putting up for sale in a patter of ceaseless rapidity. We joined this central crowd.

I had only meant to buy one animal; a pony for one of my daughters. A two-year-old Shetland gelding called Snip seemed exactly the sort of pony we were after. (The name may have derived from a fondness for chewing buttons, but as with so many problems of etymology, this solution is open to doubt.) He had a late number in the catalogue. Once we had decided that Snip's reference, qualities and appearance were satisfactory, there only remained the question of his price.

In due course, he was led into the ring. A bid was made: I topped it: another was made: I topped it again. Suddenly I felt full of a curious exhilaration. The fact that every lift of my catalogue meant parting with an extra guinea ceased to have any real meaning for me. I wanted Snip, and meant to have him. Fortunately my rival's resolve slackened after another bid, and I acquired my first pony at a still reasonable price.

But the sense of exhilaration persisted. The next pony came into the ring—a four-month-old Exmoor called Bruntsie. (He had been bred on Edinburgh's Bruntsfield links.) Bruntsie had a soft nose, a shaggy mane, and big, appealing eyes. He also carried a prize-winner's ticket. Once again the bidding started. Once again I raised my catalogue: more discreetly now, because I noticed that my wife had joined the crowd, and was standing at the other side of the ring.

"Knocked down to the gentleman in the kilt," declaimed the auctioneer in stentorian tones. At this, my wife's eyes searched me out, a look of horror draining away her previous expression of interested amiability.

However, "facts are chiels that winna ding". In spite of wifely recriminations, there was really little to be said; the only problem now was how to get two ponies from Kelso to Loch Lomondside. I was astonished and relieved to discover that British Railways had anticipated such requirements, and had, in fact, laid on a horse-box which could work the ponies' transportation over-night.

I was thus more experienced the following year when I went back to Kelso to buy a horse for myself. Two of the beasts I fancied quickly soared into price-realms where no amount of exhilaration could possibly support me. Another turned out to be a shambling stumbler. A fourth had all the virtues, so far as I or my friend The Expert could discover, but had been withdrawn from the ring because he had failed to make his reserved price. I was frightened out of buying him privately by the blarney of the broguing Irishman rolling out the beast's merits. Finally, I bought a staid Highland garron, whom I promptly re-christened Cimarosa, but who refused to answer to any other name than the one he came with, Mousie. With Mousie, I made my way once more up to the station.

A huge blood stallion was about to be put into a waiting horse-box. When the horse-box was made ready, the stallion decided upon a policy of non-co-operation. It took a deal of dangerous pulling, coaxing and sweating to get the reluctant stallion safely emboxed. The whole performance filled me with superior amusement. I glanced at my garron's shaggy mane and solemn eye, and remarked to my friend, The Expert, that a horse as difficult to handle as that stallion must be an insufferable nuisance to its owner. The Expert only smiled.

Another horse-box was made ready. I led Cimarosa/Mousie to the foot of the ramp. In an instant, he reached a verdict similar to the stallion's. Mousie's resistance was more prolonged and, perhaps an account of his Highland blood, more doggedly determined. Twice as much pulling, pushing, coaxing and sweating were called for before our object was achieved. I could hardly conceal my embarrassment from my friend, but The Expert only smiled.

At Fir Tree Cottage I had to be content with a narrow lean-to study which I had built against the back wall of the house. In this I wrote the first version of my study of Burns, and a considerable number of poems. The first edition of *Robert Burns: The Man; His Work; The Legend* contained several inaccuracies, and I was glad to have the opportunity of substantially rewriting it before other publishers took it over for second and subsequent editions.

So much has been written about Scotland's national bard, and so deeply is a folk-apprehension of his life and work absorbed into the blood-stream of the Scots people even if they never actually read his poetry, that an author who rushes into the field of Burnsiana without the fullest and most detailed study is indeed unwise.

More books about Burns have been produced than about any author except Shakespeare. This inherited popularity, embracing some fact and much myth, once again faced me when I was invited six months before that event to compile a *Burns Encyclopedia* for the 1959 bi-centenary. I worked at feverish speed with a great deal of help from my wife, then carrying our fourth child, to ensure that my copy met the required date-line. Under such conditions errors inevitably crept in. One set of galley proofs containing corrections for two letters of the alphabet got lost in the post between Gartocharn and London. Much additional research for the second and third editions enabled me not only to put things right, but to produce a companion to the reading of Burns's life and work which David Daiches, writing in *The Scottish Review* in 1980 was kind enough to describe as "one of the most useful books about Burns ever published"

The publicity resulting from the Lallans controversy had brought me into contact with virtually every Scottish writer of any significance, most of whom had strong feelings on the language issue one way or the other. Following Maclellan's publication of *The Enemies of Love* (1946), my first book of poems in English (as opposed to New Apocalypseese), I had first met James Bridie (Dr Osborne Mavor), who agreed to Robert Kemp's suggestion that my name might be put forward for a Rockefeller Atlantic Award. These awards of £300 were meant to free a young writer for one year from the more pressing daily chores of earning a living, although even in the pre-inflationary days of the forties they could not support economic independence.

On 31st August 1946, Neil Gunn wrote:

"I had Bridie here a couple of weeks ago and we were talking about Gaitens.* I see he has got an Award. I know nothing about the business, but if my name is of any use to you, please use it. I would take the line that you are not only one of our promising creative writers, but that you do also possess a constructive quality in letters which has more than a personal usefulness. With so much current exclusiveness about, not to speak of sword-swallowers or flame-throwers, a certain Catholic appreciation of values, a cool Greek sanity, has its points!"

When the award was announced Douglas Young wrote:

"I was blyth tae see by The Scotsman that they hae gien ye the hantle siller that comes owre the Atlantic, or whatever way it comes. I howp ye may mak guid uis o't and the leisur it suld bring. The Scotsman's Log scryvit something about ye scryvan a novel allanerlie i the Lallans, whilk is an idea I like weel. Uisful tae wald be a libretto for an opera by Thorpe Davie, and a wheen smaaboukit novels for the diurnals and periodicals. I the makin o verse, I dinna think onibody suild be owre gleg at scryvin original wark; they suldna ettle sair at it, but juist let the blads scryve theirsels in their ain time. For the maistery of technique it wald be as well tae mak owersets frae ither leids, and namely for tunes, sae the business doesna gang splairgean aa owre the place, the wey Sydney's effusions dae."

Sydney Goodsir Smith—he of the "splairgean" effusions—sent me his "heartiest congratulations on becoming a fellow recipient". Sir Alexander Gray thought the distinction "very

---

* Edward Gaitens (1897–1966), author of the moving Glasgow novel *Dance of the Apprentices* (1948), and an earlier Atlantic Award recipient.

gratifying", and one that later on would be "a highly honourable achievement to look back upon". Joyce and I celebrated with a splendid lunch in the Victorian-tiled Oyster Bar of Edinburgh's Café Royal in the chance but pleasant company of Wilfred Taylor, then a columnist on *The Scotsman*.

I used the time thus bought not to write a novel in Scots, as the imaginative interviewer from *The Scotsman* alleged I had intended, but to attempt a verse play in Scots on one of James Macpherson's Ossianic prose poems, *Fingal and Comala*. This was twice broadcast by the BBC and later staged by James Sutherland at the Scottish Festival which I organised for the Farquharsons of Invercauld, Braemar during the summer of 1953.

Of the first night, *The Scotsman* critic observed: "The story, from an old Gaelic legend, tells of the tragic love of Fingal, heroic leader of the Fennians, and Comala, daughter of the King of Inistore (Orkney).

"Lindsay's poetic dramatisation is in very broad Scots, a medium which suits the rugged nature of his theme. If his interpretation errs at all, it is in that he seems at first to 'out-Scot the Scots'. But that may be due to the fact that the Scots tongue today is too Anglicised, or that real Scots seldom appears on the modern stage.

"The tragic theme was cleverly relieved by the introduction of an aside by three soldiers complaining in rhymed couplets of their lot in the army.

"However, the language, unaccustomed as many in the audience were to it, was easily understood. This was largely due to admirable performances by Meta Forrest, who made a convincing and fiery Comala, George Main as Fingal and Alex Scott as Hidallan."

The *Glasgow Herald* drama critic took a more academic line: "Mr T. S. Eliot, in one of his latest essays, 'Poetry and Drama', writing of the conditions poetic drama must fulfil if it is to justify itself, says—'it must justify itself dramatically, and not merely be fine poetry shaped into a dramatic form. From this it follows that no play should be written in verse for which prose is *dramatically* adequate. And from this it follows, again, that the audience, its attention held by the dramatic situation between the characters, should be too intent upon the play to be wholly conscious of the medium.'

"Mr Maurice Lindsay's 'Fingal and Comala' . . . fulfils Mr

Eliot's conditions . . . Listening to it one is, of course, conscious of the verse, but gradually the drama predominates, as it should, though it cannot be doubted that this drama is intensified by the form in which it is cast''.

On the face of it, obviously the piece was reasonably well received. Nevertheless, the play raised doubts in my mind that could not easily be removed. It was one thing to deploy a literary Scots on an ancient legend, but quite another to relate it to modern circumstances. No Scottish playwright—not even Robert Maclellan, the author of the most famous Scots play of our time, *Jamie the Saxt*—has, in fact, managed to write a play in anything like a full canon of Scots dealing with contemporary issues other than at the basic level of what is sometimes unfortunately, and archaically, dubbed ''working-class''; a level, howsoever called, certainly not that at which the great affairs of a nation are decided. Furthermore, nobody spoke like Fingal or Comala, even making due allowance for the fact that mythological hero-figures are unlikely to be encountered in Leith Walk or Sauchiehall Street.

I entered upon a period of several years during which I experienced a crisis of poetic confidence. Scots was not the tongue I spoke. Nor, for that matter, was it even the language that the Lallans ''high priest'', Hugh MacDiarmid, spoke. Though he still urged others to use it for literary purposes, he had in fact, long since ceased writing in it himself, and for similar reasons to those that troubled me; the realisation that a language whose development had been arrested at the end of the eighteenth century simply could not cope with the nuances of life in the much more complicated and technical twentieth century. MacDiarmid's arguments in favour of the future of Scots thus seemed increasingly specious. Eventually, I took a conscious decision to write only in the language I spoke daily.

Throughout the period of the Lallans controversy the Orcadian Eric Linklater remained amiably sceptical about the future of the language. The Highlander Neil Gunn was completely convinced that it simply did not have any. Bridie never committed himself publicly on the issue.

A shy man, inarticulate in company until he had something pressing or witty to say, Bridie became a near neighbour of mine at Gartocharn when he bought the estate of Finnich Malaise. He rarely stayed for more than a few years in one home. His next move was to Craigendoran, still his home at the time of his sudden and comparatively early death in Edinburgh during the summer of 1951.

I only once saw Bridie thoroughly relaxed in public. He was in the company of the Glasgow novelists Guy McCrone and George Blake at a British Council lunch in Glasgow's Central Hotel in honour of an Italian critic, Dr Bachelli. McCrone a charming man and an enthusiastic singer with a cast in one eye and rather an effete manner, had somewhat improbably, played Aeneas in Erik Chisolm's British pioneering quasi-amateur production of Berlioz's *The Trojans* in Glasgow in March 1935. Guy took to novel-writing late in life and never wholly overcame a certain slip-shoddiness in his literary style, although his trilogy, *Wax Fruit*, together with its sequels, captures the "feel" of the rise and fall of Glasgow's industrial prosperity with an evocative sense of atmosphere unequalled by any other writer on the subject.

Similar gifts were also possessed by George Blake. At that time "Beefy Blake", as MacDiarmid unkindly called him, remained a novelist unread by me because of the poet's lofty disrecommendation. Many years later I discovered that Blake's saga of Garvel—his thin disguise for the town of Greenock—is an even more remarkable account of the development and decline of Clydeside life from the days of the sailing ship to the advent of the Second World War. McCrone achieved memorability and distinction because of the organisation and background veracity of the subject-matter of his stories rather than through the manner of the telling. Blake, though also at times a little off-hand in matters of style, made a serious literary contribution to the Scottish Renaissance Movement and was, indeed, the only significant novelist of the thirties and forties who faced up to the realities of the increasing and irreversible urbanisation of Scotland.

McCrone's Glasgow trilogy has more than once been reprinted, but Blake's novels remain out of print. A reassessment of his work is long overdue. Perhaps it will follow when Scotland's television drama producers realise that in the work of both men lies potentially compelling T.V. material.

My closest friend among the older generation of Scottish writers was Neil Gunn. He accepted the dedication of *At The Wood's Edge*, the book so much disliked by Young. Gunn read it nursing a broken right arm, and on 18th May, 1948, having recovered, wrote: "At the first reading I was particularly taken with your Bairnsongs. Seemed to me to have a rhythm and music which I would urge you to cultivate. You seem to me to have so much pith that you needn't be afraid of music. You'll never—for better or for worse—be able to sing away into sweet nothings what you have to say! So lapse into wonder and music at every inspiration."

An attack on the book by Albert Mackie in an Edinburgh paper led Neil Gunn to write, on 14th September, with his usual perception: "I was disappointed, perhaps because I grow weary of a sort of flying for its own sake. Not but that you are guilty of it yourself. The trouble is that it doesn't get us very far. From Mackie's review I got no idea of what is positive in your work— your often brilliant images, your basic strength, your tough texture . . . and your 'indispensable air of consequence'. You have the authentic mind of the poet. I salute the primary quality in you."

But he was not uncritical either, confirming both Young's adverse reactions to my ease with Lallans, and thus strengthening my impending decision that Lallans could not be my final poet's language. On one occasion Gunn protested: ". . . your strength is not coming through clearly enough. I do not think this is *altogether* a matter of my unfamiliarity with so many of the words. It's as if the words themselves were so new to you (in the sense of being rediscovered, if you like) that you've left them to do much of the transmuting or refining work that should have made you sweat in a more familiar or worn tongue . . . You are more concerned with words and thoughts than the thing that steals the senses away."

He had another, more general point of equal validity, which applied to many Scots-writing poets: "In most Lallans poetry that I have read there is a tendency to set a poem and its images against the shape of eternity . . . It becomes, when done often by so many, a sort of indulgent engiantism. Anyway, my own simple reaction is that if the poet were sufficiently concerned about, sufficiently loved, the wild flower or face of which he is singing, he would forget all about the wider spaces. If he loves sufficiently, with enough gratitude and wonder, eternity would find itself, without mention, in the face or the flower. In short, let us be simple, for it is very difficult."

I visited Neil on several occasions at his various Highland

homes. In the very early days of television, shortly before the death of his wife, Daisy, George Bruce and I made a film about Gunn's work. Later, George was to shoot a memorable film for general distribution when colour had supplanted black-and-white.

By the time I knew him, Neil had already written his best work. He was never really able to come to convincing terms with the urban scene, or with the significance of the increasing resort to violence that was already beginning to stain our society. In a sense he seemed not quite to "belong" to the post-second war world. I remember a hair-raising drive with him through Inverness during the evening rush-hour on his way to his home at North Kessock. His handling of the car was determinedly anxious. To cover up his driving shortcomings, he kept up a stream of amusing anecdotes about the Highland way of life, making his concentration on the task of driving even more tenuous. Towards the end of his life, when a widower and in declining health, he retreated behind the mysticisms of Zen Buddhism, an area into which I could not follow him.

Most of the verses in English I was now writing were quickly destroyed, usually because they arose cerebrally out of patriotic abstractions that had no basis in experienced reality. I therefore decided that the only thing to do was to lay aside poetry for a time and concentrate on discovering the Scotland that actually existed.

The opportunity came through a chance remark by James Fergusson, my old Lallans adversary. His conscience was troubling him because he had signed a contract with the publisher Robert Hale to produce for that firm's County Books series a survey of the Lowlands of Scotland. Circumstances had prevented him from fulfilling his undertaking. Might he put up my name in his stead? He did, and on his recommendation Robert Hale invited me to London to discuss the details over dinner.

Hale was a delightful man. Before setting up his own firm he had worked for Jarrolds, when he "discovered" the novelist James Leslie Mitchell, later to achieve fame as "Lewis Grassic Gibbon". Most of Mitchell's early novels were not commercially successful, but Hale believed in his potential. It was a matter of some bitterness to him that with the first taste of success, Mitchell showed his gratitude by transferring to another publisher at the first wave of a cheque book.

From my point of view the happy outcome of that dinner was the beginning of a lifelong association with the firm of Hale, after Robert Hale's death taken over by his son, John.

The Lowlands of Scotland was to be a survey taking in topography, history and literature. One could not possibly ask for a better brief to discover one's own country. For some years I had been a regular contributor to the *Scottish Field*, a popular monthly then edited by the energetic Sydney Harrison, who left the editorial chair to run his own successful printing business and a chain of Renfrewshire newspapers. A freelance journalist divides editors and producers into two categories: those who listen to an idea and then proceed to counter it with every imaginable objection; and those who seize on the idea before its exposition has been completed, already eager to propel it towards implementation. Sydney was an exhilarating example of the latter variety, and under him the *Scottish Field* achieved a breadth of interest and quality, to say nothing of a level of circulation not since matched by any of his successors.

I suggested to him that I might write a series of articles amounting to a county-by-county survey. He at once agreed. I began with those Lowland counties that had to be covered for my book, varied occasionally by a Highland county. The articles were beautifully illustrated with photographs by George Alden. In due course much expanded, they became the chapters of *The Lowlands of Scotland*. Robert Hale readily agreed that the work should run to two volumes. Twice updated, it has been continuously in print for more than thirty years.

At Fir Tree Cottage there was a happy renewal of my wartime friendship with James Pope Hennessey. In 1951, alarmed by Russian militancy, the Government of the day called up ex-servicemen for updated retraining. James and I found ourselves attending a War Office course in an 18th-century slave dealer's mansion near Devizes, Wiltshire. It was a comical situation, seasoned officers who had run the army's nerve centre during the war finding themselves being lectured on how to make the system work by youngsters who knew it only as a peacetime quasi-civil-service department.

One of the educational diversions arranged for our benefit was a visit to the School of Infantry, where we witnessed a "live" exercise called "The Battalion in Attack". This performance created conditions of so much explosive noise, smell, smoke and

flames as would have taxed beyond endurance the aural resilience of all except the teenage discotheque habitué. We sat
together in bemused distress on wooden benches. Suddenly, a
lull in the infernal racket was broken by James's languid drawl:

"Maurice, I've come to the conclusion that I don't much like the
brutal and licentious soldiery."

James came to stay in our tiny cottage at Gartocharn, near Loch
Lomondside, when my wife and I then had two small children.
For years he had relied every night on sleeping pills. My
daughters found him delightful. Protesting good-humouredly,
he romped about, displaying unsuspected invention and energy
in devising ways to amuse them; so much so, in fact, that as he
was leaving us, he confessed that for the first time in years,
physical exhaustion had made his sleeping pills unnecessary.

Sadly, as the years passed he took increasingly to drink. His
study of Trollope showed all his accustomed sensitivity and
critical perception, but he was unable to revise the final draft of
his book on Stevenson, published posthumously, for he was
found, brutally murdered, in his London home on Burns Day,
1974.

During the late forties and early fifties I saw a great deal of the
composer Francis George Scott. I had busied myself finding grant
assistance for the volume of his work published by the Saltire
Society under the title *Thirty-five Scottish Songs*, and with helping
to secure a sufficient number of subscribers. In these days there
were many merry evenings at Munro Road, with Scott singing
and shouting his way through his latest songs, sometimes after
his nephew by marriage, George Bruce, and I had recorded
something from him for our programme *Scottish Life and Letters*. It
is a matter of great regret that the only recording preserved by the
B.B.C. was the final one made not long before Scott entered into
the mental decline that increasingly distanced him from the
world around him.

During the fifties—and indeed, until she settled in America—I
also knew, and worked with, the composer Thea Musgrave.

I first met her while she was living during vacations with her
mother in Edinburgh, where mostly she had been brought up,
and studying with Nadia Boulanger in Paris. Like so many
Boulanger pupils, Thea's early style had a decidedly bright Gallic
edge part of which was a dryly attractive lyricism. It was
employed most effectively in her setting for soprano voice and

piano of some of my verses for children, *A Suite of Bairnsangs,* which Margaret Fraser first sang at the Braemar Festival, and which is now in the repertoire of many British sopranos, albeit often with the Englished version of the words.

Musical journalism still provided my regular bread and butter. The tabloid pictorial family paper *The Bulletin,* whose music critic I had become in 1946, had been founded in 1916 as a companion paper to the *Glasgow Herald* particularly directed at the views of women readers. It covered a wide range of interests in easily assimilable form, and by the nineteen-forties had as many men readers as women.

There is obviously a need for academic scholarship and the leisured criticism of the denizens of the campus. Art cannot survive, however, unless it has popular support. Popularisers who widen the imagination of readers, listeners or viewers fill the unofficial role of "teachers" of the masses. Although only a comparative minority may pay attention, or benefit, the increasing minority who love the arts must be added to the gathering, historical majority in reckoning response. Since 1786, for instance, there can have been few nights when Mozart's *The Marriage of Figaro* has not been playing somewhere in the world. Add to the sum total of these un-countable audiences the even greater number of people listening to broadcasts or recordings of the work in our own century, and the sheer indefinable size of the historical majority becomes obvious. It is, indeed, a majority that puts the true statistical significance of millionth "golden disc" pop hits, with at most a life of a few weeks or months, into proper perspective. Even by pop standards, none other than Joseph Haydn hit the target of the millionth disc a few years ago with the Decca company's recording of his complete symphonies under Antal Dorati.

As music critic of a popular daily paper, a television presenter, literary historian, journalist and conservationist, throughout my professional life I have been an unashamed populariser. There are, of course, two kinds of popularisers, and it is important to distinguish between them. There are those who think the achieving of popularity for their product more important in itself than the integrity of what they are seeking to popularise; and those who regard the work of popularisation as a matter of packaging and presentation, insisting that the qualitative standards inherent in the material must remain inviolate. It is to this latter category that I belong.

Soon after I became music critic of *The Bulletin*, I found myself in conflict with outworn traditions and the complacent acceptance of the third rate. Percy Gordon, my former teacher of the thirties, was then still music critic of the *Glasgow Herald*, a post he had held for more than quarter of a century. He disapproved strongly of his pupil's appointment to the *Herald*'s sister paper on the grounds that a critic should have behind him a long and wide experience of listening. He was not, of course, aware of the extent to which I had made use of my wartime opportunities for hearing music. Undoubtedly, though, he had point. To set against it there was, however, my refusal to acquiesce in his acceptance of what I called "the tradition of pretence".

A famous pianist gave a recital in St Andrew's Hall, during the course of which not one but three strings of the instrument broke. Next morning, I suggested in *The Bulletin* that it was high time Glasgow secured for itself a concert grand that measured up to international standards. A director of Paterson's, the firm of piano sellers who hired the instrument, wrote to the paper protesting that I had broken a long-standing convention "whereby the instrument itself is never mentioned". Percy Gordon shook his head sadly and hoped that I would soon "learn".

There was worse to come. The old Scottish Orchestra, precursor of the present Scottish National Orchestra, could keep itself in existence for only six months of the year. It was completely impossible for a part-time orchestra of this sort to achieve standards comparable to those maintained by any of the great permanent English orchestras. An occasion arrived when the Scottish Orchestra gave its usual Saturday concert in St Andrew's Hall to be followed on the next Monday by the touring Hallé Orchestra playing an almost identical programme. I drew a comparison between the two performances, much to the native orchestra's disadvantage.

The directors of the Scottish Orchestra were furious. (Years later, one of them told me that in those days they "would willingly have paid me to stay away!") Percy Gordon wrote sententiously to say that had I been within reach, he would have liked to take me over his knee and spank me! "Any fool can see that the Hallé is a better orchestra than the Scottish, but it doesn't help our own orchestra for you to say so in *The Bulletin*."

I was not in the least interested in "helping our own orchestra" preserve its poor standard; only in helping to shape public opinion towards demanding its replacement by a permanent orchestra; and to this end I waged a steady campaign in *The Bulletin*."

Scotland's acceptance of a second-rate orchestra, coupled with an outdated but persistently snobbish preference for musicians with a mittel-European name, led to the appointment after the war of a succession of second-rate conductors. The best of them was probably Karl Rankl, the first post-war conductor at Covent Garden Opera House and a good orchestral trainer. He had major but unattainable ambitions as a composer, in which role he deployed a kind of Mahlerian/early Schönberg harmonic palate. Together, Rankl and I made a train journey from Glasgow to Aberdeen. There, between rehearsals, he was to record a radio interview for a series called "The Conductor Speaks". We chatted amiably during the first part of the journey. As the train approached Brechin, suddenly he leant forward, placed a heavy hand on my knee and said: "Meester Leensay, I want you to write me a life of Chreest." "Chreest?" I said, momentarily puzzled. Then the enormity of the suggestion dawned, and with what I am sure was quite the wrong inflection, replied, "Oh Christ!" The vision of a rival "Messiah" from the pen of the man responsible for the gargantuanly boring symphony I had sat through the previous week appalled me. Politely I excused myself as being quite unfit for so elevated a task.

Apart, therefore, from the question of the orchestra, a subsidiary campaign had to be fought for the acceptance of a Scottish conductor. This, too, was achieved in 1959, with the appointment of Mr (now Sir) Alexander Gibson, whom I first got to know when he was assistant conductor with the B.B.C. Scottish Orchestra. Looking back on all that this gifted, charming and unspoiled man has done for Scottish music-making—not only in building up the Scottish National Orchestra to international concert-giving and recording standards, but also in the creation of Scottish Opera—I do not think that the aggressive brashness I showed in *The Bulletin* was altogether misplaced.

Critics constantly come under attack for their opinions or pronouncements. By what "right" does a critic praise or condemn? And anyway, is the critic really necessary?

The daily reviewer, as opposed to the more leisured academic critic, has an immediate duty to the readers of the newspaper that employs him. Readers want to know whether such-and-such a production or a performance is, in the critic's opinion, worth expending the price of a seat upon, and how near or how far from the playwright's or composer's intention the staging of a play or the playing of a symphony may have been.

We are passing through a phase in which the wishes of even the greatest dead dramatist or composer may be set aside as mere raw material for a trendy producer or a virtuoso conductor to wreak his irrelevant phantasies upon. In the playhouse, I have seen Hamlet turned into a gibbering idiot, heard long stretches of Shakespeare's lines maimed or rewritten, and watched Rosenkrantz and Gildenstern metamorphosed into pawing homosexuals. In the opera house, I have witnessed the Baron in *Traviata* meaninglessly empurpled into a cardinal amid scenes of simulated debauchery distracting attention from the music; *Fidelio*, that grand salute to the concept of freedom turned into a Marxist hymn; Rigoletto made to jest in a transvestite brothel and Mussolini produce his lowering and improbable appearance in the church scene in *Tosca*; all in the sacred name of interpretation!

Perhaps there is nothing inherently new in the misplaced exhibitionism of producers. Fashion goes in waves. In eighteenth-century England, Shakespeare's plays were systematically bowdlerised to suit its powdered and pomaded tastes, and in the nineteenth, pious people sought to purge Mozart's operas of their fancied sexual improprieties. I have always been convinced that the critic's first duty is to stand apart from such trivialising oddities, and uphold the intentions of the dead playwright or composer, no longer in a position to defend himself. The good critic should occupy that area of judgement in which creative integrity is the ultimate touchstone.

In dealing with acknowledged masterpieces the critic, by virtue of study and experience, should know what he is talking about. Where the first performance of a new work is concerned, especially if it is a symphony rather than a play—literature's dependence on the current tools of everyday speech usually keeps playwrights moderately in touch with meaningful terms of reference—a critic can only hope to offer a first impression, which he may very well wish to modify, one way or the other, after subsequent hearings.

The recurrent question of whether or not critics are really

"necessary" is really of little consequence. They are there, and have been almost since Daniel Defoe established the concept of the modern newspaper. Much of what passes for reviewing in the more openly popular Press is undoubtedly uninformed, but few of the readers of the bare-breasted tabloids are likely to be much interested in artistic criticism anyway.

The views of a critic, competent or otherwise, remain no more than one man's opinion; useful if the man is known to be perceptive, but about as influential as the buzzing of a mosquito if he is not. Unsigned reviews are nearly always worthless, however well written, since (in Scotland at any rate) they are too often simply vehicles designed to carry the hostility of an opponent or the puffing of a friend. An opinion is only worth as much as the known standing, impartiality and authority of whomsoever utters it.

My early days as a music critic involved me in the heady delights of the newly-formed Edinburgh International Festival of Music and Drama, founded in 1947 as a late-summer three week cultural celebration. It is impossible to exaggerate the impact the Festival made upon us in that long-ago sunny summer, when Europe was still in the process of dragging itself out of the shadows of war. Here, in prim, grey Edinburgh, civilisation had once again found courage triumphantly to reassert itself; at the highest level, through such delights as the magical *Marriage of Figaro* presented by the Glyndebourne company; at a more mundane level, in the surprisingly imaginative pre-war standard of cuisine offered by the Festival Club, for more than thirty-five years located in the elegant eighteenth-century Assembly Rooms in George Street, but now, alas, elsewhere!

There were those—and at the time, up to a point, I sympathised with them—who argued vehemently that the introduction of such a concentration of alien music and drama must have a deleterious effect on the native product. Almost forty years on, such fears can be seen to have been unfounded. The betartaned bagpipes-and-Gaelic haggis-only brigade have long since been routed. Instead, we have enjoyed memorable Festival productions from Scottish Opera and the Citizens' Theatre; seen Scottish plays by Sir David Lyndsay and James Bridie; and heard the music of Francis George Scott, Thea Musgrave and Iain Hamilton, all of it holding its head high in an international context.

A few weeks after Tyrone Guthrie's first triumphant production of *The Thrie Estatis*, I was persuaded into the green room at the Stevenson Hall, Glasgow, to be introduced to a Mexican pianist who had expressed a wish to see me.

"Sir David Leensay," said she, wringing my hand, "I thought your play was wuunderful. I am so glad to meet you."

"Well . . . er . . . I'm not actually Sir David," said I: "he died about four hundred years ago, I'm Maurice Lindsay."

"Ah . . . so! Then Sir David was one of your ancestors?"

"I know of no evidence to the contrary," was the best I could manage.

Since catching my Mahlerian enthusiasm from Alec Robertson, I found myself increasingly at odds with the current patronising view of this composer as a vapid splurger around in an overstocked musical paint-store. When my festival elders and betters—and they usually made sure we locals knew fully the extent of the betterment their journeying from London to "the provinces" conferred—were still pursuing this line, I proclaimed in the modest pages of *The Bulletin*: "Mahler marvellously captures the *angst* of the post-atomic generation, and will, in time, become as popular a composer as Tchaikovsky or Dvořák." He has, and he is.

Another of my enthusiasms was for the music of Carl Nielsen, discovered through the arrival in our household of a charming and cultivated *au pair* Danish girl, a happy event that also led in due course to long years of friendship with her and her husband and family, the Nellemans.

In those days, British music-lovers with ears attuned to a Nordic sound could only accept the plaintive bitter-sweetness of Grieg's miniatures, or the sombrely exultant brooding of Sibelius. I became a Nielsen champion long before the generous musical open-heartedness and forceful inventiveness of the Danish composer led to his acceptance as a figure of world stature. After the Festival appearance of the Danish State Radio Orchestra on August 29th, 1950, a visit sponsored by the enlightened Carlsberg Foundation during which three concerts were given, at the third of which Nielsen's Fifth Symphony was played for the first time in Scotland, I had the double satisfaction of hailing it in *The Bulletin*, and of recording the Festival audience's enthusiasm (and my own) in a second notice hurriedly translated into Danish by a waiting interpreter to be phoned to Copenhagen for next day's *Berlingske Tidende*.

The essential qualities a music critic must possess, after knowledge and listening experience, are catholicity of taste, perennially fresh ears and a talent for writing, the latter an adjunct less common than might be supposed. It is no use your critic hating Sullivan for not being Schubert, or Tchaikovsky for wearing his heart on his sleeve more obviously than Byrd. No matter how often a critic may find himself listening to Schubert's "Unfinished" or Beethoven's Fifth, he should never allow repetition to lull the edge from his listening. It is always the first overwhelming revelation for someone in the audience, and the stale critic has no right to denigrate what for others is properly a momentous happening.

Sooner or later most critics do lapse into a posture of self-conferred superiority. The sensitive critic who feels this occupational illness creeping up on him should lay aside the practice of the craft and do something else; teach, perhaps; or take up musicology; or gastronomy.

After listening and writing almost nightly for fourteen years as music critic of *The Bulletin*, a salutary change of direction was imposed upon me. The development of television gradually rendered pictorial tabloids and illustrated magazines unprofitable, and in 1960 *The Bulletin* ceased publication. For a further year I wrote music notices on Glasgow concerts for Edinburgh's newspaper, *The Scotsman*. Thereafter, throughout the next decade or so, I occupied a personally paid-for seat at every concert I attended.

In my more tolerant declining years I have had the pleasure of returning to the critical scene in Glasgow, giving "second-line" assistance to my good friend Malcolm Rayment, music critic of the *Glasgow Herald* and virtually the leading authority in the English-speaking world on contemporary Czech and Polish music.

During my years with *The Bulletin* my career as a broadcaster had also been developing. My earliest regular "appearances" on the air were mostly concerned with programmes relating to the arts. Among the gifted Scots actors and actresses with whom I thus associated were Harold Wightman—whose Burns readings, fortunately recorded, I have never heard surpassed—Duncan Macrae, Brydon Murdoch, Ian Stewart, Ian Gilmour, Jean Taylor Smith and Meta Forest. Sometimes, other writers also took part in these programmes.

After a *Chapbook* broadcast in which Sydney Goodsir Smith had been participating, the poet asked Ian Stewart, the producer Robert Kemp and myself, back to his home. Sydney then lived at 50, Craigmillar Park, a gaunt Victorian mansion in the Edinburgh suburb of Liberton. We had already visited the Abbotsford pub in Rose Street, then the howf of the Edinburgh literati, and Sydney had downed more than the rest of us put together. He was exuberantly oozing geniality when, somewhere around the midnight hour, he ushered us into his lounge, then staggered off to his kitchen to collect glasses. In due course he reappeared, balancing a tower of glasses on one swaying finger. Unfortunately, he caught his foot on a rug in the doorway, and down crashed the glasses. To Sydney, it was a huge joke. We were afraid the commotion might disturb his household; which, indeed, it did. As Ian Stewart was considerately brushing up the wreckage, down swept Dr Marion, the poet's first wife. With no ado whatever she boxed the actor's ears for, as she trenchantly put it, leading her husband astray, before retreating magisterially upstairs without waiting either for explanation or apology. This struck Sydney as funnier than ever.

I had known Sydney since about 1943, though in these early days our friendship developed through letters.

He had hailed my first attempts at writing in Scots with a curiously unsound prediction:

"I am very glad to see that you are bursting out into Scots. Nothing can prevent this gradual conquest. When we are old men (not a very far off date by the way I am feeling just now) the whole of Scottish literature of any value will be written in Scots or Gaelic."

When first we met, he was concerned about the fact that the greater part of Scots and Gaelic literature was a closed book, and might as well never have existed, for all the influence it exercised.

"I am trying to get as many people as possible to tackle translations from the Ancient Gaelic lyrics. These, when done at all into English, are done by Gaelic speakers but not by poets. The result is hell. Sean O'Faolain once edited a book called *The Silver Branch* which consisted of translations into English from Irish by himself, Frank O'Connor and Robin Flower, chiefly, and a few odd other ones. Unfortunately, not many of us know Gaelic, but if you've got an absolutely literal English version it is quite possible to work on that . . . I want to put this great literature into the hands of non-Gaelic Scots. If you ever think of tackling something of the kind, do send it along. I aim rather higher, poetically, then the O'Faolain book, which . . . made little attempt at recognising either rhyme or rhythm."

We once had an argument about his imagery, which I rather tactlessly called "outworn".

"You know, I don't agree with you at all about that business. It depends so very much on how you use the said imagery. Anyway, a lot too much fuss is made about imagery. It becomes all too easily a search for novelty, and leads you eventually into the sort of mess Hendry* is in. Plenty of images, but he doesn't seem to know what the hell to do with them. The same fault in Dylan Thomas's early stuff and, I think, and to be caddish, consequently, in Sydney Graham, whom I met the other night and liked very much. Thomas has got around at least to organising the abunesaid imagery . . . However, it doesn't matter very much. The poetry that will live will live and what will die will die."

He had fun with my difficulty in remembering the number of people's houses.

"Your letter" . . . was addressed to 40 . . . my good Maurice, get it firmly fixed in your skull that I live in 50. FIFTY. Five Nothing. OKAY? The number 40 must have some powerful and disturbing meaning for you because you even gave your own address as 40 Jedburgh Gardens and then changed it to 10. All very mysterious."

He had tried to persuade me to print Elegy xiii from *Under the Eildon Tree* in *Poetry Scotland Four*, "the one Westwater† read 'amid mixed feelings' at the end of the P.E.N. meeting at which you spoke. I do wish you would."

Unfortunately, it was too long, and I could not, although I have featured it in several anthologies since. In his next letter the poet was in despair over finding a Scottish publisher, Maclellan having lost his impetus and the confidence of so many of his writers.

"I do not know what to do with 'Eildon Tree'—and am beginning not to care. I think I shall just Roneo it and distribute it

* J. F. Hendry, a leader of the New Apocalypse movement.
† The painter R. H. Westwater (1905–1962) a brilliant broadcaster and a close friend of Smith's. The P.E.N. delegates could not understand Scots.

to my friends." Happily, this did not prove to be necessary. But he worried about the Scottish Renaissance as a whole. "If somebody really capable does not appear within the next year or two the movement will just fizzle out. Folk will continue writing without hope of publication, but literature qua literature does not exist until it is public property."

Scottish publishing languished, however, until after Sydney's comparatively early death, a sad loss to the gaiety of Scotland.

His philosophy of writing, and perhaps the secret of his success in *Under the Eildon Tree*, "The Riggins o' Chelsea" and his other markedly individual pieces, he himself saw as the quality of ease. " 'Ease' is a silly word . . . 'Fluency' is an equally bad word. It is a quality rare in all the arts today, especially in poetry and even more, I think in modern music. If we can produce the effects we wish without any feeling of straining after them and can do this in all the arts, then the Renaissance is in 'sauf keep', for we shall be doing what is not being done anywhere in Europe or the U.S.A. today, and what is pre-eminently the mark of the best work done in past centuries. Always provided, of course, that the standard is high. It is easy to be 'easy' on a low level . . ."

'The quality of ease!' The composer Delius called it 'flow.' Ease of flow; without it, no art survives.

Sydney was a character the dimensions of whose personality were really something of an anachronism in our penny-pinching age. For one thing, he was that rare being, a poet without a drop of real malice in his veins. I have happy memories of one particular evening which my wife and I spent in his company listening to him extolling with equal enthusiasm the merits of the prose of Sir Thomas Urquhart of Cromarty, his own latest poems and the varied qualities of Edinburgh's pubs and whores, before he eventually released us to bed in an attic boxroom littered with ancient trunks and broken toys.

Years later, making a film of the Edinburgh Festival for Border Television, I invited Sydney to contribute a piece on the main art exhibition of the year. He refused to rehearse but settled himself comfortably behind the big untidy desk in the study of his Drummond Street flat. When the camera was rolling he leant forward and began expansively:

"Now about this bloke Delacroix."

What followed, delivered extemporarily, was a witty and

perceptive appreciation of the great French romantic painter which, for mellow roundness of judgement and compelling communication, I have not heard equalled.

Among the new writers I got to know during my Gartocharn days was Iain Crichton Smith, whose talents and perception as poet, Gaelic playwright and translator of Gaelic verse, short-story writer and critic give him an uncommon versatility. Iain was then teaching in Clydebank, and George Bruce and I went to his home one Saturday morning to record a first of several such contributions. Although his background is Gaelic, and he comes, of all places, from the Isle of Lewis, where outworn traditions and bigotries are most vigorously defended, I felt an immediate empathy with the man that was to extend to his work as it appeared over the years. From the subtlety of his critical comments on my own work, perhaps that empathy has been shared.

Since he moved to the vicinity of Oban in 1955, our opportunities for meeting have been few and far between; but whether at a Gaelic Mod in his adopted Oban, from which I was introducing a series of television programmes intended for non-Gaelic viewers, or sharing the platform with him at a week-end seminar at Dundee University, I have always greatly relished his company.

Above all, though, I have consistently enjoyed and felt an empathy with his work, with its vivid reflection of strong reaction against the crippling superstitions of Free Church religion, the marvellously inventive ellipsis of his poetic thinking, often resulting in startling associations of imagery, and his constant awareness of the inevitable penetration of Lowland urban cultural values into the once-isolated culture of the Gael.

As the forties drew to their close, radio in England was already under threat from the expansion of television, although in Scotland throughout the early fifties it still remained the dominant source of entertainment and information.

My radio experience was to achieve a dramatic widening when one day the Scottish News Editor, James Kemp, stopped me in a corridor of Broadcasting House, Glasgow, and said: "Why are you too high and mighty to do news and current affairs broadcasting?"

"I'm not," I said.

"Then why don't you?"

"Nobody's asked me."

"I'm asking you now."

"Good. Then I shall."

So began for me more than ten years of news reporting, taking me on the air several times a week. For six of these years I also put together the Scottish news bulletin on Saturdays, there then being too small a news staff to sustain a rota system. I loved every minute of it. News is about people, and people make up life.

There were awkward moments, as when I was interviewing a little girl who had never seen the sea before, and whose answers were throughout monosyllabic. A series of "Noes" and "Yeses" do not give an interviewer much time to think up his next question. There were tragic moments too, like the scene at an Ayrshire mining disaster when another little girl wandered up to me and asked: "Have you seen my Daddy?", and I wept inside, knowing that neither she nor anyone else would ever see her Daddy again. There were also unintentionally comic moments. On one occasion I was giving a descriptive word-picture of a submarine stranded on Davaar Island, in the Firth of Clyde, for a programme called *Radio Newsreel*. Rashly, I tried to say: "There she lay, stranded on a spit of shingle", but committed a spoonerism. On such occasions the only thing to do is to hurry on, leaving the listener wondering whether you really said what he thought you did.

There were also the regular carefully staged annual set-pieces: the Scottish Trades Union Congress, where brotherly love was spread thinly over the proceedings, and anyway often seemed like rancid margarine; the annual Mod of An Comun Gaidhealach, that brave attempt to hoist to its feet by worn-out bootstrings of Victorian manufacture an almost moribund ancient culture; and the General Assembly of the Church of Scotland, which liked to practise the rhetoric of a Scottish Parliament without possessing any of the substance. I think I enjoyed best of all the Perth bull sales, where at least the central participants did not pretend.

It was through the Gaelic Mod, however, that I made my first entry into television. By 1952 I had reached the inescapable conclusion that if I wished to continue earning a major part of my living as a broadcaster I should have to get into the television. I therefore sought an interview with the Head of Scottish Programmes, Gordon Gildard, who received me greyly beneath a photograph of the destroyer he had commanded during the war. He had been a brilliant radio producer. Such was—and perhaps still is—the system of promotional ascent within the B.B.C. that a brilliant producer could easily be transmogrified upwards into a second-rate administrator.

Gildard listened to what I had to say, then asked: "How can you do television when you've no experience?" I retorted: "How can I get experience if I don't do some television?" "That," said he with the air of a philosopher hitting upon a truth he believes irrefutable, "is the paradox." I stormed out of the room, rudely slamming the door with a force that must have shaken the destroyer's pictorial timbers, and resolved to forget about the phoney mystique of television and address myself to the task of finding other ways of securing my income. To my astonishment, a few days later I was summoned back to Gildard's office. "Look," he said, "we've got to make a film of the Gaelic Mod at Inverness. I've arranged for you to go up there with a producer and a film crew and try your hand. You'll probably make a mess of it, but it won't much matter." Thus encouraged, I thanked him profusely and left, this time closing the door with suitably respectful gentleness.

The film contained an interview with the Duke of Montrose, then a keen supporter of the Gaelic cause. "Your Grace," I began. He interrupted: "Just call me Montrose," a term of address the use of which no doubt contributed to the lukewarm reception accorded the film by Gildard when I met him in a lavatory in Broadcasting House the morning after transmission. "Just as I expected," he said. "Not much good." I drove my way home through the thickness of the black depression in which discouragement usually engulfs me.

Next morning, the phone rang again. Once again it was Gildard. Once again he wanted to see me. This time, when I presented myself, he was smiling amiably. In an official sort of voice he announced: "The Chairman of the Broadcasting Council for Scotland, Sir Alexander King, saw your film the other night, and has rung up to say how much he enjoyed it, and how good he thought it was. I may say that I agree with him. Now about those ideas of yours for a Magazine of the Arts . . .!"

It was undoubtedly fortunate for me that a man from the world of show business (Sir Alexander was then chairman of a group of Glasgow cinemas) happened at that time to be Chairman of the

Broadcasting Council, then as now a supposedly representative body of people chosen by the Secretary of State for Scotland apparently for their complete absence of knowledge of anything connected with the craft of communication, and thus presumably easily manipulatable by the B.B.C.'s senior officials.

The immediate outcome was my debut on 25th January, 1954, introducing the first full-scale studio television drama production ever to be transmitted from Scotland; Burns's dramatic cantata, *The Jolly Beggars*. This glowing portrayal of a group of beggars celebrating a kind of freedom—the freedom that comes from possessing neither worldly goods nor social responsibilities—was left by Burns in an unperformable state. The "Cantata", as he called it, consists of a series of verse-songs, one for each of his beggar characters, set to a named folk-tune. These songs are linked by passages of verse marked "recitativo".

Various composers, notably Sir Henry Bishop of "Home, Sweet Home" fame, have set the piece for large forces, using a different singer for each song, orchestrating the folk tunes and providing original opera-style recitative for the linking passages. Such large-scale settings are nowadays economically unperformable, since we no longer favour theatrically curtain-raisers or interludes in otherwise unrelated operas, as was the common practice in earlier centuries.

Faced with the task of mounting a Scottish festival in Braemar during the summer of 1953, with limited resources at my disposal and the tiny stage of a theatre converted from a "Wee Free" church—a touch of poetic justice I greatly relished!—I had the idea of making four costume singers act out all the character parts simply by changing their roles and minor accessories as if performing for their own entertainment. The accompaniment would be provided, not by a full orchestra, but by chamber music forces, thus anticipating the cult of the chamber opera practised in the sixties and seventies by Thea Musgrave and others. Cedric Thorpe Davie eagerly approved the idea, and was commissioned to provide the score. The result was a delightful realisation that was an instant success. It has been broadcast and televised many times, commercially recorded and performed in theatres and village halls up and down the length and breadth of Scotland. It even achieved the status of a late-night show in the Royal Lyceum Theatre in the official programme of the Edinburgh Festival in 1959, the Burns bi-centenary year.

This, then, was the work chosen to be B.B.C. Scotland's first televised musical-dramatic production fresh, so to say, from its stage triumph in the wilds of Braemar. James Sutherland, the original stage producer, was involved, as was Robin Richardson, radio's jovial teddy-bear-like Arts Producer and a loveable and widely-popular personality, and Noble Wilson, then the only designated television producer in Scotland. The venue for this re-creation of Poosie Nansie's tavern was the large studio of Broadcasting House, 5 Queen Street, Edinburgh, in pre-radio days the home of the Edinburgh Society of Musicians. My intro-ducer's spot was a screened-off corner in which I sat decked out in my Montrose doublet and kilt, and heavily made up, from ten o'clock in the morning until the transmission time, eleven o'clock at night. There was, understandably, much inexperienced con-fusion among the cameramen and floor technicians, and occasional differences of opinion among the three producers.

In these days no one in Scotland could command the use of an autocue. Lines simply had to be learned by heart. I found myself rehearsing my five-minute introduction ten times over through-out the course of that long day. Not surprisingly, by eleven o'clock I was exhausted and more than a trifle nervous. When at last the great moment came and for the first time a television camera turned its red-lidded eye on me, I began in vigorous enough style according to my script, but soon forgot my lines. Fortunately, having just completed the first draft of my book *Robert Burns: The Man: His Life: The Legend*, there was little I did not know about *The Jolly Beggars*. I therefore improvised myself back to the point where I could rejoin the agreed text. Appar-ently, this caused consternation in the control room, though, as was later evident, viewers noticed nothing amiss. I had by accident stumbled upon the two basic lessons of television: never give away by as much as the flicker of an eyelash that you are thrown if something has gone wrong; and always be ready to indulge in relevant improvisation with a show of ease.

The Jolly Beggars was an isolated production. When the full television service for Scotland was launched in August 1957, there was an official ceremony followed by a celebratory pro-gramme.

The first three television news reporters were John Lindsay—real name John Lindsay Watson, no relation of mine and sub-sequently the Independent Broadcasting Authority's officer for

Central Scotland—the well-known character film actor and broadcaster Jamieson Clark, and myself. For technical reasons never wholly clear to me, we were filmed in a sequence that was to finish with the three of us sitting on a couch. We were to be discovered "live" in the studio, on the same couch, and in exactly the same position as we had been shown at the end of the film. Unfortunately, in the week that ensued between the filming and the "live" transmission, I was thrown from an over-enthusiastic horse while playing an equestrian game at our local agricultural show. I broke my upper arm, which for several weeks was painfully suspended in a sling. On the day of the programme a large and luxurious limousine was sent to transport me from Gartocharn to Broadcasting House, Glasgow. There, in some discomfort, I was eased into position on the couch, minus my sling.

In the early days of television in Scotland much that was done was makeshift and, retrospectively, slightly absurd. There was, however, a marvellous sense of fun and enthusiastic adventure, much of which inevitably disappeared with the necessary evolution of routine professionalism.

The early cameras were unable to digest sharply contrasted colours, particularly black against what the commercials on the other channel called "whiter than white". Those who turned up in offending clothes, no matter how eminent, were asked to change their shirts, being loaned a stock tinted garment in the correct size from the B.B.C.'s wardrobe.

For many years, too, the news on television and the sound news went out almost simultaneously, yet carried similar live interviews. Politicians, civic leaders, academics and businessmen had therefore to be tip-toed out of the television studio, having said their usual say, and rushed off to the lift. They usually arrived breathing heavily in the radio studio on the third floor, where they had immediately to give an unseen repeat performance.

Meanwhile, *Scottish Life and Letters* went on its way, though from 1956, when George Bruce left Aberdeen, it was transmitted from the Edinburgh studios of the B.B.C. It had its moments of tension. The most serious, however, had a happy outcome.

It had been our practice in the early editions to place Scottish letters in a wider context. Accordingly, we had included among our guest speakers the Irish poet James Stephens—who looked as wrinkled as a walnut—Stephen Spender and C. Day-Lewis, all of whose contributions, incidentally, are preserved in the B.B.C. archives. In 1954, Sir William Walton's opera *Troilus and Cressida* was premièred, and as part of the process of widening our approach we included an interview with the composer I recorded in London. This brought down on our editorial heads the wrath of the B.B.C's Head of Music in Scotland, Harold Thomson, a pallid little man whose only real claim to distinction was his preparation for the press of W. Gillies Whitaker's great book on Bach's cantatas, published posthumously. George Bruce and I simply refused to pay any attention to parochial who-does-what nonsense of this sort. Thomson, however, bided his time. In search of an original radio tapestry of music and verse, *For a Summer's Day*, George invited Thea Musgrave to compose a score for which I was to select lyrics. The composer and I discussed various ways of approaching the idea, and decided, with George's approval, that what was really needed was a through-composed work with a narrator's part spoken over music. Further to emphasise the agelessness of summer, stanzas from Alexander Hume's late mediaeval poem "Of the Day Estivall" were to be interspersed with specially written lyrical passages of my own. With the exception of an already existing Bairnsang, my words did not attempt anything beyond the purpose for which they were devised; the provision of words for music.

There was, of course, no reason for them to have a poetic life of their own. A poem is an entity complete in itself, producing its own interrelated and unified impact of image, sound and sense. The first thing a composer about to make a setting has to do is to dissect these ingredients and dismantle the sound of the poet's words, replacing it with the sound of the music. For this reason, it makes very little difference whether a composer sets a good poem or a bad one, provided the words are not absolutely bathetic. Many of Schubert's finest songs are settings of German lyrics that could not possibly stand up on their own. On the other hand Benjamin Britten, who rarely set a bad poem, played such havoc with some of Shakespeare's beautiful lines in *A Midsummer Night's Dream* that I can scarcely bear to sit the opera through. The words, in this case, are sometimes finer than the music.

In the end, what Thea and I came up with was her *Cantata for a Summer's Day* that played for forty minutes. After the first performance, Thomson went wild. We had usurped his authority.

He would complain to the Programme Controller. We had commissioned a musical work, a thing we had no right to do. I inquired how many musical works his department had ever commissioned. "None," he replied: "but that is not the point." The "point" remained unclear to me, reminding me of a story—perhaps, though not necessarily, apocryphal—of a new B.B.C. Head of Administration who, during his first week in office, pinned on Corporation Notice boards an instruction that began: "While it is true that the B.B.C. has a duty to produce programmes, that is not its only function. Good administration is also important."

Thea was anxious to write an opera, and I was keen to try my hand at a libretto. In his vague half-way, Robin Richardson, fresh from his involvement with the television production of *The Jolly Beggars*, led us to believe that we could regard ourselves commissioned to write a forty-five-minute comic opera for television. We searched around for a subject and eventually found one in Wilson's *Tales of the Borders*. It was a Scottish re-telling of the story the Italian version of which Puccini had used for his one-act opera *Gianni Schicchi*. I saw no harm in this, since in previous centuries countless composers have shared stories, and even re-used identical librettos; nor did Thea object, since her dryly individual early style certainly did not put her in the nineteenth century *verisimo* business. The outcome was a rhyming libretto from which she composed *The Abbot of Drymock*. It received its first performance at Morley College, London in 1962, with a then unknown singer, Benjamin Luxon, in the title role.

Opera presents the librettist with a number of challenges. A libretto must make both visual and dramatic sense if it is to work on the stage, even though ultimately it is the music that counts. Because it takes so much longer to sing a syllable than speak it, except perhaps in comic patter songs, there must not be too many words. Opera heightens moments of drama or comedy by adding to the sung words an additional element that music alone can provide. While basic emotion can thus be intensified, action cannot be qualified, as in a play. It is thus impossible for opera to encompass more than the simplest of counterplots.

After many meetings, leading to much re-writing and the cutting of my text, Thea produced a delicately-textured, witty score, which was duly delivered to Robin Richardson. Unfortunately, since he had first suggested the idea there had been one of those shifts of power that characterise the worlds of film and television. The genial but slap-happy Robin had fallen from grace with the powers that be. Unfortunately he had been replaced by a producer with little interest in the arts who thought Thea's music too "difficult" for a television audience; a man in the mainstream of the television tradition of underestimating the intelligence of the audience.

There was little to be done. Robin, whose expenses were once said to resemble a statement of the national debt, was clearly on his way out of the B.B.C. In these days there was little London interest in Scottish affairs. The opera had therefore to wait for its London performance to be launched on its way.

A year or two later Thea decided that she wanted to write a full-length opera on a large scale. She suggested Tolkien's Hobbit as a subject, an idea that dismayed me—and, as an investigative private visit to Tolkien in Oxford revealed, dismayed him too—since creatures of the fancy gather only grossness when represented on the stage by actors. That most delightful of children's stories by a Scots-born author, *The Wind in the Willows*, loses much of its poetry when the immortal Ratty and Moley, to say nothing of the self-important Mr Toad, become galumphing humans.

Many subjects were discussed and rejected over several months, until at last Thea came up with a good idea. Television scriptwriter Ken Taylor had written a feature about a miner brought up alive after having been trapped underground for twenty-three days. Round this slender thread I wove a dramatic story. The personable young miner had become the secret lover of the wife of the cold and unpopular mine manager, and their affair had been found out. There was therefore a double reason for the manager to call off rescue efforts to save the miner, since already all the known technical methods had been deployed unsuccessfully. To carry on would seem merely to be endangering other men's lives in what most probably would have been a futile operation. The moral pressures thus created dictated the title, *The Decision*. The opera was given several performances in the Sadlers Wells Theatre by the New Opera Company, being premiered on 30th March, 1967. It was translated into German under the title *Die Entscheidung*, and considered for production by at least one Geman company. The size of the forces required, however, has proved as much a deterrent to German opera houses as so far it has to British.

I must confess that the diminished respect in which miners as a group are currently held as a result of their recurrent pressurising of the community over wage claims not necessarily in the national interest, would make me feel uneasy about an immediate revival of the opera. Sooner or later, however, society must surely devise a fairer means of settling wage claims than a flexing of Trade Union muscle, and there will come a more favourable climate for the opera's revival. Thea's score is certainly a powerful one, and I have no doubt that the piece will eventually be professionally staged.

The lesson to be drawn from the failure to get *The Decision* taken up was not lost upon the composer. For her later operas she employed a limited cast of singers and modest orchestral resources. By the time Scottish Opera commissioned her to write *Mary, Queen of Scots* Thea had married the musician Peter Marks and settled in California. She announced to me by letter her acceptance of this commission, regretting that there seemed no possibility of us collaborating six thousand miles apart. The libretto was begun by a South American poetess, but completed by the composer herself. A similar partnership lay initially behind *The Voice of Ariadne* but in both these libretti there are, I feel, regrettable lapses into verbal banality, although Thea's music has deepened and matured. Her most popular opera, *A Christmas Carol*, glows with a warm humanity that makes it immediately accessible to audiences of all ages. I greatly regretted that distance and circumstance made our continued collaboration impracticable.

I was invited to write one other opera libretto, this time on the theme of Columba, and for Kenneth Leighton. I declined, feeling the little we know of the Saint's life to be insufficient to enable a dramatic structure to be constructed from it. In any case, I was sure that such a subject would be better handled by a Christian writer. My friend Edwin Morgan, for whose wide-ranging poetry and vivid re-creations from foreign poets I have the highest admiration, boldly tackled the task. In the spring of 1980, when the piece was staged by the students of the Royal Scottish Academy of Music in Glasgow's Theatre Royal, I am afraid I felt that my reservations had been fully justified.

My wish to found a television arts programme was also soon

granted. Entitled *Counterpoint*—a fashionable title for the time—I co-edited it with George Bruce. It was directed for television by a volatile Welshman, Alan Rees. The first programme was scheduled for transmission on 12 December, 1958, and the participants were the President of The Royal Scottish Academy, Sir W. G. Hutchinson—"varnished by God", Robin Philipson once wisecracked at a Royal Scottish Academy opening night as we stood before Hutchinson's portrait of the newspaper tycoon, Roy (later Lord) Thomson—my old friend the distinguished and witty economist and poet-translator, Sir Alexander Gray, and the sculptor Benno Schotz, who was to mould a head of the poet Hugh MacDiarmid while I interviewed both poet and sculptor.

Self-confidence was in these days a scarce and precious commodity, since all of us were equally inexperienced and technically so much could go wrong. Four minutes before we were due to take the air Alan Rees popped his head round the door and said: "Do your best, old boy. It's going to be awful, but do your best." It was several months before I learned to immunise myself against this recurring projection on to me of his own lack of self-confidence. At the end of the programme, however, his boyish delight that all had not in the event, turned out to be "awful" was equally infectious.

The first edition of *Counterpoint*, though far from being "awful" in its outcome, provided me with a singularly unpleasant experience. One minute before we were to go on the air—and a minute in the final run-up to a television programme or, for that matter the rising of a theatre curtain, is a very long time indeed!—an ashen-faced Alan was by my side again. "Camera One's gone down," he said: "play it by ear." There was little time to wonder how to play a camera by ear, because before he had got back to the control room, Camera Two had also gone down, the worried cameraman peering helplessly into its wiry interior.

"Forget the other two, keep on one shot and ask for a lens change to get on to MacDiarmid", came the whispered message through the floor manager. We embarked on the first televised programme of the arts to be transmitted from Scotland with only one camera. I introduced the programme without mentioning the painter or the poet-translator, and the surviving camera pulled back to reveal the three of us, MacDiarmid posing, Benno shaping the poet's head and me talking to Benno. "Now I'm going to ask the camera to change lens, and we'll talk to Mr

MacDiarmid", said I. There was a whirring blur on the screen, out of which MacDiarmid appeared in close-up. Half an hour and eight fussy public lens changes later, we reached the end. "Why did our turn never come?" asked Sir Alexander plaintively. I left George and Alan to explain, and rushed off to my dressing room to recover.

There was, however, a happy outcome to all this. Having half an hour instead of eight minutes in which to do his modelling, Benno Schotz managed to complete a head of MacDiarmid so vigorously assured that the B.B.C. bought the bronze cast. It stands to-day in the entrance hall of Glasgow's Broadcasting House carrying a plate that records the name and date of the programme in which it was so dramatically formed.

During the run of *Counterpoint* there were other achievements which I look back on with satisfaction; Robin Philipson—about whose life and work I was later to write an illustrated monograph for Edinburgh University Press—demonstrating the development of a theme during the fighting-cock period of his painting; James Cumming discussing the claim of some "avant garde" *savant* of the time that an ape trained to ride a bicycle through wet paint would be producing works of art, Cumming debunking this briefly fashionable nonsense with devastating understatement; and Alexander Gibson illustrating the baton language of the conductor by using the camera as if it were his orchestra, though the sound was coming from a gramophone record.

Black-and-white television could do little enough for painting, though the advent of colour television was, in due course to spread the public enjoyment of the visual arts in much the same way as radio widened the appreciation of music in the twenties. Emilio Coia suffered no such diminution through the absence of colour when he appeared in *Counterpoint* to talk about the cartoonist's art. While I interviewed him he produced a cartoon of me in view of the camera, a device other less skilful cartoonists were to repeat with me in later years. All of this now perhaps seems "old hat", but in the early fifties it was being done in Scotland for the first time. We were certainly enacting Ezra Pound's injunction to "make it new".

Although in 1959 I went over from news to interviewing in current affairs programmes—my first colleague was Bill (later Lord) Barnetson; my second, Professor Esmond Wright, eventually Chairman of Border Television—*Counterpoint* appeared sporadically until late 1960. An incident connected with it precipitated my departure from the B.B.C., with whom I had for several years been working under an "exclusivity contract" which, in return for a guaranteed income, prevented me from appearing on the other channel.

For the night of the London premier of the film of John Buchan's *The Thirty-nine Steps*, starring that most engaging of English actors Kenneth More and the Finnish actress Taina Elg, we had arranged that *Counterpoint* should carry a pre-filmed interview with the hero of the story, which I recorded in London. Because the premier did not begin until an hour or so before our programme was due to be transmitted, Rank insisted that they should choose the four-minute clip to go out with the interview, and that we should only receive it late on the afternoon of our evening show. As *The Thirty-nine Steps* was a "U" film, this seemed a safe enough arrangement.

The clip chosen by the distributors began with the closing moments of the chase over the moor before hero and heroine find shelter in a lonely cottage. It ended with Miss Elg, handcuffed to More, peeling off her wet stockings. More's hand was several inches away from the girl's leg, his fingers turned outwards. It was all very decorous, a scene unlikely to arouse the faintest flicker of eroticism in even the most priapic teenager.

Next morning, however, both the editors and the directors were summoned individually to the presence of the Controller, Andrew Stewart—he who had objected to the London broadcast of Francis George Scott's songs fifteen years before—and more or less accused of polluting the Scottish air.

It is difficult now to visualise the narrow climate in which broadcasting in Scotland contrived to flourish as recently as the fifties. One radio producer who found himself faced on a Sunday night with a script in which a swear-word occurred had to ring the Assistant Head of Programmes and get official clearance before a dangerous "damn" could be loosed on Sabbatarian ears. In the case of the peeled stockings, I pointed out that a "U" film was deemed by the censors to be thought fit for anyone to see, only to be told that so far as television was concerned, he, the Controller, was the judge of what was, or was not, fit to go over the Scottish air.

I decided the time had come to seek more liberal pastures, and wrote off at once to the two new independent television companies in process of formation, Grampian in Aberdeen and Border in Carlisle. Border Television had connection with George Outram, the founding proprietors of the *Glasgow Herald* who had also been the owners of *The Bulletin*. It was therefore to the *Herald* office that in due course I went to be interviewed, aware that the outcome might well bring about one of those sharp divisions that alter the whole direction of one's life. I was introduced to Robin Gill, a New Zealander who was eventually to come very close to the top in the once-powerful Grade entertainment organisation before, like his later namesake, Jack, falling from favour. In due course I was offered the job of Programme Controller of the new station. I had some misgivings, not about my ability to get the station on the air, but about my understanding of how to relate to a managerial tycoon. They were misgivings eventually to prove justified. The job accepted, however, our pleasant days by Loch Lomond were numbered and we began to plan our move to the Border country.

We went with regret. Though the years ahead were to hold more challenges, surprises and satisfactions, I was never again to experience the sheerly joyful physicality of life that I had known throughout the Innellan and Gartocharn years. The fact was, of course, that I had well and truly entered middle age. The exuberance of youth had sunk beyond a lost horizon.

CHAPTER 7

A TEMPORARY BORDERER

Dumfriesshire was a county with which I had remote family connections. My mother's cousin was the daughter of a former General Officer Commanding, Scottish Command, Lieutenant General Sir Spencer Ewart. She was referred to by my mother as Aunt Robin. To us children she was the mysterious lady from Langholm who charmingly failed to realise that children grow up, and who still sent us toys for Christmas long after we had put aside childish things. Sir Hector Munro, the General's grandson, Member of Parliament for Dumfriesshire and first minister for Sport in Mrs Thatcher's government, is thus my second cousin. His farm, Williamwood, lies a mile or two from the town of Annan. When he learned that we were planning to move into his home county, almost immediately he found us "Greenbank", a splendid red sandstone late eighteenth century house, added to in Victorian times standing in two acres. It has its own lodge and an open view to the south-west across the River Annan.

"Greenbank" turns its back on the edge of the flat plateau of ground on which the town had been built. A much wider valley than the bed the River Annan now occupies, carved by ice-age glaciers, winds past the front of the house, so our large garden sloped steeply towards the sandy banks of the river, a frequently-flooded field away. Throughout the growing months, cutting the grass with a rotary machine on the steep slopes of the front garden was a weekly exercise in toe-preservation.

To the right of the house lay a terraced fruit and vegetable garden. The apple trees more often benefited wall-climbing local children than the owners of the orchard. To the left, a grassed-over valley, once a drove road, threads its way towards a former ford through the river. In Spring, the far bank of this domesticated declivity became a trumpeted yellow triumph of daffodils, grouped in as thick a profusion as ever I have seen.

Until it became ours, "Greenbank" had been in the hands of one local family, the Roddicks, whose ancestors, indeed, had built it. We needed its ten-room spaciousness, because my parents-in-law were anxious to move in with us. Though they were not yet very old, neither were we any longer young. We soon discovered that "crabbed age and youth cannot live together," even when the extremities are not fully stretched. My wife and I were easy-going, impatient with over-emphasised trivialities, the undue observance of out-dated formalities and attitudes, and the parents of four noisily vigorous young children. Our house partners had spent much of their life in the East, accustomed to servants. To some degree they embodied many of the characteristics of the ruling race in an occupied country familiar to readers of Somerset Maugham. Furthermore, at a lower level of enforced association, our mellow basset hound did not greatly admire their mincing poodle. Our three years at Annan were not therefore an unqualified domestic success, although by no means without enjoyments and achievements.

The town itself has several curious features. Apart from a handsome Regency-period Bank of Scotland building (which, years later, I found myself involved in successfully defending against a demolition threat), the centre of the town has been heavily Victorianised. Warm, red local sandstone gives the place a comforting glow, even in wet weather. Nor is there any lack of open, warm-hearted social gatherings, the most important of which is the annual ceremony of the Riding of the Marches, held each year in June, and to which virtually all the townsfolk contribute in one way or another.

Nevertheless, Annan society, at least when we lived there, was curiously stratified. At the upper end were the local lairds, many of them bearing the names of ancestors known to (but not always liked by) Burns. Since most of them were land-owners living a little outside the town, they were in a sense doubly distanced from the rest of the community. Most of the population of five thousand or so was made up of shopkeepers and tradesmen whose families had been Annanites for generation.

We found ourselves grouped with the doctors, dentists, lawyers, bankers and other professional people who were usually incomers, mostly from Glasgow or Edinburgh. Such, however, was the fascination at that time of locally-based television that we were eagerly welcomed, even sought after, by each of these self-contained groups.

The weather around the Solway estuary turned out to be milder than that on Loch Lomondside. Annan lies exposed to the prevailing south-westerly wind, and rarely experiences weather extremes, cold or warm. In spite of this greyish middle climate, we did enjoy the occasional high summer days, and reaped much pleasure from our impossibly large garden.

Not that I had much time to devote to it, since my task on arrival was the setting up of a programme structure for Border Television to meet an opening deadline six months ahead. From Robin Gill, to whom I was directly answerable, I learned a curious kind of ruthlessness; no doubt a necessary ingredient in the make-up of those who aspire to top management. It did me little enough good, for I have rarely had the heart to apply it, doubtless often to my own worldly disadvantage.

The Company's first office was in an 18th-century house, scheduled for demolition, near the centre of Carlisle. There, we planned the operation while our studios were being completed at Harraby; that "hill of Harrabie" of the ballads, where the reiving English hanged Scots luckless enough to fall into their grasp.

I had to engage programme staff and construct a news gathering network in both the Scottish section of our hybrid area and the much more heavily populated English territory. My six years as Saturday news editor for B.B.C. radio stood me in good stead. Our bailiwick covered the breadth of Scotland south of the Southern Uplands, and the north-western corner of England, taking in Westmorland to the south and Hexham, Northumberland, to the east. Later, the Isle of Man was added to this curious amalgam of races and cultures.

The actress Mary Marquis Caughie, a girl of outstanding beauty and intelligent charm, joined us. Fearful that the English might stumble over the Caughie, we agreed that she should drop her surname to become Mary Marquis. After more than two years with Border Television she moved to B.B.C. Scotland, from which ever since she has won the admiration of viewers and listeners. Derek Batey, later of *Mr and Mrs* fame, was another of our early recruits, drawn from the B.B.C. programme *Come Dancing*. Later still, a guitar-playing schoolboy began to appear regularly on our programmes. In due course he asked me for a job, but his father wanted him to read law. I have always taken the view that television glamour is a false currency, so I supported his father. Three years later, a degree safely in his pocket, back the young man came with exactly the same request. This time we succumbed. His name was Michael Rodd, soon to become widely know through the B.B.C.'s *Tomorrow's World*, and other networked programmes.

We went on the air on 1st September, 1961. The hours leading up to such an occasion, by its nature unique, are bound to be fraught with uncertainties and anxieties. Things were not made easier for me in that I had already discovered my personality and that of my boss were more or less incompatible. "The programme had better be good", he remarked menacingly a few hours before we opened up, adding: "Don't forget what you're starting tonight will go on more or less forever." Much the same thing, in less ferocious terms, had been said when B.B.C. opened up its television transmission in Scotland. Fortunately, perhaps, I have never been over-awed by any part of the "forever" syndrome, except that tiny fragment of it which actively involves me!

By the standards of 1961 the programme was, I suppose, reasonably good. Apart from well-known local light entertainment artists, the cast included the Carlisle soprano Ena Mitchell, then still at the height of her oratorio-circuit career, and my wartime friend, the Dumfries-born actor John Laurie. We were well and truly blessed. Gill insisted on the presence in the studio of the Bishop of Carlisle. Like a good Presbyterian agnostic, I therefore insisted on having the Reverend Dr George (later Lord) MacLeod, as a kind of insurance policy on behalf of the Scots side of the heaven-seeking business.

One of the most rewarding aspects of the early days of B.B.C. television in Scotland had been the strong sense of camaraderie it generated. In tiny Border Television programme and engineering staff mixed in a manner unthinkable inside the B.B.C. colossus. The camaraderie lasted over our first Christmas. With David Main, our first programme director, I wrote a seasonal pantomime, and union technicians of the Association of Cinematograph and Theatrical Technicians enthusiastically appeared as "extras", something unimaginable a mere matter of weeks later, when the goodwill "honeymoon" period was over. Then, exasperated by an inter-union squabble as to who should pull out a wall plug, I did it myself, but had to put it back and await the solemn resolution of the dispute to avoid a general union walk-out.

Like all the I.T.V. stations Border Television was affected by the A.C.T.T. strike of 1962. Gill assembled the entire staff and told them in the bluntest terms that if the technicians struck and thereby closed the station, that would be the end of the struggling young company. The technicians struck, but allowed the station to be run by the management to ensure survival. Between appearing in programmes, I found myself acting as a sound-mixer or as a cameraman, the latter an experience I thoroughly enjoyed.

By 1964, my relationship with Gill had become so strained that I decided to resign from Border Television and return to the risky but much more agreeable life of a freelance in Scotland. One Saturday morning the chairman of the company, John (now Sir John) Burgess, opened the *Cumberland News*, one of the group of newspapers he owned, to read that I had resigned, and that his Managing Director had accepted an appointment with Associated Television, then the "flagship" of the Grade entertainment empire. The to-ings and fro-ings that filled that day are of little interest now, but when the next edition of the *Carlisle Journal*, the rival local newspaper, appeared it carried the heading "Gill goes—Lindsay stays." Since Gill was, indeed, "going", but to a "plum" job, the inference was somewhat ridiculous, Nevertheless, at the time the headline amused and gratified me.

I remained with Border Television for a further three years under the more genial direction of Gill's successor, a charming Irishman, James Bredin. By then, the proliferation of responsibilities had resulted in the role of Programme Controller being split. As my interest was not in exercising Border Television's tiny lungs amid the bellicose rivalries of the network's roaring boys, I opted to stay with the production side of the business, making programmes rather than scheduling those of other people.

There were, of course, one or two especially satisfying experiences during my Border years. To raise production standards and encourage morale, I took the view that from time to time those outside the Border area must see our best work. We therefore networked a specially-commissioned verse play for Christmas *No Star on the Way Back*, by that richly evocative Cumbrian poet and most kindly man, Norman Nicholson, for which Thea Musgrave wrote incidental music. I have always regretted that Norman did not adapt his script for stage performance, since it would undoubtedly have become popular in schools. Both he and the composer published separately the words and the music of the songs included in the play.

Other memorable enjoyments for me included my *Borderline* series of half-hour long "in depth" interviews—a jargon-phrase conjuring up feats of intellectual aquatic virtuosity!—partially networked outside London. My subjects included Lieutenant General Sir Brian Horrocks, The Reverend Dr George MacLeod, Stirling Moss, Kingsley Amis, Dame Sybil Thorndyke, Sir Bernard Fergusson (later Lord Ballantrae) and Sir Compton Mackenzie.

For a senior military man, successful in battle, Sir Brian Horrocks had a surprisingly warm personality and a ready wit, yet there was no mistaking his steely core. My *Borderline* programme with him was recorded in the Glasgow studios of Scottish Television. Half way through the recording the proceedings inexplicably came to a halt, the studio staff walking off the floor. A shop steward then appeared and declared:

"Mr Lindsay, the boys refuse to go on working, because neither you nor the director you've brought from Border Television are members of the union."

"You are completely wrong," said I. "David Main, the director . . ."

"They're not boys, they're grown men—or supposed to be!," growled Horrocks.

"The lads . . ." began the shop steward.

"The men," insisted Horrocks.

Fortunately, I managed at that point to get back into the act.

"I'm a member of Border Television's management," I pointed out: "and David Main is most certainly a fully paid up member of the A.C.T.T. Have you tried asking him?"

The shop steward turned on his heels. As suddenly as they had departed, the studio crew came slouching back and the recording continued.

I had known the Reverend Dr Geoge MacLeod—a baronet who did not use his title, but became a life peer, Baron MacLeod of Fuinary (in Morven), in 1967—by repute since before the war but personally only since my B.B.C. news reporting days. As long ago as 1937 my current girl-friend "got" religion, and persuaded me to take her to Govan Old Parish Church, where George MacLeod was packing the pews by his preaching. When we arrived inside the porch, the men were being sent to one side, the girls to the other, a Paulian gesture that annoyed us both. Nevertheless, I greatly admired MacLeod's powers as a speaker and the persistence with which he carried forward the restoration of Iona Abbey. To mark the eight hundredth anniversary of the founding of the abbey, the B.B.C. invited me to present a television feature. The producer was the B.B.C.'s Head of Religious Broadcasting, Dr Ronald Falconer, a kindly and tolerant man who felt that so far as religious programmes were concerned, technical competence on the part of the operatives was more to be desired than orthodox religious belief. Naturally, after the abbey itself, George MacLeod was the supporting star.

We drove from Glasgow to Oban, and embarked for Mull aboard a hired motor boat skippered by a weather-beaten leathery-looking woman who was something of a local character, but renowned for her seamanship! Before we had sailed very far we found ourselves pitching and yawing in seas so heavy that I very much doubted if we should ever set foot on land again. At the height of our troubles, George MacLeod gathered his black cloak around him, stood up at the front of the little cockpit in which we were huddled, splashed and cold, and embarked on a succession of hilariously funny stories. It was impossible to feel in the least frightened in the presence of such masterful, almost theatrical, imperturbability.

On Iona, we stayed at first in the Abbey buildings, but the domestic round and the all pervading presence of MacLeod himself made it difficult to sustain the objectivity essential when making a programme. I therefore withdrew to the local hotel, run at that time by one Mrs Campbell. She was not an admirer of George MacLeod. While the coolness was probably mutual, George always spoke of her in a more kindly manner than she of him. It was this same Mrs Campbell who, on an earlier visit, had somewhat startled my father by bursting into the breakfast room and angrily demanding: "Who's had a bath?"

"I have," my father owned up.

"You silly old goat," scolded Mrs Campbell. "Don't you know that on Iona you either stink or swim?"

The newly retired Scottish Manager of the National Provident Institution for Mutual Life Assurance had never publicly been called a silly old goat before. He took it in good part as, indeed, did most of those who felt the eccentric edge of Mrs Campbell's forthright tongue.

When I asked George MacLeod to take part in *Borderline*, he first wanted to know if this was a series dealing with those on the verge of insanity. On being assured that it was simply the reflection of a line expounded by speakers whilst visiting the Borders, he agreed. In the event, he delivered himself of his clutch of vigorous prejudices with incredible charm and skill.

The last time I met him was at a Garden Party in the grounds of Holyrood House in the summer of 1981, when he was in his 87th year.

"I've just come back from Russia again," he announced, "and I'm more than ever convinced that the Russian social system is the only possible one for the future."

"I absolutely and totally disagree," I replied, tautologically, though with equal vigour.

He fixed me with his engaging smile. "Then that brings the conversation to an end, does it not?" he said. "Nice seeing you."

Of my other *Borderline* subjects, only two were disappointments—Stirling Moss seemed to have only superficial interests away from motor racing; Kingsley Amis never emerged from behind a curtain of hostile superiority, looking throughout as if everything around him, including me, emanated a bad smell. He may have hated being interviewed on television, but like all the others he had signed a contract and, in due course, took the money.

Only two women appeared in the series. The more senior was Dame Sybil Thorndyke. I lunched her in a Jermyn Street restaurant to discuss the programme. Even the business of ordering from the menu was a delightful exercise in intense high camp. Though then a very old lady, she was still making frequent appearances on the stage and on television.

"When do you think you might want to retire?" I asked her.

"Never," she asserted with an extra burst of vigour: "At least, only when people no longer ask me to do things."

Happily, they never did, right up to the time of her death.

Sir Compton Mackenzie, having been one of our earliest house-guests, was an old friend. We had begun corresponding as a result of his preface to the first *Poetry Scotland*, and the friendship developed after he moved into his beautiful flat in

Edinburgh's New Town. Between times, he had introduced me
to the delights of Irish whiskey at Ireland's enterprising Wexford
Festival, of which he was President.

He was by far the most compelling raconteur under whose
spell I have happily succumbed. A Catholic convert, he appeared
to enjoy an enviable serenity based on unquestionable faith. The
subject of religion came up between us only once, when he
declared: "There's no need to talk about that. It's all settled. Let's
discuss something that isn't."

On several occasions he claimed that a Scottish National Party
rally in the 1920s he had spoken the words subsequently
"chopped into lines by Chris Grieve in his 'Little White Rose of
Scotland'." As Mackenzie grew older, he was liable to forget
what he had already told you and repeat stories several times
over in the course of an evening. I heard the "Little White Rose"
story on at least three separate occasions. Eventually, it was to
involve me in a distressing altercation. On Alexander Scott's
mistaken advice that MacDiarmid had "disowned" the poem*,
under pressure of time, without checking (as I should have done)
and remembering Mackenzie's claim, I wrongly re-attributed the
lines to the novelist. The poem uses a phrase by Yeats, "the rose
of all the world," and the thought and most of the remaining
words are Mackenzie's. But the arrangement of the poem,and its
telling   word-changes,   quite   clearly   make   the   piece
MacDiarmid's. I greatly regretted the distress my innocent,
though careless, misattribution caused the poet. Monty, as he
was affectionately known, came of an acting/family and, it has
sometimes been alleged, in his youth saw the cause of Scottish
Nationalism as a drama in which he might play the glamorous
lead role. He kept up his flair for acting to the end of his days. For
several years he had featured in a television advertisement for a
well-known brand of Scotch whisky. On one of my visits he
offered me a drink, reeling off, as was his custom, a list of
available malts. "I thought you would be offering me so-and-so,"
said I, naming the blend with which his handsome features had
become associated. "Good heavens, no," he laughed; "You don't
think I'd let that stuff pass my lips?"

He suffered greatly from sciatica in his later years. When I
arrived to discuss with him the shape of my proposed *Borderline*

---

* MacDiarmid had, in fact, temporarily disowned, under pressure, another poem, "Perfect", a
word-for-word versification of a prose passage by a Welsh writer.

programme he received me in his four-poster bed, propped up by pillows. "Do you know why I've lived such a long life?" he asked me rhetorically. "The recipe's simple. Never stand up when you can sit down, and never sit down when you can lie down."

He was sitting down throughout the opening night of the Royal Scottish Academy during the last year of his life when my wife and I came upon him. We rested beside him. Once again he demonstrated his gift of total recall with astonishing lucidity. "I visited you in 1948 at—let me see—a flat near the University—a close—one up—the door on the left hand side. Chris Grieve was there—so was John Glaister*—and we ate fish."

A few months later I called on him for the last time. He had agreed to address The Nomads, a Glasgow dining and discussion club limited to thirteen elected members of which my father had been one of the founders, and of which Sir Compton was then President. Monty felt too frail to fulfil the engagement. He nominated me to take his place and commanded me to wait upon him to receive the text of his address. None existed. He talked as eloquently as ever; of the early days of the Scottish National Party, and of his youthful hopes for Scottish Independence; hopes that had not been fulfilled. Once again, he repeated his "Little White Rose" story, leaving me in no doubt whatever that basically he thought himself the real author. He talked of the founding days of *The Gramophone* magazine, that enormously successful monthly review for record collectors in which he still retained a profitable interest. Yet I found his attitude to music strange. Passionately devoted to it though he was, he claimed to have written many of his novels against the sound of his records, a practice oddly insulting to the thoughts of the great composers. He talked, too, of what he regarded as the destructive sexual over-explicitness of the modern novel, blaming D. H. Lawrence for the start of the "rot". "Sexual mechanics are not in the least interesting," he declared. "What matters are the emotional involvements that may, or may not, bring them about."

A few weeks later that witty tongue was silenced. His body was flown to the island of Barra in a severe rain storm. An elderly piper friend insisted on playing by the graveside, an exposure which brought about his own collapse and death. In a curious

---

* Professor of Forensic Medicine at the University of Glasgow and like his father before him, a famous character. The son was always known as "Young John".

way it seemed a fittingly dramatic manner for Monty to take his final leave of us.

Current critical opinion dismisses virtually everything Mackenzie wrote as being of little lasting worth; but a more balanced view will sooner or later prevail. The early novels, especially *Carnival, Sinister Street,* and *Guy and Pauline,* have in them the stuff of period permanence, while the long series of Ben Nevis farces contain a laughter-potential ingredient bound to re-erupt for the delight of some future generation, and disturb once again the apparently indispensable ferment of stodgy, starchy Scottish hypocrisy in the doing.

But to return to *Borderline.* Among the politicians who appeared was Jo Grimond.

"People say you are much too nice to be a politician?" I put to him.

"If that's the worst they can say of me, I don't think I need mind too much," he laughed.

Another to appear was Iain MacLeod, then the recent author of an incredibly dull book on Neville Chamberlain. Both at lunch the week before the recording and in the morning we spent together in the studio, I found MacLeod one of the most boring men I had ever met, surpassed in narrowness of interest only by George Woodcock, the T.U.C. General Secretary, whom I once took on an obviously unappreciated tour of the Lake District when a line failure threw him into my company for ten empty hours. Not so Hugh Gaitskell, who exuded a warmth, an intellectual liveliness and an open frankness of manner which made it impossible not to succumb to his charisma.

Entertainers usually appear on television to earn money, not votes. Dame Gracie Fields was therefore a harder fish to land in our frail little Border net. In response to my invitation, her redoubtable woman agent wrote saying that Miss Fields had never done an interview programme before. For reasons that eluded the writer, Miss Fields, however, had decided to accept my invitation, for a fee that ended in several noughts. I telephoned the agent.

"You'll need to knock off the last two noughts to meet our tiny budget," I replied, somewhat cheekily.

A pause for consultation at the other end.

"Done," came the unexpected answer.

The programme was recorded in studios at Teddington. After a brief outline rehearsal we went into adjacent cubicles to be made up. As the make-up girl was getting to work on my features, the door suddenly burst open and there was Gracie, a dust-sheet hanging from her neck. "Don't make him look more beautiful than me, luv," she threatened in broad Lancashire, "or I'll kill you!"

Poets and politicians, scientists and pop stars, painters and academics, serious policemen and petty criminals; all of them turn up in the interviewer's guest chair. One of the most singular was an often-jailed Mr Z, who felt a Messianic urge to help lower the crime rate by extolling to the criminal fraternity the virtues of going "straight". To an enthralled television audience he delivered himself of an impassioned plea on behalf of the attractions of honesty and the need for upright members of the community to help ex-criminals rehabilitate themselves. It brought a lump even to my hardened throat and a tear to my cynical eye. As soon as we came off the air and the studio door was opened, two policemen walked in to arrest Mr Z for driving away his stolen car without paying for the petrol he had taken from the garage across the road.

To mark his seventieth birthday, we organised a half-hour programme with Hugh MacDiarmid. James Bredin sent his car to Biggar to fetch the poet and his wife for lunch in the board room beforehand.

Over the years my relationship with MacDiarmid had been disrupted, but more or less repaired again. In a long-since defunct magazine, *The Saltire Review*, I had had the temerity to express less than total admiration for the quotation-laden chopped-up prose of his *In Memoriam James Joyce*, and had been furiously attacked in one of his more extended and sillier outbursts of invective, a book inaccurately entitled *Burns Today and Tomorrow*, most of it being about MacDiarmid yesterday.

In my capacity as music critic of *The Bulletin*, I had also been duty bound to criticise him for driving away the leading London music critics from an important London recital designed to make more widely known the songs of Francis George Scott. Unwisely, the publisher Maclellan, who organised the occasion, had invited MacDiarmid to deliver an introduction. What materialised was an absurd whisky-blurred forty-five-minutes'-worth of nationalistic nonsense; a débâcle that led to three London music critics, one of them Eric Blom, leaving the hall, thus setting back Scott's chance of serious English recognition by many years.*

Such episodes suggested that criticism of any kind was simply not acceptable to MacDiarmid. Ultimately, personal friendship had thus to be hero-worship or nothing, as even a life-long older friend like F. G. Scott was to discover.

The day-to-day running of a television station, especially outside London, does not, of course, bring one into hourly contact with the famous or the great. Much of the work, though exacting, is boringly routine. In the early days of television there was a common belief that a career in television must be not only glamorous, but also a long succession of amusing incidents. If this were really so, then the ceaseless machine would scarcely run as smoothly as obviously it does. Accidents do from time to time occur, and sometimes they can seem funny, at any rate retrospectively. I had my share of them.

In the middle of a programme for children which I was introducing, Mary Marquis was addressing a baby chimpanzee sitting on a table beside her. Suddenly, one of the studio lights exploded with an enormous bang, and the terrified chimp leapt at Mary, flinging its arms tightly round her neck. Staggering under its strangling weight, loudly and clearly Mary gasped out: "Jesus Christ!" It is probably the only occasion when Mary has been caught off guard in front of a camera.

I managed to persuade a well-known poet who had never before appeared on television to make his debut with a solo piece about his own work in our nightly magazine programme *Look-around*. As soon as I had finished my introduction, I realised that my poet had been smitten with stage-fright and was not going to open his mouth. I therefore dashed across the studio with the intention of turning his solo into an interview. Unfortunately, I forgot that I was wearing a microphone linked by cable to a point in the wall. Consequently, the cable and I went round opposite sides of a studio prop, an elegant stucco Grecian pillar, bringing it crashing down a foot or so behind the startled poet's head just as I reached him, and causing him to utter an unscripted invocation to the deity that suddenly loosened his tongue.

There was, too, the case of the celebrated Scottish musician

---

* The details of this episode, and of MacDiarmid's other well-intentioned but disastrous interventions damaging to Scott's musical interests, are to be found in my book *Francis George Scott and the Scottish Renaissance* (1980).

who had made her name with a talented double turn. She appeared in the first part of a concert as a solo pianist, and in the second as a solo violinist. When visiting Carlisle I got her to record the piano part of a Handel sonata movement before we went on the air. During transmission, she accompanied her piano recording on the violin. The performance over, I began my interview by asking: "Miss So-and-So, when did you first start playing with yourself?" Neither she nor I could understand why the cameramen suddenly fell about the floor silently laughing.

There was also the occasion when I found myself interviewing the bird's-nest-hatted chairman of a branch of the Mother's Union. It had just expelled an unfortunate woman for being the innocent party in a divorce action.

"Is it the case," I asked, "that the Mothers' Union is a Christian organisation?"

"Certainly."

"So it follows the precepts and teachings of the church's founder, Jesus Christ?"

"Of course."

"Where, then, in the teachings of Jesus Christ is there any justification for punishing the innocent?"

For a long slow second the bird feathers quivered as if about to take off: then the good Christian mother, as purple with rage as her hat, leant forward, and in full close-up view of the camera resoundingly slapped my face.

"Thank you for so complete an answer," said I.

On another occasion I was about to sign off a half-hour discussion programme by thanking the participants, a Cumbrian Member of Parliament, a famous designer and a contributor then popularly known by his nickname of "Mr Newcastle."

"And there we'll have to leave it tonight," said I, facing the camera. "Thank you Joe Symonds, Bernat Klein and Dan . . . Dan . . ." At which point my mind went blank.

"Smith," hissed Bernat Klein into my ear, leaning well into the camera shot.

"Smith," I laughed, "Of course, how silly of me!"

Another lean-in and Klein added: "A very difficult surname to remember." At which point we went off the air.

From then, until the arrival at Border Television of auto-cue, I saw to it that there was always a large idiot board within easy eye-reach carrying the names of all the contributors to my programmes.

In spite of our awkward audience-mix of nationalities, many who visited Border Television's studios thought the organisation a curiously successful combination of B.B.C. and Independent Television characteristics. One of those who viewed our efforts favourably was Magnus Magnusson, then writing a weekly feature, "Magnus on Monday," for *The Scotsman*. Of Border's screen effort he wrote:

"What sort of image do they want to project? Brisk and brash? Solid and rural? Busy and urban? It is not the programme schedules that matter so much, ultimately, as the mood you inject into them.

"I was discussing this problem last week with the man who actually was faced with it when Border Television started up— Maurice Lindsay, first Programme Controller and now Production Controller. Lindsay is one of the most experienced broadcasters in Scotland, both on radio and television, and he has put his stamp very thoroughly on the fledgling station.

"As was to be expected, he found the challenge immensely stimulating and exciting, if somewhat disconcerting at times— when you are used to the wide resources of a big established organisation, resources that you have come to take for granted, it comes as a mild shock to be suddenly bereft of them; no pronunciation department to fall back on for all these funny Cumbrian place-names, no library, no automatic source of information, that most precious of all commodities.

"But there are compensations, of course. Within the limits imposed by the budget, you can give your own interests fairly free play; and what Lindsay has achieved in his two years at the helm, apart from giving the programme presentation a much greater degree of sophistication than one would expect from so young an organisation, is a most noteworthy balance of practical and cultural interests. Living in the West as I do, I do not often have the opportunity of seeing Border T.V.; but those "Focus" programmes that I have managed to glimpse have all been distinguished by an easy, unforced blending of activities; carting and art exhibitions, Territorial camps and books, council affairs and music.

"Most people in Scotland will have had the chance of seeing a programme series called *Borderline* in which Lindsay interviewed distinguished personalities from many fields. This was net-worked to other stations, and is Border's main non-regional prestige programme. Apart from the exceptionally adroit inter-viewing, what stands out in my mind was the complete implicit rejection of any distinction between life and letters as it were—between men of affairs and men of letters. In the same way, when Border T.V. engages in a programme designed to display local talents a budding opera singer will get just as much screen-time as a young pop crooner.

"No doubt Border viewers will have their own feelings about this, but to me this seems an important achievement. No nonsense about seeking the lowest common denominator in order to show a profit . . ."

Soon after his unsolicited encomium the Director General of the B.B.C., Sir Hugh Carlton Greene, became an unexpected subject for my interviewing. Robin Gill persuaded him to do a half-hour interview programme for Border Television. Sir Hugh laid down one condition; the programme must not be shown on Granada, for which, apparently, he harboured considerable dislike.

Sir Hugh was, in my view, a Director General not much lower in stature than Sir John Reith, who had laid down the founding principles of integrity and impartiality on which the B.B.C.'s subsequent reputation was to be built. At a critical juncture in its history, Sir Hugh faced up to the thankless task of liberalising the B.B.C. to take account of changing social and artistic attitudes, and to permit satirical comment on people and affairs of public concern essential for the health of a free modern democratic society. He achieved this difficult task wisely and well in the face of much gadfly protest from such representatives of the forces of reaction as the so-called Festival of Light and that mildly ridi-culous headline-seeker, Mrs Mary Whitehouse.

I called on Sir Hugh at Broadcasting House to discuss the shape of the programme. That settled, from his higher chair the sharp eyes above the mischievous grin fixed me. He said:

"There are some people in this building who do not approve of what I am doing. However, I think you can safely leave me to take care of them."

"Quite," said I, thankful that I was not of their number.

During the programme he spoke freely about the differing roles and responsibilities of the B.B.C. and the independent companies as he saw them, and of the constant pitfalls surrounding democratic communicators in the mass media. He appeared to enjoy himself; certainly, I did. The programme was screened by several regional independent companies. In Scotland, however, it was transmitted by the B.B.C., thus creating something of a fraternal record.

I had first met Benjamin Britten in 1960, at Haddo House, Aberdeen, where June Gordon, now Lady Aberdeen, had for many years run an early summer festival to which famous musicians were happy to come. On one of these occasions, three years previously I met and interviewed the elderly Vaughan Williams, whose *Sea Symphony* was being rehearsed. Characteristically, he would only talk about Parry, whose *Blest Pair of Sirens* was also included in the programme, and which the old man was to conduct. On the other occasion, attending privately, I observed a B.B.C. Scotland film team filming the festival, the centre-piece of which was Britten's *Spring Symphony*, and noted that the interviewer was a newsman with absolutely no knowledge of music. Over lunch on the second day my assistance was urgently sought by the producer. The composer had refused to collaborate with the news interviewer. Could I possibly help?

Obviously, I could hardly suddenly appear in a film where the interviewer was someone else. After a chat with Britten, somewhat to my surprise he agreed that I should shout suitably amended questions over a quadrangle. My questions would then subsequently be edited out, leaving only his answers to be linked into a statement.

A few years later I recorded for Border Television a discussion with him at Sir Miki Sekers's private theatre, Rosehill, near Whitehaven. In the middle of the morning Sekers appeared and announced:

"Ben, coffee is ready in the house. Mr Lindsay, you and your men can have it in the kitchen."

"No," said Britten firmly. "Either we all have it together, Miki, or we don't have it at all."

With rather bad grace, Sekers gave in.

After three years in Annan the tensions of attempting to harmonise the generation mix became too great, particularly for my wife, who had to bear the brunt of them during the day. An unsatisfactory situation had also developed at Annan Academy which, by the flourish of a bureaucratic pen, had been jumped up from Junior Secondary status to become on paper a Comprehensive school.

My wife's parents decided to move to a flat of their own in Stirling. In order to be nearer better schooling, we bought a house in Head's Nook, a village within sight of the long spine of the Pennines, almost halfway between Carlisle and Brampton. The place got its curious name—"Pook's Nook", Douglas Young took pleasure in miscalling it!—after a Liverpool shipping tycoon who had built himself a high-Victorian pseudo-Gothic mansion there, the village developing to meet his domestic requirements.

"Woodlands" was the end house in a little red sandstone terrace. It faced open fields and a prospect of distant hills. It backed on to the large and beautiful garden of a bungalow at the foot of which ran a brook sheltered beneath a thick belt of trees. Three old ladies lived next door, all suffering from deafness in varying degrees; which was just as well, because I like to play my hi-fi at performance level, firmly believing in Berlioz's precept that music should be felt as well as heard.

Our two senior daughters now travelled daily to St Gabriel's, a convent school in Carlisle, then still a private establishment with a remarkably high academic record. There was no attempt at religious proselytising, the only blow-back of indignation coming from my second daughter after she had been authoritatively informed by a well-meaning nun that the soul was located between the molecules of the spine.

Life in a village offers rewarding pleasures. We had experienced them at Gartocharn, and were to enjoy them again at Head's Nook. There is the feeling of belonging to an entity whose boundaries and qualities are clearly defined. Simple occasions, like village fairs, sports or Guy Fawkes night celebrations take on a significance, and yield a satisfaction, they would be unlikely to generate in the sophisticated context of a city. Village life is perhaps the nearest we can get to re-creating the slower intimacy of past ages without having to accept their incurable ailments, unhygienic smells and general discomfort.

I remember one Head's Nook Guy Fawkes night in particular, a crisp evening with the smell of frost and mouldering leaves crinkling the air's edge. On *Lookaround*, our early evening television magazine programme, I had uttered earnest warnings, as was my annual custom, on the importance of care in handling fireworks. A few hours later, near the bonfire on our village green, I stooped to light a miniature rocket. It had a defective fuse and went off prematurely, striking me half an inch below my right eye with such force that I was thrown on my back. By the time I boarded the night sleeper for London, the eye had completely closed. When the sleeping-car attendant brought my early morning tea, I looked up at him blearily.

"You been fighting, sir?" he enquired politely.

"Certainly not," I replied indignantly. "I was hit by a firework."

"Quite, sir," said he, laying down the tray.

By this time, increasingly I found myself questioning many aspects of television's social responsibilities. Some of the answers, or non-answers, seemed profoundly disturbing. The focus of my younger days as a professional broadcaster had been public service radio. I had sensed from the start of my subsequent television experience that in terms of career advancement, for me television had come a decade too late. London is, and remains, however regrettably, the goal that must be achieved, in this as in much else, if you mean to "get to the top." It is difficult to uproot yourself and move to London when your children are at critical stages of their education. That apart, I had become far from sure I really wanted to spend the rest of my life in front of television cameras anywhere.

Both radio and television provide useful ways of enabling a poet to earn his bread and butter, so long as his interests are varied, his talents adaptable and his tongue and pen sufficiently fluent. Two nine-month spells as a newspaper leader-writer during my *Bulletin* days had brought home to me the deadening drag of shaping words and phrases round an editor's ideas. In broadcasting, however, the shaping is usually personal and largely verbal. To me at any rate, it was more or less effortless.

Early in my broadcasting career I became fascinated by the craft of interviewing. The measure of success an interviewer achieves lies in how well he succeeds in bringing out the essence of his interviewee's story. Interviewing should normally have one thing in common with dentistry: both should achieve painless extraction; except of course, in dealing with politicians and others reluctant, or unable for whatever reason, to tell the truth. More than most, perhaps, poets ought to like to talk to people. Ultimately, television is about people.

My news work and current affairs reporting gave me the same

kind of sense of involvement with the random variety of life that working in the War Office had done, years before and on a much wider scale. One became slightly knowledgeable about a great many subjects, though an expert in none; at least in very few, outside the region of one's own disciplines.

My desire to present opportunities for viewers to widen their imaginative horizons—perhaps the educationalist manqué in me—gave me a rationale, an additional justification for my involvement with the media beyond the immediate purpose of earning my bread and butter. However idealistic one may be— and few that I met during my sojourn in the world of Independent Television, the companies of which are in business primarily, and quite properly, to make money, suffered from an excess of that quality!—the controller of a television channel has a fundamental duty to give people what they want, so that imaginations may be satisfied at all levels. Nevertheless, horizon-widening has steadily improved, both in range and adventurousness, at any rate in metropolitan-based television, though the introduction of cable television could reverse the process.

Not all the centralised constraints on programming seemed sensible to me then; or, indeed, do now. I entirely favour the insistence by the Independent Broadcasting Authority on the local acceptance of national news bulletins at fixed times, edited and presented in accordance with the highest standards of objectivity and professionalism. There is also some control by the Authority, though perhaps not always exercised rigorously enough, over the truthfulness of advertising, and a necessary care for the propriety of its purposes. Sillier constraints include mandatory party political broadcasts, which still are, and always have been, the signal for the flushing of innumerable lavatories— perhaps not a wholly inappropriate gesture, in view of the half-truths, if not downright lies, frequently put across—or the switching on of electric kettles. Equally silly is the official determination to continue to impose compulsory Christianity on our multi-racial society through the use of regular Sunday propaganda time-slots. Politicians and preachers seem unable to accept the simple fact that creating boredom converts no one.

But what worried me most then—and, indeed, still does—was the immeasurable impact of repeated nightly demonstrations of violence sustained over an indefinite period; much more damaging, surely, than the stultifying effect of the more or less harmless, if mindless, trivia that necessarily makes up so much programming, yet appears disproportionately to worry the authors of such academic (and largely ignored) government-sponsored documents as the Pilkington and Annan Reports.

Is it really safe to assume that the genteel official method of measuring degrees of violence, the more ferocious moments being reserved for post-nine-o'clock viewing when all the little kiddiewinks are supposed to be tucked up in bed, is protection enough against the erosion of behavioural standards in society by repeated dulling example? Is the nightly dose of Cowboys and Indians truly so unreal that the deaths of the Indians—part, after all, of the great American genocide conscience-troubler, about which some of that country's more sensitive citizens still harbour a guilt complex—remain unrelated to real death to addicts of the *genre*? Is the fact that even the most extravagantly incredible detective usually gets his man a sufficient assertion of the moral aspect of right over wrong—in fiction, at any rate, though often, unfortunately, not so in life—enough of a visual counter to the recurring and frequently lavish glorification of male macho? Or should we simply accept that the world is so naturally violent and inherently evil a place that overmuch worry about such concerns is beside all practical point?

My trouble was that middle age had not calloused my caring, even though the sheer extent and magnitude of suffering and poverty, nowadays more clearly revealed than ever through television's nightly peep-window, created a feeling of hopelessness which working for the medium did little to ameliorate.

I had long since ceased to have any involvement with current affairs programmes. Indeed, circumstances during the mid-sixties had combined to focus much of my producing and per-forming efforts on Arts programmes, designed either for local Border Television consumption, or for a mini-network of the Independent stations outside London. Increasingly, therefore, I turned to poetry for easement of spirit; escapism, I suppose, as some might turn to weekend sport, betting or drink. But on the amateur level, these pastimes call for a comparatively modest effort. In practice, there is no such thing as an amateur poet. Poetry requires total commitment.

I have often been asked why a poet bothers to write at all, since his audience is scarcely measurable in terms of circulation success. "Poetry," T. S. Eliot once pertinently observed, "is a mug's game." Why, then, be a mug?

There are varying degrees of muggishness. I have never had much patience with pseudo-bohemians who protest loudly that society owes them a living so that they may develop their usually totally non-evident "genius", behaving the while like layabouts protected by some imaginary social right. Nor do I believe much in the existence of "mute, inglorious Miltons", a belief the poor artistic return from the Arts Council's literary bursaries seems to substantiate.

There have been few poets able and determined to devote their entire energies to the practice of their craft. Most of those have had private incomes and few were of the first rank. The great poets engaged fully with life. Chaucer was a diplomat, Shakespeare a man of the theatre. Dunbar was a clerical courtier, Henryson a schoolmaster in Dunfermline. Burns was, first, a farmer, and then an exciseman. Even MacDiarmid produced virtually all his best work while in the settled employment of provincial journalism. Those who have had little else to do but turn out verse, good, bad or indifferent, have either been rich by inheritance, like Byron, or in receipt of a competency from a relative, an admirer, or as in Wordsworth's case, the State. Even good poets with nothing to do but versify, however fine their best things—and fortunately, only a poet's best things count in the end!—have usually merely added hugely to the pages of unread and often unreadable matter on the dustier shelves of libraries. I am convinced that nowadays a poet should involve himself in the day-to-day affairs of ordinary folk, so long as his bread-winning activities leave him time enough to think, write and revise, and are not of such a nature as to blunt the edge of his sensibilities.

In my own case, the conditions of being, so to say, "with poem", results in a state of unease—almost of malaise—that is only resolved when the poem is a draft on paper. That draft will then be revised and re-revised, until it is as good as I think I can make it. There usually comes a point when further immediate revision proves fruitless, and the draft has to be laid aside. Coming upon such a draft weeks, even months, later the block in the subconscious can mysteriously loosen, delivering an image or other instant solution to some apparently unresolvable technical problem. In a sense, therefore, I would agree with Louis MacNeice's theory that from the point of view of the poet, the writing of poetry is partly a therapeutic activity. But only partly. The inescapable compulsion remains.

An even more frequent question is: "How on earth do you set about writing a poem?" occasionally varied to: "Where does a poem come from?" Answer to such questions can only relate to one's personal experience, though doubtless most poets cope with the creative process in a manner broadly similar.

For me at any rate, a poem often begins with an image, a phrase of conversation, a line in a newspaper or novel, or, less frequently, an apprehended concept. The words of a phrase shift about somewhere in the subconscious, like submerged stones moving under the motion of the sea, eventually compelling me to identify them, rescue them and write them down. Sometimes the phrase or image drags along with it a related image. Sometimes the original fragment has to wait in my notebook for days, perhaps weeks, before a re-reading of it can stimulate the subconscious to deliver again. Sooner or later, these mysterious undemandable scraps, these unsolicited donneés, become numerous enough to suggest the direction in which the poem is tentatively shaping itself. Once that stage has been reached technique comes into play and there is nothing for it but to get down to what Robert Graves calls "the anvil work". If the imagination's fire keeps the material being forged molten enough, a presentable artefact may soon begin to show. If for any reason the fire goes cold, nothing will happen, except a fashioning of sterile words dead upon the page.

I clearly recall the way in which a little poem called "Poet" came into being, itself dealing with the question of why poets write. I was sitting alone one frosty morning in the leathery lounge of a London club. That afternoon, I had to attend an important meeting. In front of me, however, were a few free hours, a blank page in my poetry notebook, and the original fragments of a poem that some months before had gone cold upon the anvil.

It takes a great deal of effort and self-discipline to force oneself to concentrate upon the difficult business of writing a poem. It is so much easier to remember a phone call that must instantly be made, or succumb to the lure of a newspaper or magazine lying invitingly open.

In the process of thus disciplining myself, my eye lighted on a headline of a newspaper lying on the floor. "Red Sea Danger", it proclaimed. Like most newspaper-created dangers, this one passed me by; but for some reason the phrase "Red Sea" warmed up the anvil. Why was a sea called red when it was nothing of the kind? "Dead Sea" was a little easier to accept, though not totally. Again, what about "Black Sea"? I remembered my disappointment when I first looked across the Danube and found that it was not particularly blue at all. Back to the sheet of paper in front of me. White. The white sea, out of which I might pull words, as I had pulled baggy minnows from the sea's edge fishing as a child with a twig and a bent pin, and getting my ankles bitten by midges from the marram grasses on the machair. Come to think of it, what is paper but processed grass? Usually, I caught nothing. Why, then, did I keep on fishing? Same reason as, later, I was to spend so much time working at poetry, instead of engaging more profitably on sensational journalism or sexy stories; or just idling, blethering or dozing. The fisherman's most frequent catch is hope. Hope that there, at the end of the line may be—well, what? A fish? A poem? The wonder of life, or the pity of it all?

Like one of those kaleidoscopic tubes filled with pieces of coloured glass that when shaken form themselves into ordered patterns, a strange excitement jumbled these thoughts and images into position: the position that turned out to be the poem "Poet".

> Red Sea, Dead Sea, Black Sea, Blue Danube—
> romantic designations, disappointments.
>
> I choose the white sea, paper. Here,
> I flick the mind's lines with baited pen.
>
> People ask me why. It doesn't pay.
> I'm lonely. I get stung with withered grasses.
>
> But I keep casting, now and then unhooking
> wonder or pity off a bent hope.

Obviously, "Poet" is a slight piece, though one which works, I think, within its own terms of reference. Sometimes, the process is less easy, hints from the subconscious arriving rather like a do-it yourself kit which cannot be assembled because the packer has forgotten to include all the parts, and you are forced laboriously to manufacture the missing bits yourself.

On other occasions a section of a poem comes together fairly easily, then the thing gets stuck. No amount of thinking will set it moving again. This was the case with my poem "These Two Lovers". Two sections of it lay on paper for more than a year. In this instance the poetic blockage freed itself during a railway journey from London to Carlisle. Between the courses of a boring overpriced British Rail lunch I flicked through the pages of my notebook. The unfinished torso caught my eye. By the time I had drunk my gritty coffee the poem lay all but finished on the page.

There is, or should be, an inherent satisfaction in doing a thing to the best of one's ability, be it writing a poem, making a chair, driving a car or operating a factory machine.

Nowadays the likelihood of material reward resulting from the writing of poetry is minimal. It is simply not regarded as a "necessary" social activity. The popularity of the poetry of Scott, Moore and Tennyson was a 19th-century phenomenon. The first two owed their success largely to the fact that their long poems were really verse novels. Tennyson caught in a unique manner the popular mood of the high Victorian Empire's flush of conquest and confidence. The widely felt need for justifying public events with poetic matching was itself an almost unparalleled phenomenon, though perhaps in our own less materially well-supported age of anxiety, Auden has come nearest to fulfilling a similar role.

When being interviewed in Dublin on Telefis Eireann by a man who when not a part-time television interviewer auctioned cattle, I was asked:

"Mr Lindsay, how much do you make out of a poem?"

I explained that you do not usually write poems to make money.

"Then why write them?" the auctioneer wondered.

I suppose I have always felt an insatiable desire to snatch at the "feel" of a moment, set it down in words for my own remembrancing with perhaps the hope that I may add a dimension of richness to the experience of other readers. What I have thus pursued is the lyric cry, whether moved by characters whose brief and marvellous uniqueness seemed suddenly comic or profound, or a memorable coming together of wind and sea and sky unaccountably stirring the heart. Always the meeting-place of such accidents is transcience, "the kind of touch and go that poetry makes satisfactions of," as I put it in my poem "Picking Apples." I have never really understood the anxieties of those who, demanding of life some sort of conclusive "meaning", construct religions to provide one, or search art for "messages" and "answers". Religions can offer consolation to those unable to face "the nothingness of all things homed to and obeyed." Art, on the other hand, can enrich our understanding of our own kind, and sometimes induce the Wordsworthian feeling that we are greater than we know. In the sense that a few supreme artists soar so far above the colossal burden of human stupidity and cruelty as to become a Shakespeare or a Mozart, then, indeed at least we are potentially greater than most of us know. Moving towards that knowing, by whatever means, of itself lends life a kind of third dimension. For the rest, John Dryden was probably right when, using the term in its broadest sense, he declared: "The chief, perhaps the only aim of poetry, is delight." Delight, after all, needs no self-justification, provided it is not secured at the expense of others.

During my Border Television days I produced two collections of poetry in English; *Snow Warning* (1962) and *One Later Day* (1964). *Snow Warning* contained the fruits of my Gartocharn years, and many of the poems in it survived into my *Collected Poems* (1979). *Snow Warning* reflected my interest in people and places. I drew strength from contact with the farm folk whose lives were related to the changing seasons and the soil around their homes; unlike mine, which was entirely dependent on the contrived artificialities of the media. I was not, of course, so naïve as to romanticise the farming life, or ignore the limitations posed by its unimaginative drudgery.

My own ancestors had for generations farmed in Scotland, and later in Ireland. I like to think that perhaps some of their feeling for the "speak" of the earth, and the inarticulate strengths of those who work it, found its way into some of these Gartocharn poems.

In *Snow Warning* I found my own consistent voice for the first time, though not yet a cure for my bad wartime habit of publishing too much that was insufficiently revised. What I wanted was a rough enough texture to match my subject matter, and an unrestricted thought-flow within a rhyming form. This I secured by the use of enjambment.

My feelings in the early sixties on the limitations and future of Lallans were reflected in the preface to *Snow Warning*. "During the fifties," I wrote, "the Scots tongue receded more rapidly than ever under the impact of television, and has now been reduced to a mere matter of local accent. It is utterly unthinkable that this poor wasted and abandoned speech, however rich in theory its poetic potential, can possibly express what there is to be expressed of the Scottish *ethos* in the age of the beatnik and the hydrogen bomb . . .

"We are all Anglo-Scots now, whether we like it or not. The future of Scottish literature must therefore be with English, albeit an English tempered by something of the old Scots roughness of texture. In any case, the only thing that matters is what is being said in relation to the human dilemma."

This preface brought down fury on my head from several quarters. My good friend Alexander Scott (who had, indeed, a few notable unfired Scots arrows still in his quiver) thundered roundly against the error of my ways. So did Sydney Goodsir Smith—"The Riggins o' Chelsea" and a few other good things still unwritten—who likened my changed views to "les trahisons des clercs." But time, I believe, has since shown that I was right, though perhaps I should not have pontificated quite so firmly. Very little written on Scots since 1962 has disproved my claim. Twenty years on there is not a single Scots-writing poet under fifty producing work of real distinction in the old tongue.

The example of Gaelic is sometimes quoted indirectly to refute such pessimism. True, no one could have foreseen in the early thirties that by the end of the decade Gaelic would be producing poets of such outstanding ability as Sorley Maclean, George Campbell Hay and, a little later, Derick Thomson and Iain Crichton Smith. Unfortunately, what they write rides high above the head of the average Gaelic speaker. At best, therefore, Gaelic might be said to be resting briefly on a plateau along the irreversible journey of its centuries-long decline.

I certainly wish well to those who can manage to convince themselves that Gaelic literature will carry its creativity into the twenty-first century, and hope they may be proved right. No one will cheer more loudly than I should a major, or even a good minor, Scots-writing poet sail bravely up over tomorrow's horizon.

The poems in *One Later Day* were mostly written at Annan. Like its predecessor, this book came from a small rural English publisher who did not remain very long in business, though both books quickly sold out their small editions of five hundred copies. When *One Later Day* was ready to go to press I wrote to Hugh

MacDiarmid asking if I might dedicate the collection to him. On 5th May, 1966 he replied:

"It is good of you to wish to dedicate your new book of poems to me and I have much pleasure in accepting—especially now I have read the proofs. I think it will be one of your best [books] of poems. A number of critics recently have complained that I had too narrow a view of poetry, and have pleaded for a freer tackling of all sorts of subjects, especially subjects of human interest. This is in line with a growing reaction against bards donning the sacred robes before they sing, and against high falutin' poetic diction and the idea that everyday subject matter is unsuitable for poetry, which calls for elevated themes and treatment. You seem in these poems to have solved this problem in a very successful way. Many of the poems show keen observation and sympathetic understanding of matters pertaining to common humanity. Though apparently simple and even casual in expression, they are of course nothing of the kind, but expressed in an easy idiom and with engaging rhythms that are in fact far from easy to come by."

When the book itself reached him, he acknowledged it on 21st November: "Many thanks for *One Later Day*. I have read the poems again and that confirms my belief that this is one of your best books and opens up a distinctive line along which you will reap further rich harvests . . . Thanks again for the dedication, which I appreciate greatly."

Certainly, when, as I have mentioned, Alexander Scott agreed to put together my *Collected Poems*—a task my own habitual self-doubting made me reluctant to undertake unadvised—the number of poems chosen by him increased with the advancing chronology of my volumes. This I take to indicate some sort of poetic progress.

Movements and groups perform a useful supportive function for the young writer, giving him the spread of shared confidence. Yet they are only the props beneath a ship on the slips before the final launching. Once I had broken away from MacDiarmid's Lallans group I became, and have since remained, very much a loner. I have thus never been a "cult" poet—nor, for that matter, an "in" one—possibly because of my frequently expressed distrust of extraneous extremism of any kind. "You and your damned B.B.C. impartiality!" an irate Marxist once growled at me when I reminded him of Dr Johnson's belief in the improbability of any one political party holding a monopoly of the truth.

Another, and perhaps more significant, reason for my comparative literary isolation has been the fact that I have always done more than one thing. With my mother's artistic ancestry and my father's background of hard-headed business practicality, I embody a kind of personal dichotomy to satisfy which I have needed both the leisure necessary for creative effort yet also, though less urgent, from time to time the responsibilities of administration. Consequently, having been poet, music critic, radio and television news reporter, programme controller of a television station and, latterly, environmentalist, in the eyes of many I come automatically under the strong suspicion of being a jack of all trades. "Do more than one thing tolerably well in Scotland and they hate you," I once exaggeratedly remarked to the colourful Nicholas Fairbairn, Scotland's first Solicitor General in Mrs Thatcher's government.

"My dear Maurice," he drawled; "do *one* thing tolerably well in Scotland and they hate you!" In a country where, football apart, unassuming mediocrity is now regarded as a major social virtue, perhaps he had a point.

Somehow, no matter how wounding the neglect I have from time to time fancied I suffered, or temporarily lacerating, destructive or partisan a review has felt, my muse has so far always managed to struggle to her feet again. Robert Kemp once remarked that to be a writer in Scotland it was necessary not only to have talent, but also to possess the constitution and resilience of a prize-fighter.

Poetry may not have been the only interest in my life, but it has always been by far the most insistent. In my own eyes my activities in broadcasting, journalism and administration have occupied a supportive role to my conviction that poetry matters supremely, and for its own sake, however it may fare with current fashion. Fortunately, when the cliques and the claques fall finally silent, posterity undertakes its own unhurried assessments and pronounces measured judgements against which, changing tastes apart, there is no appeal. Before that prospect I rest content.

My last two years at Border Television brought me into working contact with Douglas Hurn, a producer who had borne the hectic heat of the early days of the highly competitive light

entertainment side of television, and in consequence had suffered a nervous breakdown. He had become a Catholic convert.
In spite of our fundamental difference in outlook, we respected
each other as craftsmen and enjoyed each other's company.
Together we ran *Kaleidoscope,* a regionally networked programme
of the arts. For it, I talked on film with the Irish poet W. R. Rogers,
who recollected his long friendship with Louis MacNeice and
read a beautiful elegy for his fellow-countryman. Later I was
deeply moved watching our cameraman film MacNeice's grave in
an Armagh cemetery. MacNeice's fluent colloquial verse had
captured so many of the complex moods of the thirties that it was
difficult to think of so lively a mind mouldered beneath the
mound of grass by which we so awkwardly stood, clumsily
breaking the peace with a clapperboard.

Though Rogers' elegy is, indeed, a fine poem, he never quite
fulfilled the promise his early work suggested. He had been a
senior B.B.C. official, but had committed the unforgivable sin in
that organisation's code; not of being hopelessly incompetent at
his job; but by running away with the wife of a still more senior
official! In his later years he published little. When I met him he
seemed tired and defeated.

Collecting material for *Kaleidoscope* involved a rumbustious
Cardiff session with Richard Burton, who recorded Dylan
Thomas's "A Child's Christmas in Wales," and a fascinating
afternoon in Biggar with MacDiarmid planning the *Kaleidoscope*
film *Rebel with a Cause.* It was later screened several times daily by
the National Library of Scotland during the 1967 Edinburgh
International Festival as part of an exhibition marking the poet's
seventy-fifth birthday.

When making the film I was unaware of the controversy that
had arisen in 1965 over MacDiarmid's poem "Perfect". A
Welshman, Glyn Jones, had claimed it to be merely a chopped-
up version of a prose passage of his own, a charge which
MacDiarmid publicly admitted. Subsequently, on the ethically
curious but factually accurate grounds that without his re-
chopping no one would ever have heard of the lines, the poet
withdrew his disclaimer and repossessed the piece.

Much of our filming was done in Shetland, and "Perfect" was
included in this context. In Lerwick, it proved to be impossible to
find a game-dealer's shop where we could buy a pigeon, easily
enough obtainable in a city. Douglas Hurn therefore borrowed a

gun and shot an unfortunate pigeon that happened to be roosting in the rafters of a storage shed at Lerwick harbour. Back at the hotel, he boiled the head by means I was too squeamish to enquire into, till the bubble-brained bone-casing reached a suitable whiteness to match the poet's image. I avoided soup on the hotel menu for several days thereafter, just to be on the safe side!

The "cause" to which I attributed MacDiarmid's "rebellion" was, of course, his belief in the need for Scotland to regain her independence. Later, I came to realise that basically, he was simply a psychological rebel, as the extraordinarily revealing "Ode to All Rebels" confirms. That film repaid whatever debt I felt I might still owe MacDiarmid for the enthusiasms he had inspired in me during my Lallans diversion twenty years before.

Some months before I left Border Television my wife and I visited Manchester to tape a programme with the astronomer Sir Bernard Lovell. A technical hitch developed, and we had to spend some hours together before it was overcome. Sir Bernard explained why we would never discover the nature of the receding uncaused cause, no matter how powerful a telescope was invented; and how, in his view, music had gone "wrong" after Bach.

On our way back to Carlisle we made a detour through Biggar to take MacDiarmid and his wife to dinner. We had a pleasant meal in a former mansion house converted to a country hotel. MacDiarmid was at his most gallantly engaging. Over coffee Valda suddenly said:

"I can't think why I'm accepting your bloody middle-class hospitality."

"I don't think you need worry too much," I laughed. "You've already eaten it."

As usual on such occasions, the poet looked embarrassed and annoyed.

No one I have met was as singular and intriguing a puzzle as MacDiarmid. Certainly, no other poet I can think of has produced a considerable quantity of poetry of the highest genius, yet also a vast outpouring of verse far below that level—some of it, to be blunt, little better than doggerel—and yet has seemingly been unable to notice the difference.

There was, too, another dichotomy; that between his contempt for proletarian values and his insistence that if "the people"

eventually succeeded in creating "higher" values, they would
automatically turn themselves into a privileged class:

> Civilisation has hitherto consisted in the diffusion and dilution
> of habits arising in privileged centres. It has not sprung from the
>   people.
> It has arisen in their midst by a variation from them
> And it has afterwards imposed itself on them from above.
> A state composed exclusively of such workers and peasants
> As make up most modern nations would be utterly barbarous.
> Every liberal tradition would perish in it. The national and historic
> Essence of patriotism itself would be lost, though the emotion no
>   doubt
> Would endure, for it is not generosity that people lack.
> They possess every impulse; it is experience they cannot gather
> For in gathering it they would be constituting the higher organs
> That make up an aristocratic society. Day, the surrounding world, the
>   life of men
> Is entangled and meaningless; society is the endless human
>   triviality . . .*

Unfortunately, though, it is all we have got! Just as, in the
wonderful lyrics of *Sangschaw* and *Pennywheep*, and in his great
masterpiece *A Drunk Man Looks at the Thistle*, MacDiarmid often
seems to make use of Lenin as a kind of God-substitute, so the
poet's idea of the unattainable higher perfection sometimes
appears to resemble the stasis of that Victorian heaven where,
beside God on His throne:

> . . . children crowned
> All in white shall wait around.

Neil Gunn, that most positively life-affirming spirit among
twentieth-century Scottish writers, asserted that the poet suffered a personality change after his fall from a London bus in the
twenties, and that as a result of his later serious illness he experienced a drying-up of his lyric impulse. Thereafter, he seems to
have been overmastered by the desire to extend his poetic reputation at any cost, borrowing ideas and even extending passages
from innumerable sources in an attempt to achieve a universal
synthesis his gifts could not encompass (and which, in any case,
may well be beyond the purpose and power of poetry). The
growth of megalomania, the seeds of which were no doubt sown
in the isolation of his Shetland years, drove him as he grew older

---

* *Stony Limits and Other Poems (1934).*

increasingly to adopt stances and attitudes as absurd as they were publicly tiresome. Eventually, he became the prisoner of his own political extremism, defending the crushing by the Russians of the freedom of the individual in Hungary and Czechoslovakia.

There was undoubtedly a mean and vindictive streak in the nature of the man, of which in later years I occasionally found myself the butt. More significantly, it led him, for non-literary reasons, to exclude the work of the gentle Edwin Muir from his *Golden Treasury of Scottish Verse* (and shamefully to pillory and persecute Muir in the Press). It was glimpsed and cruelly caught by the Glasgow artist William Crosbie, in his portrait of the poet, now in the Kelvingrove Art Gallery. Yet until he gave his open support to military aggression, I revered, even loved, the man.

During my six years with Border Television, several times I turned over in my mind the desirability of reviving *Poetry Scotland* to encourage a new generation of poets whose emergence would be essential if the so-called *Scottish Renaissance* movement was to have any follow-through, and to demonstrate that at least some of the writers of the "second wind" generation still had something of interest to say in their middle years. There were, however, two fundamental difficulties. I had become increasingly aware of the suspicion of those who think it quite in order for a poet to be a university lecturer, a school teacher, or a boarding-house keeper, but not at all acceptable to be a poet and a television executive. It was, in any case, the policy of the Scottish Arts Council at that time to encourage collective rather than individual editing. I therefore felt that to be solely in charge of the venture might leave my editorial judgement exposed on both flanks.

I discussed these notions with George Bruce, who approached Edinburgh University Press. They were immediately attracted by the idea, but felt that we should aim for a regular Scottish verse annual rather than a sporadic magazine.

Once you have rejected one as the ideal number for an editorial committee, three become essential if decisions are to be reached. George and I therefore approached Edwin Morgan, who agreed to join us. He, however, opposed the revival of the title *Poetry Scotland*, on the grounds that it was too strongly redolent of the forties. With my strong instinct for continuity I would have preferred the resuscitation of the old title, but agreed to the simple though accurate title *Scottish Poetry*, followed by the appropriate year.

For the first issue much thought was given to deciding the order in which the chosen poems might best be placed. From the second issue onwards a simple alphabetical arrangement was adopted. After the second issue, which acknowledged Mac-Diarmid's seventy-fifth birthday, Edinburgh University Press's production schedule began to slip, *Scottish Poetry* always having to be slotted into vacant machine time between the printing of academic publications. As a result, longer and longer intervals stretched between the appearance of our supposedly annual issues. Consequently, our association with the Press ceased after publication of the sixth issue. The seventh issue was published by Glasgow University Press, an organisation delightful to work with, but unfortunately without any effective means of selling its products. The two final issues came from Michael Schmidt's Carcanet Press in Manchester, a publisher devoted to the cause of poetry but lacking any specifically Scottish ties.

In all, *Scottish Poetry* spanned a decade of new writing. Half way through its run Roderick Watson replaced Edwin Morgan on the editorial board, Morgan's heavier teaching commitments and growing personal reputation as a poet and translator making increasing inroads on his time.

Our working method was for each of the editors to read all the material submitted, dividing it into three categories; accept, discuss, reject. There was never disagreement about the third category, and rarely much discussion over the first. Two out of three votes rescued contributions from the limbo of the second category.

I hesitate to claim any of the contributions we published as "discoveries" of the quality thrown up by *Poetry Scotland* in the forties. *Scottish Poetry* did, however, publish what was obviously outstanding early work by Douglas Dunn, a poet who has since established his own distinctive urban voice; and, perhaps to her surprisingly, it included two effective poems by Valda Grieve, the wife of Hugh MacDiarmid.

By the time we were working on *Scottish Poetry 9*, it had become increasingly apparent that, Dunn apart, no new voices of real importance were sounding forth. Worse still, the standard of the general run of submitted work was falling. We therefore decided that the ninth issue should be our last.

I have long been convinced that it is useless to teach children Botticelli, Beethoven and Browning if you do not also encourage their awareness of both the natural and man-made heritage which surround them. The arts, our buildings and what we do to our environment are the products of our social attitudes, and our heritage is thus indivisible.

Arising out of this conviction I founded and edited, latterly with the assistance of Alexander Scott, *The Scottish Review*, a non-sectarian apolitical quarterly supported from its beginnings by the Scottish Arts Council. It bore the subtitle "Arts and Environment". It too provided, and at the moment of writing, more than twelve years later, still provides, a platform for young as well as for established Scottish writers and looks critically at many aspects of Scottish life and the arts despite the necessary restraint of remaining apolitical (such being the operational terms of its sponsors, The Scottish Civic Trust, The National Trust for Scotland and The Saltire Society, whose representatives, among them George Bruce, formed an advisory editorial committee).

In some quarters it was thought to be "toothless", an organ of "The Establishment", whatever that may be. The Scottish temperament, with its unfortunate and self-destructive love of fierce polemics and its consequent frequent inability to sustain ideas and causes to a reasoned conclusion, is forever throwing up shortlived "little magazines" that thrive on this or that prejudice, then die down like weeds out of season. *The Scottish Review* aimed at critical fairness, balance and consistency, and in some measure at least managed to hold to these currently unfashionable virtues. Above all, it provided space for the kind of considered reviews for which room can now only rarely to be found in Scottish newspapers.

Like *Scottish Poetry* before it *The Scottish Review* was a labour of love. Foolishly perhaps, I turned down the one quasi-editorial opportunity that might have made me rich. A well-known West End London hotel, briefly languishing in an out-of-fashion interregnum between providing a traditional playground for the inherited rich and a refurbished haven for the possessors of oil shekels, was for a few years an agreeable place for ordinary folk to stay in, at a cost—then reasonable, though now unimaginable—of five pounds a night for bed and continental breakfast. This bought the use of a bedroom luxuriously appointed in the manner of the twenties and a marbled wash-basin and bath with elaborate taps once, no doubt, turned by the hands of a vanished aristocracy. Step out of line and order ham and eggs for breakfast, or thirst after a late night lager, and the bargain element immediately soared upwards through the price-ceiling!

One evening, sitting in the gilded lounge with the proofs of a book spread over my knees, a heavily made-up girl sat herself opposite me.

"You a writer?" she enquired cryptically.

"In a manner of speaking," I said, rather less so.

"Then buy me a drink," she demanded.

Curiosity aroused, I searched for, and eventually found a bell. In due course a poker-faced waiter appeared. I thought I detected a suspicion of recognition flicker his features as my self-invited guest ordered a brandy and soda. That delivered, and after an appreciative swallow, she put the glass on the table, looked me straight in the eye, and said: "I'm in the trade."

Obviously, she was not engaged in any of the more conventional forms of commerce. "Oh!" I said, adding after a suitable pause: "I don't really think . . ."

"You in a suite?" she interrupted.

"No," I said, mildly flattered that I even looked as if I might be.

"Then you couldn't have me anyway," she declared. "They watch you like hawks in this joint. People in bedrooms are out, but they can't say a thing when I visit gentlemen who have a suite."

Before I had fully digested this insight into the administration of a high-class hotel, she continued: "Besides, that's not what I'm after. A gentleman's just left me. I want to write a book; only I'm no good at writing. My life story, you know. I'm a call girl. You could write it for me if I told you what to say. I love the work, and have plenty to tell. Never a dull moment, you know, and plenty of famous names."

The prospect of adorning the bookshops of Soho as an anonymously disembodied ghost, even if no other complications were to arise, did not much appeal to me; so politely, I declined.

"What sort of stuff d'you write anyway?" she asked.

"Oh, poetry! Books about literature, Scotland. That sort of thing."

"Sure you won't do it, then?" she tried again.

I declined again, more firmly.

"Well, thanks for the drink anyway," she said, bouncing to her feet through a cloud of scent that seemed suddenly to have gone on the offensive. "Nice meeting you."

I watched her wiggling bottom recede. "Cheerio, Charlie'", she called to the waiter as she wafted my chance of a ghoster's fortune through the revolving door.

I rang the bell again. "Do you know that young woman?" I asked. "Which young woman, sir?" said Charlie, still poker-faced. "There would appear to be several in the lounge at the moment." I ordered another brandy and soda, this time for myself.

After living for three years just across the English side of the Border I was beginning to long once more for Scotland. True, at Head's Nook I only had to walk a mile or so to a small rise, and there to the north sprawled the Scottish shores of the Solway and the foothills of the Southern Uplands.

Apart from my unease about the medium itself, there were several practical reasons for my gathering dissatisfaction. A station as small as Border Television held few further possibilities of development in programme terms. I had become increasingly aware that my by now wide-ranging television skills were un-likely ever again to be welcomed by B.B.C. Scotland, since in these days changing channels was regarded as little short of apostasy. I was also becoming anxious about the schooling of our children. However uneasy a Scot may feel about the short-comings of the modern Scottish educational system, he is bound to hesitate before irrevocably committing his children to the English system, and the consequent likelihood that, at any rate where daughters are concerned, there may well follow an English marriage.

I am a passionate admirer of what remains unspoiled of England's once green and pleasant land—if rather less so her crumbling dark satanic mills—and a devotee of her literature, music and painting. The fact is, however, that although I like many of the English as individuals, in collective English company I am rarely for long able to forget that I am not of their kind.

Joyce and I had several times been the guests of John Noble of Ardkinglass and his wife, Elizabeth, at their annual mid-summer musical house parties gathered together in their splendid Sir

Robert Lorimer home by the shores of Loch Fyne. Guests assembled on Friday afternoon and left on Monday morning. They were regaled each evening with music by chamber ensembles imported by John for the occasion, wonderful food prepared by Elizabeth, and a happy mixture of agreeable company. During the weekend of June 1966 John was full of a venture to be set up in Glasgow under the chairmanship of his old friend, Jack Maclay, a former Secretary of State for Scotland and now Viscount Muirshiel.

I had met Maclay (as he then was) once before, briefly, on the platform of Glasgow's Central Station when both of us were about to board overnight London sleepers. The Secretary of State for Scotland was clutching the then newly published book of mine, *By Yon Bonnie Banks**, in which I had advanced somewhat controversial views about Scotland's future. "What a pity we're in different trains," he said. "I'd love to have argued over some of the things you've said in the book." As things turned out, he had to wait seven years to be able to do so. By then, I had come to appreciate his wit and innate charm, the wisdom of his long practical experience, and also that keen edge of reason that made him one of the longest serving and most successful of Scotland's post-war Secretaries of State.

John told me the new body Lord Muirshiel was founding was to be a charitable organisation called The Scottish Civic Trust. Its task would be to stimulate and engage public interest in the preservation of historic buildings and the betterment of the Scottish environment.

"It's an architect they'll be wanting," I said.

"Not at all," John insisted: "In fact, quite the wrong sort of person. You *must* apply."

"But . . .," I protested.

"No buts," said John. "Just apply."

By Monday morning he had got me to promise that I would, indeed, apply when the advertisement for a director appeared, though without further commitment on my part. In due course, to make quite sure I should not miss it, he sent me a cutting of the advertisement clipped from the *Glasgow Herald*. I fulfilled my promise, then forgot about it, there being something more urgent to brood upon.

* Hutchinson, London, 1961.

An outcome of the worries and strains of my early years at Border Television had been the appearance of a rash that refused to go away. Eventually, the cause was diagnosed as a combination of stress and an allergy to man-made fabrics. For a time ointments of various kinds kept this nuisance under control. I was then given a new drug believed to be a cure for this trouble. It was; but almost immediately, I developed a duodenal ulcer that failed to respond to dietary treatment.

In July 1966 we holidayed at Gartocharn, staying in the village hotel almost next door to our former home. My mother-in-law had suffered a heart attack, and had recently come home from Stirling Hospital. We wanted to be within visiting distance. In the middle of the holiday she suddenly died.

On the day after her death, my wife had much to attend to, and asked me to keep the children out of her way. It was a warm high-summer Saturday. We caught the paddle-steamer *Caledonia* at Craigendoran, and sailed down the Firth of Clyde; past the Cowal hills that fringe with blue the Western Highlands; past Innellan, sadly decayed; then into Rothesay Bay and round the Isle of Bute. It was one of the most perfect sailing days imaginable. I had never seen the Kyles of Bute looking more lovely. It was also a valedictory experience. Already, the demand for car ferries had led to the disappearance of such splendid Clyde steamers as the elegant turbine *Duchess of Montrose* and that one-time flier among paddle-steamers, the *Jeanie Deans*. Soon, the *Caledonia* would also be paid off and sold to a London brewer. Moored against the Thames Embankment and humiliatingly renamed *Old Caledonia*, she did duty for a few years as a pub until fire gutted her interior, warping her hull and dooming her to the breaker's yard.

In the autumn, I underwent a stomach operation for the removal of my ulcer. While this was happening, a "palace revolution" occurred at Border Television. Once the dust had settled, I felt that the opportunities for continuing to make the kind of programmes that interested me would probably be more limited. While convalescing, I received a letter inviting me to present myself for interview in Glasgow in connection with the job of director of The Scottish Civic Trust, for which John Noble had persuaded me to apply. Somehow or other I got myself up, and down again, on the train. When my wife met me at Carlisle

Station I assured her that we could forget the whole business. My answers had been much too blunt. I would certainly not be chosen.

George Bruce came to stay for the weekend. Over dinner on Friday evening, I was seized with such an intense pain that I had to excuse myself and crawl to bed. Early next morning I found myself back in my former room in Carlisle Infirmary, where a pulmonary embolism was diagnosed. From a drugged far-away world I overheard a house-doctor tell a nurse that I had perhaps a "fifty-fifty chance".

Happily for me, the livelier fifty prevailed. On her first visit to me in hospital Joyce told me that Viscount Muirshiel had rung up. I had been chosen for the job. They would hold it open until I recovered. Given all the circumstances, it seemed an offer I could not reasonably refuse.

As chairman of the putative Scottish Civic Trust, Muirshiel had a seat on the board of the parent Civic Trust in London. Years later, he told me that at a London meeting, before the final decision to appoint me was taken, he remarked to Sir Hartley (later Lord) Shawcross that the choice of a Scottish Director lay between a poet and an architect. "For heavens sake don't take the poet," advised Sir Hartley; advice that, fortunately for me, Muirshiel disregarded.

I had thoroughly enjoyed my fourteen years in television, but it is essentially a young man's game. I was no longer young, had doubts about the social responsibility accepted by this newest but already most influential branch of the media, and in any case had no wish to grow old vegetating down a Cumbrian by-way. On 1st April, 1967, six years to the day after I arrived, I pointed the nose of my car away from the Borders and headed back to Glasgow.

CHAPTER 8

GLASGOW ONCE MORE

Our return to Scotland presented topographical problems. Ideally, I would have liked to settle finally in Gartocharn but no suitable house was for sale. There was, too, the practical difficulty of a family of six commuting to Glasgow, at necessarily different times. Besides, my wife and I had doubts about the wisdom of returning to a place where we had once been so happy. In life there is really no going back, and it is probably unwise to pretend that things are otherwise. We therefore decided to live in Glasgow.

My last two weeks with Border Television were singularly hectic. With Douglas Hurn I was making a television film to support the English National Trust's "Operation Neptune" campaign, focusing attention on the horrifying ravages wrought on England's much-abused coastline. I also had to audition the candidates who aspired to succeed me in my before-the-camera role.

House-hunting in Glasgow from Head's Nook was a frustrating experience. An enticing advertisement would appear in the *Glasgow Herald*. We would ring up the solicitor or estate agent handling the sale and ask for particulars, then drive the hundred miles to Glasgow only to find that the seller's opinion and our own did not coincide, or the house had just been sold. In the end it was my wife, following a lead of her own, who discovered the ground-floor flat of a converted mansion in the palace-like range of Great Western Terrace which was to be our home for nine years.

I settled back in Glasgow on a somewhat inauspicious date for the beginning of a new enterprise, the first of April. Because of school commitments the family could not follow until the end of the summer term. I stayed for a time in the family home, but it had become a museum of dusty ghosts. The dining-room, where as children we had celebrated high days and holidays, and where for so many years we had listened on Sunday to my father's mandatory after-lunch gramophone-record hour, had been turned into a bedroom. Though the glorious horse-chestnut tree outside the window still flared its pink flambeaux as brilliantly as ever, the once strip-sheened lawn and the tennis court, neither of which ever fully recovered from their wartime conversion to a barrage-balloon site, had coarsened into an urban meadow.

Like so many forceful people in later life my father, by this time seventy-six, had fallen back upon his eccentricities, making our daily relationship a difficult one. I therefore moved to the Automobile Club in Blythswood Square, the southern approaches to which after dusk provided amusing cameos of the world's oldest profession in action.

Once I took myself off, relations with my father immediately improved and remained warmly cordial for the rest of his days. He himself had at one time played a part in the conservation movement, campaigning vigorously, though vainly, against the needless destruction by Glasgow Corporation of the Peel of Drumry, in Drumchapel, and of David Dale's house, in Glasgow. For many years, too, he was an outstandingly active chairman of the Glasgow Treelovers' Association. I admired his business acumen, his staunch championing in Scotland throughout the twenties of the League of Nations Union, his unflagging personal courage and the effective determination with which he took upon himself after retirement the daunting burden of supporting financially the upbringing of several grandchildren following the divorce of one of my sisters. On the other hand, I never fully came to terms with his inability to display affection, or his wary distrust of the senses; a distrust which, as a poet, obviously I did not share.

During his final years he lived in the converted dining-room to save himself climbing the stairs. He died in his sleep after dictating notes for what he proposed to say at a family Burns supper. After the long convalescence that followed his 1918 war wound, the doctors warned him not to expect to live much beyond his fiftieth birthday. His death occurred a few months short of his eighty-fifth.

He felt that much of my early poetry was "too damned

downturn," a view he also expressed about the poetry of Yeats, putting me in good company! I like to think that at least he would have enjoyed my later light verse, and might even have approved of the poem I composed in his memory, an elegy about which Hugh MacDiarmid wrote: "I thought your poem about your Father very moving indeed, and well worthy of a place with the best of such elegies written this century by any British poet."*

Since I have recorded the difficulties I experienced with my father, I hope I may be forgiven for including the tribute to him which MacDiarmid so much admired.

> You might have died so many kinds of death
> as you drove yourself through eighty-four Novembers.
>
> 1916. The Cameronian officer
> keeping the Lewis gun he commanded chattering
> over the seething mud, that the enemy
> should be told only in terms of bulky bodies,
> for which, oak leaves, a mention in dispatches.
>
> 1918. The fragment of a shell
> leaving one side of a jaw and no speech,
> the bone graft from the hip. Shakespeare mouthed
> (most of the others asserting silences)
> over and over again, till the old words
> shaped themselves into audibility.
>
> 1921. An eighty-per-cent
> disability pension, fifty the limit of life
> expectancy, a determination of courage
> that framed the public man, the ready maker
> of witty dinner speeches, the League of Nations,
> the benefits of insurance, the private man
> shut in his nightly study, unapproachable,
> sufficient leader of sporting tournaments,
> debates and the placing of goodwill greetings in clubs.
>
> 1935. Now safely past
> the doctors' prophecies. Four children, a popular
> outward man wearing maturity,
> top of his business tree, when the sap falters
> and the soon-to-be again confounded doctors
> pronounce a world-wide cruise the only hope,
> not knowing hope was all he ever needed
> or counted on to have to reckon with.
>
> 1940 to 50. Wartime fears
> not for himself but for his family,

---

* Letter dated 27/9/71, in Edinburgh University Library

the public disappointments and the private
disasters written off with stock quotations
from Shakespeare or Fitzgerald, perhaps to prove
the well-known commonness of experience,
the enemy across the mud, old age.

1959. It was necessary
at seventy-five, to show he couldn't be taken
by enfilading weaknesses. A horse
raised his defiance up. It threw him merely
to Russia on a stretcher, with two sticks
to lean beginner's Russian upon.

1969. The end of a decade
of surgeons, paling blindness, heart attacks,
all beaten with familiar literature
bent into philosophic platitudes,
to the January day in his dressing-gown
when he sat recording plans for a last Burns Supper.

You might have died so many kinds of death
as you drove yourself through eighty-four Novembers
till you fell from your bed, apologised for such foolishness,
and from your sleep rode out where no man goes.

The move from Head's Nook to Glasgow was a backbreaking
affair, mainly because of my library of some four thousand books
and two thousand gramophone records. My study, intended by
the architect to be the dining-room of the house, was a decorative
essay in opulent high-Victorian splendour.

Great Western Terrace, by whose railings I had wept so many
years ago when the family Nanny told me Uncle Doan was
getting married, had been completed in 1870 by Alexander
"Greek" Thomson, Glasgow's greatest architect after Charles
Rennie Mackintosh. Thomson's impressive urban range provided houses whose original magnificence could only have been
challenged by those that crowned the hill-top above Kelvingrove
with Charles Wilson's Park Circus. When first erected, Great
Western Terrace lay outside the City boundaries. As the minute
book of the original Association of Proprietors records, for five
years a night watchman had to be employed privately, until the
Glasgow police area was extended to take in Kelvinside.

After a generation or so, the rich merchant princes who had
been the original occupants of these houses—among them Sir
William Burrell, donor of the magnificent Burrell collection of
pictures, tapestries and *objets d'art*—were gradually succeeded by

less affluent Glaswegians. In 1910, a year of severe financial hardship for Scotland, the construction of stately terraces and tenement blocks was abandoned, leaving many of them permanently unfinished, edged with jagged, protruding keystones. In that year, Number Eleven Great Western Terrace was divided into four flats, permission to break the single occupancy clause of the title deeds having to be procured from the House of Lords. The house thus became among the first of the great city mansions to be flatted, a process post-1914-war economic changes soon made common practice.

The immediately previous occupants of our new home had been the grandchildren of the painter Tom McEwan, a member of the Ben-and-Glen school with a particular penchant for the browns of autumn, whose studio had been in Blythswood Square. Many of his pictures adorned the walls of his descendants' flat. I attended the auction at which they were sold, hoping to buy one or two pictures to preserve some sort of continuity. By then, however, the Ben-and-Glen school had already risen well above its wartime level of disfavour, and the prices soared far beyond the limits of my pocket.

We soon discovered that a tentative scheme for the restoration of Great Western Terrace had been prepared, but lacked the necessary impetus to carry it into practice. Before long, I found myself in charge of its realisation. In the event, negotiations with thirty-two proprietors simply to reach the point at which the scheme could go out to tender took nine years, during which costs greatly increased. The restoration eventually used up the best part of £250,000. About half of this amount was found by the owners themselves, the other half coming from the government through the Historic Buildings Council for Scotland, a body on which I was later to serve, and the local authority. The countless thousands who daily use Great Western Road in the course of their lawful occasions certainly get good value for this particular expenditure of public money. The terrace is a delight to look upon, and the restoration has established beyond question its status as one of the greatest pieces in the still undervalued gallery of Glasgow's architectural heritage.

For the next few years my time was almost wholly devoted to establishing The Scottish Civic Trust. Though an offshoot of the parent body in London—The Civic Trust, founded by Duncan Sandys (later Lord Duncan-Sandys) in 1957—The Scottish Civic

Trust is an independent organisation responsible for raising its own financial support. With Viscount Muirshiel as its first chairman, the Trust was officially launched on May 27th, 1967 at a ceremony in the Bute Hall of the University of Glasgow, presided over by its Vice-Chancellor, Charles (later Sir Charles) Wilson. As we left the platform Sir Robert Matthew, one of the founder Trustees, murmured to me:

"We'll need to do something about the New Town of Edinburgh."

"Indeed," I agreed, not then having the faintest idea of the scope of the operation that would turn out to be necessary.

During the preparatory weeks between my arrival in our empty office with my enthusiastic secretary, Margaret Miller, and the Trust's official inauguration, we had already been forced into action by a cry of help from an *ad hoc* local group in Stranraer. During my Border Television days a previous Town Council had distinguished itself by wanting to pull down the town's Dutch-style town hall and a nearby eighteenth-century mansion used as local authority offices. By mustering public opinion through television, I had been partly instrumental in getting that threat averted. This same council had employed consultant architects to draw up plans for the redevelopment of the old centre of the town the charm of which consisted almost entirely of its casually winding streets. At their centre stood the sixteenth-century Castle Kennedy. The Council's latest bright idea was to get rid of the castle to make way for shops.

Being only a few weeks old, the Trust had no architect on its staff. I therefore enlisted the help of Curtis Wolfe, an architect who practised in Gatehouse of Fleet and was widely known for his sensitivity where the restoration and restitution of old buildings was concerned. Together, we crawled over the castle and quickly agreed that on no account should it be destroyed. An on-the-spot argument then developed with a local councillor, sent to support the views of his destructively-minded colleagues.

"What right have you to interfere with the decision of the elected local representative?" he demanded.

"The right of democracy," I replied, my impudence buttressed by some hasty homework. "You were certainly elected; but only twenty per cent of the electorate bothered to vote at all, and a mere twelve per cent of that minority plumped for you!" He tried another tack.

"Ma ancestors were tortured in yon castle," was his startling retort. "An that's why I want to see it dinged doon."

"On these grounds," said I, "you could claim that Edinburgh Castle ought also to be dinged doon and replaced with a car park."

"Ah'd be in favour o' that," said the elected representative.

Fortunately, his attitude proved to be a last ditch example of a mindless anti-conservation prejudice common in Scotland since the middle of the nineteenth century. Later that year the Civic Amenities Act was passed—and the concept of the designated and protected Conservation Area was created. Demolition proposals for the private profit of developers, or for the rating benefit of local authorities, may very well be environmentally misguided. Prior to 1967 they had often to be resisted by public-spirited individuals and local groups with no official encouragement whatever. Nowadays, most local councillors are much more mindful of their responsibilities towards our irreplaceable heritage.

Castle Kennedy, Stranraer's Town House and its eighteenth-century near-neighbour were all saved, though unfortunately much needlessly unsympathetic town centre redevelopment went ahead.

As recently as twenty years ago the basic case for conservation had constantly to be argued, public opinion being slow to absorb "education". Local groups of enthusiasts had to be formed throughout Scotland. When The Scottish Civic Trust came on the scene there were about twenty-seven civic or amenity societies throughout the country. Within the first decade of the Trust's existence this total was built up to around one hundred-and-fifty. Some societies became highly organised, democratically well conducted, technically informed and undeniably effective in carrying through useful local projects and expressing to planning authorities an informed, and therefore much appreciated, view on local environmental matters. Others in areas relatively free from development pressures concerned themselves mainly with such minor, though locally important, matters as ensuring that the village green was properly maintained.

To some extent the National Trust for Scotland, through its increasingly significant ownership and management of land of outstanding beauty and buildings of historical or architectural importance on behalf of the nation, had been carrying out this educational process since its inception more than fifty years ago. It catered in its early days, however, mainly for leisure-seekers, and, perhaps understandably, surrounded itself with a slightly upper-class aura. Its appeal was thus to the converted. Unlike the National Trust, The Scottish Civic Trust has no members, relying for its "grass roots" contacts on those locally independent, though loosely affiliated, civic or amenity societies which now cover the length and breadth of Scotland.

The earliest new Civic Societies to come into being after the establishment of The Scottish Civic Trust had to be cajoled into existence. Later societies evolved spontaneously out of local needs.

Aberdeen, the third largest Scottish city, had no amenity organisation in 1967. It therefore seemed an obvious place for the Trust to make a start. A public meeting was organised with the aid of Aberdeen's Junior Chamber of Commerce. At first, Viscount Muirshiel and I appeared together on platforms of this kind. We set out in my car for Aberdeen. At noon, I suggested we might stop off at a Brechin hotel for lunch, but Muirshiel was keen that we should push on beyond Angus. Before moving to his final Renfrewshire seat, he had been Member of Parliament for the Montrose district, and still found it difficult to enjoy an undisturbed meal in his old constituency. Roadworks so delayed us, however, that by the time we reached Brechin we had either to eat there or forgo lunch altogether. We decided to stop. Inside the hotel, the barman advanced towards us effusively. Hand held out in our direction, he said:

"Mr Maurice Lindsay, I'm so delighted to meet you. I've often enjoyed your television programmes. What can I do for you and your friend?"

The former Secretary of State for Scotland, one of the most charming and urbane of men, took this demonstration of the ubiquitous power of television in great good part.

As it happened, the account was soon squared. A few weeks later, when we were engaged on a similar operation in Greenock, some of his one-time political opponents had infiltrated the audience and, for no reason obvious to me, proceeded to heckle us. I found this disturbance irrational and irritating. Muirshiel laughed it off. Heckling, had nothing to do with reason, and anyway, it was a normal part of every politician's experience.

I have heard it claimed that the Civic Society movement built up throughout the United Kingdom during the sixties and seventies was composed almost exclusively of "middle-class pressure groups". Leaving aside the obnoxious snobbery implied, so far as Scotland is concerned this was certainly quite untrue. Civic societies came into being in "underprivileged" Glasgow districts like Maryhill, Springburn and Govan; areas undergoing massive redevelopment and possessing very few listed buildings. Local people clearly felt the need of an independent body to express their concern that the development of their district should, as far as possible, reflect their hopes and wishes, and not just the latest fashionable whims of the central planners. Even with the establishment of elected but often party-motivated community councils there is still a real need for responsible civic or amenity societies. The present style "all or nothing," take-it-or-leave-it political manifestos rarely concern themselves much with environmental issues. Organisations like civic societies, dealing exclusively with one particular, though major, aspect of life, can still perform a vital watch-dog function, even although their only power is that of persuasion.

The Scottish Civic Trust's first major project was the setting up of organisational machinery to carry through a survey of all the five thousand or so homes in the Georgian New Town of Edinburgh. In this it had the expert partnership of the Edinburgh Architectural Association. More than one hundred and forty architects, surveyors, civil engineers, photographers and devoted secretarially-minded citizens, over a period of eighteen months produced a detailed account of the troubles affecting, or likely soon to affect, the two-hundred-year old New Town of Edinburgh, the most extensive compact piece of eighteenth-century town planning to be found anywhere in Europe. The results of this massive survey, the details of what was then a unique exercise in public participation, and the outcome, are recorded in *The Conservation of Georgian Edinburgh.**

The Edinburgh New Town Conservation Committee was established under the chairmanship of a former Lord Provost of Edinburgh, John Grieg Dunbar, with the architect Desmond Hodges as its first Director, and a start was then made on the work of repair and restoration, a task that may well prove to be never-ending, though of inestimable benefit not only to

* Edinburgh University Press (1972).

Scotland's heritage but also to her important, if not always sufficiently conservation-minded, tourist industry.

The initiator of all this, and, later, its presiding genius was, as I have indicated, Sir Robert Matthew, the architect of London's New Zealand House and Royal Festival Hall. I had first met Robert in the early fifties, when he was architect to London County Council and Chairman of the London branch of the Saltire Society. It invited me to London to talk about contemporary Scottish literature and to read my own poetry. I stayed with the Matthews, and quickly became aware not only of the warmth of Robert's personality, but also of his ability to master what were important points in the context of an argument, a technique I was later to watch him practise many times over during the months when our Edinburgh venture was evolving from its brave but uncharted beginnings towards the culminating public event presaging practical action.

This was a one-day international conference held in Edinburgh's Georgian Assembly Rooms on a warm Saturday in June 1970. The speakers included the then Minister of State, Lord Hughes, the Lord Provost of Edinburgh, Neil Mackay, Count Sforza, at that time Deputy Secretary General to the Council of Europe, Lord Holford, Sir Colin Buchanan (though not yet knighted), François Sorlin, who had successfully restored several major "hotels" in the Marais district of Paris for General de Gaulle, and Sir John Betjeman, who played the popularising role in what was fundamentally a major publicity effort to persuade the folk of Edinburgh that their New Town really was unique and as worth saving as the experts claimed.

One daft incident diversified the day. Tickets for the eleven hundred seats in the Music Hall of the Assembly Rooms had been bought and duly occupied. Significantly, the audience was made up mainly of New Town residents, the people concerned. They listened to the speeches and debated the implications from ten in the morning until five in the afternoon. During the lunch break, two student interlopers managed to join the company. At the final question time they did their best to lobby a so-called alternative project, the need for a sewage works in Edinburgh, then apparently still discharging untreated effluent into the Firth of Forth. When the concluding vote was taken, eleven hundred people supported the motion placing upon The Scottish Civic Trust the task of proceeding (with Government and Local

Authority support and financial aid) to establish a New Town Conservation Committee. There were two votes against. In announcing the motion carried by a large majority, the conference chairman, Viscount Muirshiel, in his characteristic friendly manner made it plain that while a sewage works was undoubtedly of the first importance to Edinburgh, so was the New Town; but the sewage debate was for different experts and another time and place. In spite of the usual shortage of money, the Edinburgh New Town Conservation Committee is now an established force for the Capital's and Scotland's benefit.

So, too, though perhaps more improbably and with a more limited objective, has been the conservation of, and revival of life in, the eighteenth-century model village of New Lanark. This industrial centre on the upper Clyde, unique in Scotland, was founded by David Dale and further developed by his son-in-law, Robert Owen. The belief was that if the workers in their cotton mills were provided with good accommodation by the standards of the day, a co-operative shop (well before the founding of the Scottish Co-operative movement), a church, an institution for moral improvement and recreational facilities, together with schooling for the children, output would rise. The cotton industry closed down in the middle of the nineteenth century and the Gourock Rope Works took over. By the 1960s, however, nylon had made conventional rope-making an obsolete process. The village went into a steep decline and seemed likely to face abandonment and dereliction. The Scottish Civic Trust therefore coordinated the setting up of a Committee under the chairmanship of a former Provost of Lanark, Harry S. Smith, and a full-time director, James Arnold, to reverse the decline in New Lanark's fortunes following the disappearence of its industrial purpose. In reaching agreement to set up this arrangement there was invaluable support, not only from Provost Smith, who helped to foster the project from the start, but also from Charles Gray, then chairman of the Planning Committee of Lanark County Council, who admitted to having been converted by the arguments in favour of saving the place. To me he remains unique, in that he is the only politician I have ever met who admitted to responding to reason rather than party dogma.

There was, once again, essential support from the Historic Buildings Council for Scotland and its enthusiastic secretary at the time, Harry Graham. Again, as with the New Town of

Edinburgh, the promise of local authority and governmental financial support made the critical transformation a practical possibility. Again, too, the Trust acted as the initial catalyst and co-ordinator, without whose efforts it is probably unlikely that work to save the fabric and the spirit of the place could have been begun in time.

If there had been nothing else to show from my years as The Scottish Civic Trust's first director but the saving of the New Town of Edinburgh and the village of New Lanark, I think I should feel well satisfied. Other things were, of course, achieved, including the saving from destruction and the adaptation for new uses of a large number of listed buildings of major architectural importance. Experience has shown on more than one occasion that the credit for exercising decisive influence in cases of this sort is frequently claimed by others only peripherally involved. All that ultimately matters, however, is that a worthwhile building has been saved, whoever thinks the credit should be his!

But this is not a history of The Scottish Civic Trust. I will therefore mention only one other project where our involvement was crucial, and our success not without its amusing aspects.

Papdale House, on the mainland of Orkney, is a small eighteenth-century mansion that was the birthplace of the Laing brothers, one of whom, Malcolm, made the first English translation of the Icelandic saga *Heimskringla* for the Everyman Library. The house could not have claimed particular importance had it stood on the outskirts of, say, Kilmacolm or Kirkintilloch rather than Kirkwall; but in the Orkney context, and because of the Laing connection, its proposed destruction had to be fought.

The local education committee acquired the Papdale estate and built a new school and hostel on it. They then wanted to pull down the original house. Our task was to persuade them to change their collective mind. A deputation of three flew to Orkney; Muirshiel, whose role was to explain the philosophical principles of conservation; the Glasgow architect Archie Doak, who had drawn up plans to convert Papdale House into a home for the school's rector; and me. I had to outline possible grant aid sources and deal with the financial aspects of the proposed conversion. After being heard out with that polite suspicion which is an Orkney characteristic wherever money is concerned, we were asked to adjourn to allow the committee to deliberate. Before we were summoned back there was a break for tea, during which an elected member, a former service officer of high rank, came over to me, cup in hand, and said:

"Damn funny thing a bloody poet talking about finance."

"I hope that's not literary criticism," I observed.

"What's that you say?" he bellowed, evidently hard of hearing.

"I said I think that's a very neat witticism," I bellowed back.

"Yes, isn't it," he agreed.

Our ideas were accepted, and Papdale House was saved. Although as always on such occasions many people helped in various ways, especially the Orkney Heritage Society led by the late gentle Ernest Marwick and the energetic Laura Grimond, The Scottish Civic Trust again acted as catalyst and co-ordinator. Because of my pre-war love of Orkney, this particular success gave me great personal satisfaction. Consequently, when I was invited to fly up for the opening ceremony and asked to bring with me the scroll to be hung in the hall of the house, I was delighted.

On a bright sunny morning, the framed scroll carefully parcelled, I boarded the aeroplane at Abbotsinch. As is the usual practice, the Orkney passengers disembarked for a short stop-over at Inverness. The sun was brightly shining, but the stop-over became longer and longer. Finally, it was announced that a thick fog had closed in over Orkney and there was no possibility of reaching Kirkwall that day. The Papdale House ceremony went ahead without me or the scroll.

Inevitably, I have come much into contact with planners during my years with The Scottish Civic Trust. There have always been a few sensitive souls among their ranks, though in recent years a greater number of the younger planners appeared much more keenly aware of the visual as well as the aesthetic values of conservation: but, like economics, planning is necessarily an impure discipline which cannot exercise its virtues outwith the influence of politics.

Acres of Glasgow, cleared of the collapsed debris of vanished nineteenth-century prosperity, cry out for new industry; yet in these job-hungry times the pressures of quick buck-makers lusting after green-field sites could prove hard for politicians and planners to resist.

The universal benefits that planning was supposed to confer upon the quality of our lives when it was first imposed on us after the Second World War have proved to be largely illusory. No doubt its propagandists set our expectations too high. No doubt the craft of planning carries at least its fair share of stolidly unimaginative practitioners; possible an even larger share than the older and still more highly respected profession of architecture, whose members in the end must bear responsibility for the spread of the dehumanised post-war style known as "brutalism". Yet in spite of innumerable small, and not so small, planning successes, the grand failures have been all too many.

Some blame undoubtedly lies with our democratic system, through which local and national elections often throw up a large proportion of garrulous, dogma-ridden functional illiterates on whose narrow shoulders rests the burden of decision-making on behalf of us all. Admittedly, I know of no better, or at least of no less unreliable, system. It is often claimed that the composition of our local authorities and, indeed, our governments, reflects more or less the broad cross-section of the kind of people we are. Looking back over British history it is difficult to avoid the conclusion that economic success in Elizabethan and Victorian times depended largely on our ability to plunder and exploit with greater energy than our rivals the natural resources and enforceable cheap labour of backward nations. In a world where such conduct in no longer acceptable, or practically possible, we stand forth in another light; a people uncompetitive, lazy and resentful. To all intents and purposes Scotland was knocked out of the colonising competition with the failure of the Darien Scheme, just before the Union of the Crowns. In practical terms she probably gave up her struggle for nationhood soon after the First World War. Yet even in such a context of accepted decline, I sometimes think that she seems to be afflicted with more than her fair share of those to whom objective reasoning is something of an unaccustomed exercise, and who certainly care little enough for her heritage.

Our planning and conservation laws are said to be the envy of Europe, but full use is not made of them. We are of course by no means the only people to have let much of our man-made historic heritage fall apart. Unfortunately, laws that look good on paper do not necessarily work out in practice. Too much financial responsibility threatens both local authorities and individuals who might try to act as the law allows. It is perhaps unreasonable to expect a hard-pressed local authority, even if it is sympathetically inclined towards conservation, to enforce maintenance repairs upon the reluctant owner of a listed property, and possibly end up with a large bill which it has to meet itself, or with an unsaleable property on its own hands.

Many local authorities are not, of course, sympathetically inclined. When anti-conservation authorities make up their collective minds to get rid of an historical building, as often as not that building will disappear. If it is not accidentally bulldozed—as happened notably to two buildings in the territory of one English authority during the seventies—it may be declared "unsafe" and peremptorily removed "in the public interest": failing which, it may be "murdered" by being left to crumble gently down, another victim of apparently blameless neglect. The plain fact is that where conservation issues are concerned the national purse does not open with commensurate generosity to match the declarations of the national mouth.

We cannot, of course, save everything from the past; nor should we try to. In Scotland, where the man-made heritage forms an important capital asset of our tourist trade, we are not saving enough. As the ravages of decades of unchecked decay work their slow harm on the fabric of our cities and towns, the threat to the man-made heritage spreads like an insidious disease for which lax laws, however excellent in theory, quite clearly cannot any longer be expected to produce spectacular cures. The relatively trifling financial resources made available for conservations since 1946 have done little more than rescue some of the more glamorous and famous patients from premature demise. Disaster has befallen many thousands more.

I like to think that there may yet be better times ahead. During the past twenty or so years, the young have swung in behind the conservation movement, offering some slight hope for the future. Meanwhile, though more popular, it is still not a major vote-winning topic, and so continues to lack political muscle.

Alongside my new career as an environmentalist, my return to Glasgow produced a renewed outburst of creativity. Two poetry collections, *This Business of Living* (1969) and *Comings and Goings* (1971), were put out by Duncan Glen's Akros Publications. The occasional seemingly inevitable misprint apart, both were models of book design. I had been a regular contributor to *Akros*, Glen's poetry magazine, for many years. It did much to encourage Scottish poets. As an editor, Glen was generously catholic in his taste, although occasionally apt to display a somewhat blinkered predilection for indifferent work merely because it happened to be in Scots.

This Business of Living and *Comings and Goings* contain some of my most frequently anthologised poems. Of them, James Aitchison wrote: "There is an emotional climate in the poetry of his fellow Scots, Norman MacCaig, Iain Crichton Smith and George Mackay Brown; there is also a clear sense of physical, almost regional landscape in their work . . . Lindsay does not colonise experience in this way, rather explores a wider range of ordinary experience; and he does so with an almost imperceptible technique, using his considerable craft to conceal the craft of poetry rather than declaim it. His voice is no less distinctive than those of most of his contemporaries but it is a quiet voice; it is also one that is impossible to parody."

Comings and Goings was dedicated to my wife, a gift to mark our first quarter-century of marriage. From Brownsbank, Biggar, MacDiarmid wrote: "Many thanks for the inscribed copy of 'Comings and Goings'. I think you have struck a rich vein in these pieces about everyday incidents and domestic matters . . . I was struck of course by the dedication to Joyce. Twenty-five years! It is unbelievable. I know only too well how the passing of the years accelerates as one gets older. I can only wish Joyce and you another twenty-five years of happiness together."

A prose quotation, come upon by chance when reading another author twice provided me with a rough thematic framework for a poetry collection. A remark by Marie Leneru fulfilled this purpose in *Snow Warning*, when she declared: "Wit and goodness and laughter and malice, *la toilette* and change and noise, one must love all this—*because there is nothing else*". A quotation by the American poet Archibald McLeish fulfilled a similar function for *This Business of Living*: "I have been proceeding so far on an assumption and a proposition . . . the assumption that our deepest human need is to make sense of our lives, and the proposition that poetry is one—and in some ways the most effective—of the means by which life can be brought to sense."

To help me try to make a little more sense of Scotland to myself, I decided that two tasks ought now to be undertaken. One was the compilation of a more catholic and extensive anthology of Scottish poetry and prose than had ever been brought between two covers. It was published in 1974 as *Scotland: An Anthology*, and was well reviewed, both here and in America. The American editions sold out but the British edition—though described by *The Scotsman* as "an anthology that will give much pleasure to us; a book that should be read by a roaring fire, preferably with a dram at hand" and by the *Glasgow Herald* as "a serendipity shop"—eventually achieved the somewhat melancholy distinction of being the only one of my works ever to be remaindered. By that time I had reached the conclusion, rather ruefully, that the Scots are simply no longer much interested in the great words and moments of decision that shaped their past. Having only a shadowy present and an even less substantial national future, possibly this lack of interest should not be altogether surprising.

My other self-imposed task was much more formidable; the writing of a *History of Scottish Literature*. The previous work of its kind, by J. H. Millar, appeared as long ago as 1903, and had concluded with a vigorous but rather overstated attack upon the then comparatively new Kailyard School in its historical context. Mine concluded with a consideration, albeit interim, of the Scottish Renaissance movement and a glance at what kind of literary future, if any, might lie ahead of us.

When published, the book amounted to just under five hundred pages. It was written in longhand in my study at Great Western Terrace, mostly over weekends and on weekdays late into the night.

I vowed I should write of nothing I had not read, or at least carefully inspected. This turned out to be a self-imposition that involved many hours of research in libraries and a perusal of much that was third-rate. The effort of amassing and ordering such a huge quantity of fact, and weighing it all in the balance of my own judgement—incidentally, I do not believe there is any such thing as "objective" history-telling, especially where the arts are concerned—in addition to running The Scottish Civic Trust, writing several concert notices a week for the *Glasgow Herald* and broadcasting regularly, though enjoyable, was quite considerable.

An English scholar, writing in an American academic magazine dealing with studies in Scottish literature, doubted whether, in an age of specialisation such as ours, overall histories of subjects could serve any useful purpose. It all depends, I suppose, on what is meant by "useful". If the true purpose of literature is not, in the broadest sense, to give pleasure and delight to the general reader by widening and deepening his perception of life and his understanding of human nature, then the labours of generations of poets, novelists and playwrights have been futile. Literature is certainly not intended merely to provide raw material for abstruse or eclectic doctrinal theses, or bring readily to hand an acceptable supply of dry bones with which contending academics may smite each other. Deny the validity of the pleasure principle and you rip art out by the roots.

During my nine years at Great Western Terrace another pleasant opportunity came my way. I had the welcome chance of correcting the errors of inevitable haste in my *Burns Encyclopedia* and in *Robert Burns: the Man, his Work, the Legend*, substantially rewriting both for a second edition. Not long after, the demand for a third edition, this time linked to a small American edition, gave me special satisfaction in that now, for the first time, my two Burns books appeared under Hale's imprint.

If I have achieved anything of permanent value—apart, perhaps, from the handful of poems by which most minor poets survive through anthologies—I like to think that for a time at least it may perhaps be my *History of Scottish Literature*, and for perhaps a rather longer period, my *Burns Encyclopedia*.

My admiration for Burns developed during the war. First and foremost he is, of course, a subtle poet. In addition, he caught and conserved through his verse, and to a lesser extent his vigorous letters, the "feel" of the old agrarian Scotland that had lasted more or less unchanged from mediaeval times, but in his day was trembling on the verge of dissolution before the pressures of the Industrial Revolution.

Scotland has produced no other artist so worthy of our gratitude and honour. It is small wonder that the Scots have made of him their national bard, celebrating his birthday annually with Burns suppers. Many of those who have no feeling whatever for poetry—the majority, unfortunately!—are instinctively aware of Burns' role as a unifying symbol holding together what people of widely differing sensibilities experience as their sense of Scotland. Our "National Bard" in some curious way even helps us sublimate our all-too-evident national failure in political and economic terms; the slow but steady decline of control over our own destiny that has relentlessly ebbed away Scottish self-confidence since his day. Without the impact of Burns—complemented, of course, by that of Sir Walter Scott, whose six greatest Waverley Novels popularised the main confrontation points of Scottish history—it is very possible that the North British movement of the early nineteenth century would have reduced Scotland even more rapidly to the fiery impotence of an occasionally troublesome English region.

For that reason I have come to think mistaken MacDiarmid's campaign against Burnsolatry, although in my youth I sympathised with it. Mistaken, too, was his intellectually much more justified onslaught on music-hall Scotchery. The sad fact is that we can no longer afford to encourage the further loosening of anything at all that ties up the shards of popular national sentiment, however frayed the strings or tawdry the wrappings, unless we are once-and-for-all prepared to renounce our claims to nationhood and stop pretending!

Realisation that Scotland totally lacked the political will for self-help dawned on me after I had campaigned for John MacCormack's Scottish Assembly. On 28th November, 1949 I appeared on the platform of the enthusiastic rally held in a packed St Andrews Hall, when the so-called third National Covenant was launched with the greatest enthusiasm. Unfortunately, it lost momentum almost immediately, achieving virtually nothing. MacCormack himself had been taken by surprise at its success and had failed to work out any practical follow-up which might have circumvented the vested interests of the English-dominated Tory and Labour parties against conceding even limited Home Rule within the United Kingdom framework. My subsequent roles as a communicator and as Director of The Scottish Civic Trust thereafter kept me out of any practical involvement in politics.

Truth to tell, I have never had much of a stomach for the deception and subterfuges which constitute much of its code of conduct. My belief that I could more usefully play a non-political role produced a curious confrontation with the then solitary Scottish National Party representative in Parliament, Winnie Ewing, whose patriotism, tenacity and courage I greatly admired. We had spoken at a Burns supper in Bathgate. Afterwards, she attacked me furiously for my public apolitical stance. What right had I to stand back from the battle, she demanded? Did I imagine it was fun to have to face up to the rough and tumble of practical politics at the expense of normal domestic life? I did my best to explain that, rightly or wrongly, I believed I achieved much more as a writer and broadcaster, strengthening public awareness of the Scottish heritage, than I could ever accomplish as a reluctant and inexpert practising politician. The better to stem her indignation I stressed:

"Besides, you are good at it. I wouldn't be. It's no use doing what you aren't good at."

I refrained from pointing out that, whatever either of us might feel about Home Rule, countless opinion polls over the past fifty years have made plain the absence of popular support for a policy of total separation from England. On the other hand, there had been, and still is, a fairly consistent poll majority for Home Rule within a perhaps constitutionally reorganised United Kingdom. Much as I should like to see a Scotland as proudly independent as Norway or Denmark, I have come to admit to myself that emotionalism is an unreliable touchstone by which to measure practical affairs. You cannot unscramble an egg. Two centuries and a half of willing self-abasement has in all probability made impossible the complete economic disentanglement of Scotland from the United Kingdom. The popular view that meaningful devolution is feasible and desirable therefore seems to me the right one. Never before has there been so great a need for the unification of Europe if the free world is physically to survive, let alone prosper; but that does not preclude reorganisation within its framework. Needless to say, I got nowhere at all in this argument with Winnie Ewing. Nevertheless we parted friends.

At Great Western Terrace, we had the happy experience of watching our children grow into delightful adult friends. The transition was in each case smooth, and we were spared the traumas of rejection and hostility that some parents have to endure; or, perhaps, bring upon themselves by narrow over-domination, or a reluctance, at the right time, to let go.

We had enjoyed many family holidays abroad. With our friends the Nellemanns we had several times stayed in Denmark—at first in their beautiful self-built house overlooking the lake at Lille Vaerløse, and later in their still more beautiful farm house near Frederikshavn, in North Jutland. We explored fairly thoroughly that pleasant country, its kindly people of all our European partners perhaps the most similar in temperament to ourselves.

There is also a curious literary parallel, in that Robert Burns and Hans Christian Andersen were both of peasant stock, and both were born in humble cottages that have come places of pilgrimage visited by scholars, admirers and tourists from every corner of the globe. My own visit resulted in a poem, "At Hans Christian Andersen's Birthplace", which first appeared in *Snow Warning*, a copy of which is now in the library of the birthplace at Odense.

As a family, we had also toured extensively in Belgium, Switzerland and Germany, and spent holidays in homes or villas in Austria, Holland, France and Italy. My wife and I have also made many long European explorations by car. There is a special delight in being able to choose the route and Alpine pass up which one wants to drive, and to drink in the heady coolness of its heights at leisure; to visit old towns in the mood for private discovery; or see Richard Strauss's Garmisch, or mad Ludwig's Bavarian fairy-tales in stone without the pressure of a tour guide jogging one's elbow.

"Just think, honey," said one blue-rinsed American lady to another at Neuschwannstein. "Ludwig put all this up just so that we could come and see." To which "honey" replied: "And fancy them being able to build like this all these years ago!"

From such overheard tit-bits, only occasionally amusing, the tourist in command of his own wheels can easily free himself.

A European from head to toe, I have always found the regular absorption of other aspects of that culture of which we are inextricably a part essential to keep my spiritual batteries charged. Since The Scottish Civic Trust is a member of *Europa Nostra*, the advisory body on conservation to the Council of Europe, I have also had opportunities of getting to know some less familiar parts of Europe under its auspices.

Duncan Sandys—later Lord Duncan-Sandys—who had set up the Civic Trust in London in 1956 shortly after he had moved on from being Minister of Housing and Local Government, had also been one of the prime movers in the founding of *Europa Nostra*, and since 1969 its Chairman. His energy, his clear declamatory style tinged occasionally with a touch of the Churchillian rhetorical stammer, and his ability to speak French and German, made him an outstanding success in this role.

Among his many virtues, subtle logical persuasion was not perhaps among his strongest. Since I have known him, his technique in a discussion, whether on television or so to say, "live" was not to attempt to answer the counter-arguments of an opponent, but simply to keep on reiterating his own original arguments, thus wearing the opponent down.

The most remarkable practical application of this gift for absolute insistence occurred during a *Europa Nostra* seminar in the seventies, in the Italian town of Bologna. Bologna at that time had a communist administration which had gained considerable credit in international planning and conservation circles from the publication of extensive and detailed plans for the restoration of many of its fine old buildings. During the practical part of the seminar the delegates were conducted round an exhibition thick with promise, and then taken to see the actual work on the ground. Unfortunately, the only example of civic restoration that could be shown was a group of two houses accidentally bombed by the Italian airforce during the war. Lord Duncan-Sandys thereupon demanded that we should be taken to inspect the many examples of private restoration he had noticed driving about the city. The local authority official in charge of us at first put up every possible kind of objection. About half an hour later he gave up. Collapsing down beside me in the coach just before it moved off on the desired inspection and sweating profusely, he mopped his brow, grabbed my arm and said, hoarse with feeling: "Now I see why you British won the war!"

Lord Duncan-Sandys's persistence in the cause of conservation has undoubtedly made some European impact on issues of greater consequence. More than most, he fully merited the many honours bestowed on him by several European countries.

To one who, like me, finds music almost as vital a daily necessity as breath, no country offers such associational satisfaction as Austria. In one sense visiting the shrines of writers or composers is the pursuit of illusion. Mozart, to my mind the supreme creative genius among all the world's great artists, is certainly not to be encountered behind the gilded frontage of his Salzburg birthplace, with its hygienically preserved rooms through which the grateful and curious daily file; still less in the home in the Makartplatz* (in Mozart's day the Hannibalplatz) across the river, the Mozart family's more spacious semi-detached final Salzburg home. When I first visited Salzburg, the half of the two-storey villa where the Mozart family lived had been destroyed during the war by an American bomb, and was in

---

* Thus renamed after a painter who subsequently lived there.

the process of being rebuilt. Meanwhile, the museum was
housed in the neighbouring half.

On a later visit I discovered—Oh horror!—that sure enough,
the rebuilt original Mozart half-villa was once more a museum,
but in place of the half that survived the war there now stood a
towering block of high-rise flats, destroying forever the period
graciousness of the whole surroundings. To the Mayor of
Salzburg I immediately wrote an indignant letter. He did not
reply, possibly because the postage involved in answering
similar expressions of hopeless distress would have been
considerable!

I drew consolation from the reflection that Mozart himself
thought little enough of the Salzburg civic dignitaries of his own
day. The Salzburg of the mind lives on through his music.

It was in Vienna—war-battered but miraculously free Vienna,
enough of its heart surviving to preserve its traditional image—
that much of Mozart's greatest music was written. Hard against
St Stephen's Cathedral there is the Figaro House, where the
world's greatest comedy with music was composed—to say
nothing of several more or less simultaneously written masterpieces—in the incredible space of six weeks. To stand alone in the
bare little room where those wonderful finales to the second and
fourth acts were conceived was an unforgettable experience; an
act of silent thanksgiving for perhaps the most human and
munificent of the many miracles Mozart bestowed upon man-
kind.

Possibly because the youthful flow of Mozart's genius, so
cruelly compressed between his sixth and thirty-sixth years,
seems so abundantly effortless and cosmopolitan, the impact of
his other place-associations are harder to pin down. It is much
easier, for instance, to visualise the restless Beethoven stamping
and scowling about his many Viennese homes; or sense the
presence of Schubert in the birthplace, Himmelpfortgrund No.
72 (now Mussdorferstrasse No. 54), long since hemmed in by
out-of-scale nineteenth-century office tenements; or think of him
again, in more relaxed mood, among the Weinstuben of the
Grinzig district, where he loved to relax with his friends, and
where tourists now gulp down delicately cool *heurige Wein* while
sweating waiters rush about dishing out meals for packaged
bus-loads.

The first time I followed Schubert's tracks a taxi set me down outside the home of Mozart's *Magic Flute* librettist, Emanuel Schikaneder. To my surprise, a plaque on the wall informed me that it had also been a home of Franz Lehar, whose operettas give us so delicious a twist of later Viennese musical confectionery.

Sometimes, following the tracks of a composer has led me into a blind alley. Boccherini, whose music I have admired since boyhood—and about whose life and work I even hoped to write a book had circumstances allowed—was born in the still fascinating mediaeval walled town of Lucca, in Northern Italy. In 1927, long before the current revival of interest in his music, the Luccans brought back his remains from Madrid, where he had died in 1805, and reinterred them in the Basilica di San Francisco.

During the summer of 1979, I set out in search of his birthplace, located in the Via Boccherini, according to my guide-book. After a bewildering quest down narrow streets, eventually I found it. The Via Boccherini had been renamed in the early sixties in honour of a local politician whose contribution to the fame of their town not a single Luccan I spoke to could recall!

A similar experience ended my search in Zürich for gramophone records of the music of Joachim Raff. I went into a large shop, where a Germanic-looking cigar-smoking assistant advanced to attend to me.

"Have you any Raff?" I inquired.

"Vot is Raff?" said he.

"One of your best Swiss composers," said I; "very well known at the beginning of the century."

"Swiss music no goot," he declared, emphasising the judgment with a vigorous wiggle of cigar smoke. The clanking and creaking of an over-amplified pop group made conversation exhausting.

"If I may say so," I opined politely, "that music is no good either."

"Ach," said my stout Germanic friend, "but that no goot pay."

But to return to Vienna. Though you may gaze, if you are so minded, upon the couch of Sigmund Freud, it is curiously difficult to pick up the tracks of Brahms or Mahler. My inability to raise much deep-rooted enthusiasm for the music of Schönberg and the other members of the second Viennese school at least left me free to pursue the airier ghost of Johann Strauss whose statue, violin swirling in mid-phrase, is one Viennese monument tourists never miss.

Wine, women and song! So we think of Vienna. But something seems to have happened to the city's legendary gaiety. Sitting one evening in a cafe in the Kärtnerstrasse, I was surprised to find that I was the only customer. Unlike Paris, or even London, modern Vienna, it seems, goes prosaically to bed at 10 o'clock.

Finally, great Haydn, whose house in Vienna I looked at from the outside. Much more of his spirit is to be found in the beautifully restored great hall of the Esterhazy palace at Eisenstadt, where many of his early symphonies were first performed; more still in his spacious home in the centre of the town. Standing before his marble tomb in the Eisenstadt parish church, it was odd to recall that after his death that head, for so long a generous source of invention, inspired gruesome thieves to sever it from the body before burial, the bones remaining disunited until 1932.

Deep as has been my devotion to the music of Schubert and Haydn, it is ultimately to Mozart that I always return; a composer, indeed, for every season of the heart. Throughout the war I carried in my pocket a bound copy of the miniature score of the "Jupiter" Symphony. Whatever crisis of joy or grief I have encountered, it has been Mozart who has pronounced the healing benediction. Haydn, who awakened my musical sensibilities with his "Military" Symphony when I was ten, has cheered me increasingly along the approaches to old age. His persistent refusal to allow even the smallest hint of depression to weigh him down makes him an especially revivifying companion in times as troubled as ours, and his. Somewhere in between my affection for the music of Mozart and Haydn comes the eternal longing, the yearning beyond all possibility of gratification, that Schubert sublimated. He, too, is indispensable to me.

In my later years these three Viennese masters seem really to have no equals. That is not to say, of course, that I fail to thrill to the heroic striving and triumphant assertion of Beethoven; the ardent freshness of Schumann's romanticism, a freshness doomed to sicken with the century; the mythic all-engulfing sensual experience of Wagner—indeed, after first seeing the complete cycle of *The Ring*, it was at least a fortnight before I could bring myself to deal with the daily occasions of life again!—or the sensuous ecstasy-tossing of Richard Strauss, the last of the great composers wholly to win surrender from my senses.

Nor have I been deaf to older music: the spare intensity of

plainsong; the energy of secular mediaeval music, or the cold
rough-hewn mysticism of its religious counterpart. With Byrd,
Vittoria and Palestrina, I have been lifted willingly towards that
fancied heaven so confidently imagined by the great cathedral
builders; with Bach, bridged the Protestant equation of high
religious fervour and bourgeois profit-making that somehow for
a while also won through to the source of all things; and with
Albinoni and Vivaldi felt the late reflected warmth of Renaissance
Italian joyousness. I have loved, too, the music of Berlioz,
Mahler, Delius, Elgar, Shostakovich. But why go on? Those of us
for whom music is the only known synthesiser of all human
experience thankfully acknowledge that in its presence the
unanswerable trials and tyrannies of the moment are forced for a
time to loosen their hold.

So much for personal preferences. Much of my lifetime's
listening has been done for professional reasons. Thanks to Alec
Robertson's teaching I have always been conscious of the critic's
duty to respond to a composer within his own terms of reference.
The showy rhetoric of Liszt and the sumptuous self-pitying of
Tchaikovsky put them, for me, on a very much lower plane that
that occupied by many other masters; but to despise, for
example, Sir Arthur Sullivan or Emerich Kalman because neither
measures up to Schubert provokes false comparison and dictates
a needless self-denial of the lighter pleasures. I confess, however,
that I have neither managed to come to comfortable terms with
atonality, nor achieved even partial acceptance of the fashion of
those younger composers who favour aleatoric improvisation, to
my mind nothing less than a lazy abdication of artistic responsibility. Once, coming out of an Edinburgh Festival concert where
our ears had been sorely taxed, I ran into Desmond Shawe-
Taylor, also engaged in the critic's scuttle. "Jesus! Oh God!" said
I. "I don't know about them," said Shawe-Taylor: "but I think
I've got square ears, and I'm too old for the operation."

Late twentieth-century music mainly operates mathematical
formulae of unfolding sound-patterns rather than through lyric
flow. Most of what I hear, I dislike; and so, apparently, does the
seat-paying public. As a result, the gulf between "serious" contemporary music and "pop" has become virtually an unspan-
nable chasm. Somewhere in between comes Jazz, which despite
my many efforts to get on to its wavelength, still seems to me little
more than a kind of musical skittering. As for rock, punk, heavy

metal and the rest, words completely fail me. So far as I am concerned, with the mere gestural sounds of what constitutes "Top of the Pops" we have moved from the world of music into the domain of sociology, that pseudo half-discipline which seeks a behavioural explanation for anything and everything.

All of us have our regrets. Leaving aside such major regrets as the continuing decline of Scotland and the fatuously British "us" and "them" polarisation, perpetuated by the Trade Unions, that so disastrously hampers industry—matters about which personally I can do nothing—mine include the prejudice that kept me from eating oysters until I reached late middle-age, and an altogether lamentable absence of youthful enthusiasm to visit the United States of America.

In 1973, I was invited to cross the Atlantic for the first time by Patrick Hazard, then occupying a chair for the internationalising of English at Beaver College, Glenside, Pennsylvania. I was to give readings of my poetry and be willing to discuss the place of the media in relation to the arts in Britain. I found the vigour and variety of the eastern United States marvellously rejuvenating. I loved the cosmopolitan vitality and warm-hearted openness of the Americans I met, young and old, black and white. I greatly admired, indeed envied, the general refusal to believe that problems do not automatically contain their own solution, an attribute contrasting strongly with the world-weary current British custom of pretending that problems do not exist! Above all, the generous receptiveness of my American audiences gave me a great deal of much-needed personal encouragement.

A Scottish writer becomes accustomed to finding his work totally ignored in England, and if he is a poet, acknowledged only grudgingly by his own compatriots. If, as I so often found, a poem "worked" on an audience of alert and critical young Americans, it seems not unreasonable to suppose that an absence of interest elsewhere does not necessarily indicate a deficiency in the poem itself.

I gave poetry readings at Beaver College, the centrepiece of which is a replica of Alnwick Castle built for a nineteenth-century Pittsburgh coal owner, and in colleges and schools at Trenton and Philadelphia. At a large Catholic school in Philadelphia I was promised a few senior pupils who "might have some interest in poetry". To my astonishment, I found myself facing a crowded hall filled with youngsters from fifteen to eighteen years old, accompanied by several of the nuns and priests who were their teachers. I had chosen my programme carefully to avoid giving religious offence. When I had finished a nun stood up and said:

"I would be glad if you would read your 'Glasgow Nocturne', Mr Lindsay, and then explicate it."

This poem about Glasgow violence contains a phrase frequently scrawled on city walls, "Fuck the Pope". Its subject is the attack of a gang on a pair of teenage lovers one of whom has deserted the gang to go with the girl; its theme, the ultimate mindlessness of violence.

I did as I was asked. To my surprise and delight there followed a thoroughly adult discussion about the causes of urban violence and their reflection in literature. Afterwards, over a glass of sherry, I expressed surprise at such broad-mindedness.

"Do you think we don't know what people say in the world outside?" asked the nun. "You have to face up to problems, whoever you are and whether you like it or not."

Reading to audiences made up of people with no preconceived idea what to expect, and watching them react precisely as one hoped, is a heart-warming experience. I fancy that such a clean approach, unfettered by the irrelevant prejudices which so often cumber the Scottish mind, comes nearest, in the long run, to the method by which posterity makes its distanced judgements.

Some years later, while I was resting in bed recovering from a slipped disc and alone in the house, the telephone rang. Painfully answering it I learned that "Glasgow Nocturne", included in *Voices of Our Kind*, a schools anthology compiled and published for Glasgow Corporation, had been denounced as obscene by some workshop student at a Glasgow College. The journalist wondered if I had anything to say. What I actually said was, I fear, quite unprintable! Next morning, to my astonishment, the story appeared on the front page of the *Glasgow Herald* under the heading "Row Over 'Obscene' Poem," accompanied by a picture of a young woman holding up an illegally duplicated copy of the offending verses. The story ran:

"A poem handed out to an 'O' level English night class at Glasgow College of Commerce has led to a row between the college and one of the students.

Mrs Norma Wilson, aged 30, of 45, Moorhill Road, Newton Mearns, claimed yesterday the poem—written by Maurice Lindsay, director of the Scottish Civic Trust—is 'totally obscene,' and demanded that the college take some action against the teacher who introduced it to the class.

The poem, 'Glasgow Nocturne,' was handed out to the class of 20 on Wednesday evening by a young teacher who was standing in for the usual teacher.

Mrs Wilson said last night she intended to send a copy of the poem—which describes a sexual encounter and a street fight—to the Lord Provost of Glasgow and members of Strathclyde Regional Council's education department.

She said: 'My reaction was one of total shock when I was handed the poem. It is totally obscene, and should certainly not be required reading for an 'O' level English course.'

Mrs Wilson, a secretary at Glasgow University, added that she had also contacted Mr Robert McClement, Scottish secretary of the National Association of Schoolmasters and Union of Women Teachers, to look into the matter.

The poem, which is published in a collection of poems from 1942 to 1972, was given to the class as a homework exercise.

Mr Anthony Callaghan in charge of 'O' level classes at the college, said last night: 'I understand the teacher concerned was only taking the class on a temporary basis. I have launched an inquiry into the matter'.

Mr Lindsay said last night: 'This woman's view of my poem, which was published in 1968, is childish. She should be reading Enid Blyton instead of literature.' "

Bully for Mr Anthony Callaghan, thought I, for knowing how to keep his own escape hatch open! Not surprisingly, none of the dignitaries complained; nor took the slightest notice. Not surprisingly, my wife wanted to know if the pupils in her English class really thought the poem was obscene, since it was printed in one of their official text books. So a discussion on obscenity in literature took place; after which, there was general agreement that "Glasgow Nocturne" most certainly did not come into the obscene category. The background was only too familiar to most of the pupils. However, one boy, son of a professional purveyor of religion, reported the discussion to his father, who promptly complained to the Head Teacher. The Adviser was called in.

Since the poem was—and still is—in a text book approved for school pupils, Authority was not in a position to say very much. Eventually, my wife was censoriously informed that it might have been wiser not to have allowed discussion on the subject at that particular moment and with some of the pupils in that particular school. In other words, it would have been better to have battened down the well-worn hatches of Scottish hypocrisy on the natural and timorous curiosity of inquiring young minds.

Following a lecture on "Scotland's Heritage" which I gave for the British Council in Brussels in 1975, I was invited the following winter to undertake a lecture tour in Holland. My repertoire included both "Scotland's Heritage"—an illustrated survey of our man-made heritage down the ages and the laws and institutions devised for its conservation—and a reading of my own poetry. The tour took me to parts of Holland not normally visited by the tourist, including Eindhoven, where everything and everybody seemed to be connected with Philips; and Arnhem, with its bridge over the Rhine and nearby war museum commemorating the disastrous Allied airborne raid that was meant to assist the Allied armies of liberation.

The museum saddened me. I knew some of those who died in the operation. I have never been able to make up my mind if it is really wise to preserve the memories of the cruel divisions of the past in this way, since war, however "just" or inevitable, represents the ultimate failure of human intelligence. For us in these islands who escaped the horrors of Nazi occupation, it is perhaps easier to allow the scars of memory to heal than in the countries of Western Europe.

After Auschwitz, surely the most appalling of all monuments to human degradation, the worst I have seen is that at Oslo. Having paid my entrance money, I noticed that among the piles of catalogues in various languages much the highest was the German pile.

"You don't seem to sell many of these," I quipped, nodding to the German catalogues as I picked up an English one.

"Go inside and you'll see why," the ticket lady answered grimly.

Her point was not lost on me. Most young Germans, I fancy, do not want to be horribly reminded of the barbarities practised by their fathers in upholding the Third Reich, for which they themselves feel, quite rightly, that they had no responsibility.

A fascinating aspect of foreign lecture tours is being a guest in the homes of other people. At Arnhem, the family of my host and hostess possessed a handsome basset hound. As soon as I sat down the basset hound gave me a thorough nosing, no doubt

scenting traces of Toby, our own basset hound. The Dutch dog
then signified his desire for a close encounter of the more impossible kind by attempting to jump up on my knees, basset hounds
everywhere suffering from the delusion that they are really
lapdogs. That misunderstanding sorted out, he settled reproach-
fully at my feet. In due course he followed me up to my bedroom,
another basset hound delusion being that they provide good
bedfellows for humans. In spite of an even more reproachful
look, I shut the door firmly on his woeful face. In the morning, I
found that I had to step delicately out of my room. Over breakfast
I mentioned casually to my hostess that Hans had forgotten
himself on the rug outside my bedroom door.

"He certainly did not forget himself," she assured me firmly.
"That is Hans's way of saying he loves you!"

Our eldest daughter got married on 5th July, 1975. She decided
to have the ceremony performed in the Register Office. From
early July onwards until the 12th, grown-up men in Belfast and
Glasgow put on bowler hats, drape themselves in orange sashes,
and march in quasi-military formation through the streets behind
out-of-tune bands, ostensibly to celebrate the long-ago victory of
William of Orange over James VII and II in Ireland's Battle of the
Boyne, but in reality to demonstrate their belligerent intolerance
of a form of religious superstition different from their own. Our
journey from the car park to the Register Office was not un-
eventful.

> Walking with my daughter to her wedding,
> murder came marching through the town;
> two thin ranks of policemen stayed it
> from coming into its own.
> Spread women, ugly men and little children
> dressed in the Sunday best of bigotry,
> suffered to come unto intolerance
> down orange miles of bannered frippery;
> the gadfly flutes, the goading fifes,
> the yattering side-drums of expended wars
> forcing sectarian division through
> our public streets choked back with fuming cars.
>
> Between one section's end and the next,
> led by a white-gloved prancer with a stick—
> a clown without true clowning's dignity—
> we seized our chance to get there. I said *Quick*:
> and we were through.

A piece of the thing
leapt at us, a bulge of animal red,
knuckles half-raised, *D'ya waant tae get fuckanwell killed?*
"Back now. Get Back," a policeman intervened;
the threat retreated and the rite re-filled,
folded between blue mackintoshes, held
to keep democracy safe for those who hate
for the Queen's fame, in the name of gentle Jesus.

After the reception guests had departed and Joyce and I were recuperating over a glass of wine, relating our separate conversations, our second daughter announced her intention of following the nuptial trail. Six months later that wedding took place in Westbourne Church, where we ourselves had been married. Once again, there was another reception in "Greek" Thomson's spacious rooms.

Our son and youngest daughter being now both students, it was obvious that they, too, would soon leave home. Great Western Terrace had ten sixteen-feet high rooms, and before long we would be a two-person family. A proposal that we might move to part of a divided home on the outskirts of Kilmacolm came to nothing, but the feeling that we wanted to get back to the country had us in its grip.

One Saturday morning in the early summer of 1976 we looked at two houses in the Renfrewshire village of Houston. Both proved to be disappointingly unsuitable. Over lunch and a copy of the *Glasgow Herald* we noticed a house at Milton Hill claiming to have "a splendid view over the Clyde", so we drove to the north bank of the river and up a one-in-four hill, zig-zagging through a steeply-sloping garden development, in layout vaguely reminiscent of a French mountain village. At the top of the hill we encountered the "splendid view," and at once fell in love with it. The house itself was a wooden box on stilts, but its one big main room was large enough to accommodate many of our books. There and then we decided to buy it.

Leaving Great Western Terrace was something of a wrench. I had to get rid of about a third of my library, a painfully ruthless process involving the dispatch to the sale room of books I regarded as life-long friends. Out went my copy of Fabre's *Book of Insects*, bought with pennies that almost fifty years ago should have been spent on a school meal. Out, too, went my eighteenth century copy with the long s's of Thomson's *The Seasons*, over which as a teenager I had dreamed on summer afternoons in Glasgow's Botanic Gardens. Part of my archives—correspondence, poetry notebooks and so on—had been acquired some years before by the National Library of Scotland. The remaining and larger part was now sent to the University of Edinburgh. Their departure marked another of life's divides.

On the first of August, 1976, we returned once again to Dunbartonshire, the part of the world from which my seventeenth-century ancestors had set sail for Ireland. It felt like coming home.

INDEX

Abbot of Drymock (Musgrave/Lindsay), 139
Abbotsford Place, 8, Edinburgh, 74
Abbotsford Pub, Rose Street, Edinburgh, 100, 101, 129
Aberdeen, 39, 40, 77, 91, 193
Aberdeen University, 94
Acreage of the Heart, The (Todd), 71
Act of Union, 1707, 79
"Addition to the Family, An" (Morgan), 109
Aitchison, James, 201
Akros, 200
Akros Publications, 200
d'Albert, Eugène, 18
Albinoni, Tommaso, 211
Alden, George, 37, 120
Alexander, Peter, 41
Alexander of Menstrie, Sir William, 105
Allan, John R., 101
Alnwick Castle, 212
America, 10
Amis, Kingsley, 151, 153
An Comunn Gaidhealach, 61, 133
Andersen, Hans Christian, 205
Andrews, fishmongers, 16
Ane Satyre of the Thrie Estatis (Sir David Lyndsay), 86, 127
Angus, Marion, 98
Annan, 146–8, 162
Annan Report, 166
Annan, River, 146
Anniesland, 22
Apsley Cottage, Pulborough, 65
Ardyne, River, 46
Argyll & Sutherland Highlanders, 49
Aristotle, 87
Arnhem, 52, 215

Arnold, James, 196
Army Pay Corps, 51
Arts Review, 11, 86
Ashton Terrace, 11, Glasgow, 10, 12, 14
Assembly Rooms, George Street, Edinburgh, 126, 195
Aston, B. G. ("Baggy"), 28
"At Hans Christian Andersen's Birthplace" (Lindsay), 206
Athole Gardens, 32, Glasgow, 14, 19, 24, 31, 61, 103
At the Wood's Edge (Lindsay), 102, 117
Auchenshuggle, 12
Auden, W. H., 35, 46, 170
"Aunt" Ada, 19
Auschwitz, 215
Automobile Club, Blythswood Square, Glasgow, 187

Bach, 21, 42, 211
Bach, John Christian, 42
Bachelli, Dr, 117
Baikie, Wilhelmina, 30
Balloch, 104
Bamborough, Miss, 63
Barbirolli, Sir John, 24
Barker, George, 109
Barnetson, Bill (later Lord), 143
Barr, Seona, 7
Barrie, Sir James Matthew, 21
Basilica di San Francisco, 209
Batey, Derek, 148
Bayley & Fergusson, 67
B.B.C., 25, 55, 63, 65, 68, 85, 86, 91, 121, 139, 143
B.B.C. Scotland, 11, 148, 162, 182
B.B.C. Scottish Symphony Orchestra, 124

Beaverbrook, Lord, 16
Beaver College, Glenside,
    Pennsylvania, U.S.A., 212
Bedford, Duke of, 72
Beecham, Sir Thomas, 63, 108
Beethoven, Ludwig van, 128, 134, 180,
    208, 210
Belgian Piano Quartet, 81
Bell, Henry, 34
Bell, toyshop, 17
Belloc, Hilaire, 65
Benatzky, Ralph, 29
Berlingske Tidende, 128
Berlioz, Hector, 117, 163, 211
"Berwick Thurso", *see* Blytheman,
    Maurice
Betjeman, Sir John, 79, 195
Biggar, 157, 175, 176, 201
"Birthday, A" (Muir), 59
Bishop, Sir Henry, 135
Blackwell of Oxford, 37
Blackwood, publishers, 68
Blake, George, 117
Blest Pair of Sirens (Parry), 162
Blom, Eric, 55, 64, 67, 157
"Blotto", 108
Blytheman, Maurice ("Thurso
    Berwick"), 62
Blythswood Square, Glasgow, 11, 26,
    187, 190
Blyton, Enid, 214
Boccherini, Luigi, 55, 56, 209
Bologna, 207
Book of Insects (Fabre), 217
Borderline, 151–3, 154, 156, 160
Border Television, 145, 148, 149–50,
    160–1, 162, 166, 171, 174, 176, 178,
    182, 184, 186
Botanic Gardens, Glasgow, 218
Botticelli, Sandro, 180
Bottomley, Gordon, 80
Boulanger, Nadia, 121
Bowling, 34
Brahms, Johannes, 29, 209
Brechin, 124
Bredin, James, 150, 157
"Bridie, James" (Dr O. H. Mavor), 21,
    48, 92, 114, 116–17, 126
British Council, 74, 117, 215
Britten, Benjamin, 57, 138, 162
"Brock, Gavin", *see* Lindsay, Maurice
Brock, Henrietta, ("*Teta*"), 10, 12, 14
Brock, Janey, 14
Brock, John ("*Doan*"), 10, 12–14, 49,
    189

Brontës, the, 28
Brooke, Sir Alan, 82
Brooke, Rupert, 28
Broomielaw, Glasgow, 31
Brown's, Danny, 13
Brown, George Mackay, 38, 201
Brown, Harry, 72
Brown, Miss, 18
Browning, Robert, 180
Bruce, Dr George, 7, 59, 60, 91–2, 93,
    109, 119, 121, 132, 137, 138, 142, 178,
    180, 185
"Bruntsie", 112
Brussels, 215
Buchan, John, Lord Tweedsmuir, 144
Buchanan, Sir Colin, 195
Bulletin, The, 91, 96–7, 108, 122–3, 124,
    127–9, 145, 157, 164
"Bunkum", 108
Burgess, John (later Sir), 150
Burns Encyclopedia (Lindsay), 113, 203
Burns, Robert, 28, 58, 67, 83, 86, 97,
    100, 113, 147, 167, 203, 205
Burns Today and Tomorrow
    (MacDiarmid), 157
Burrell, Sir William, 189
Burton, Richard, 175
Byrd, William, 128, 211
Byres Road, Glasgow, 16, 26
Byron, Lord, 58, 167
By Yon Bonnie Banks (Lindsay), 105, 183

Café Royal, Edinburgh, 115
Café Royal, London, 75
Caird, Sheena, 11
Caledonia, P. S., 184
Caledonian Hotel, Edinburgh, 48
Callaghan, Anthony, 214
Camberley, 60
Cameron, Morven, 7
Cameronians (Scottish Rifles) 9th
    Battalion, 44, 48, 73
Campbell, Mrs, 152–3
Cantata for a Summer's Day (Musgrave/
    Lindsay), 138
Carcanet Press, 179
Carlisle, Bishop of, 149
Carlisle Journal, 150
Carlsberg Foundation, 127
Carnival (MacKenzie), 156
Carroll, Walter, 16
Cartier, J. B., (*L'Art du violon*), 56
Castle Kennedy, 191, 192
Caughie, Mary Marquis, 148, 158
Cavatina (Raff), 25

Central Hotel, Glasgow, 117
Central Station, Glasgow, 109
Chamberlain, Neville, 46, 156
Chapbook, 86, 129
Charing Cross, Glasgow, 25
Chaucer, Geoffrey, 99, 167
Chelsea, London, 63
Chênedollé, C.-J. L. (*L'Aube du romanticisme*), 56
Cheyne Row, Chelsea, 69
Child's Christmas in Wales, A (D. Thomas), 175
Chisolm, Erik, 117
Chopin, 91
Christmas Carol, A (Musgrave), 141
Christmas Morn, Steam Drifter, 37
Churchill, Sir Winston, 49, 50, 82
Citizens' Theatre, Glasgow, 93, 99, 126
City Hall, Glasgow, 13
Civic Amenities Act, 1967, 86, 192
Civic Societies, 193
Civic Trust, London, 185, 190, 206
Claremont Street, Glasgow, 20
"Clarinda" *see* Maclehose, Mrs Agnes
Clark ("Foxy"), 26
Clark, Jamieson, 137
Clyde, River, 15, 35, 46, 47
Coia, Emilio, 143
Collected Poems (G. S. Fraser), 77
Collected Poems, 1979 (Lindsay), 35, 71, 95, 102, 103, 171, 173
College of Commerce, Glasgow, 213
Columba P.S., 31, 32
Come Dancing, 148
Comfort, Dr Alex, 87
Comings and Goings (Lindsay), 201
"Conductor Speaks, The", 124
Coningsby, Eric, 24–5
Conquest, Robert, 77
Conrad, Joseph, 28
Conservation of Georgian Edinburgh, The (ed. Lindsay), 194
Corraith, Gartocharn, 108, 109
Corraith, Innellan, 34, 46, 47, 103
Counterpoint, 142–5
Courthill, Bearsden, 29
Covent Garden Opera House, London, 124
Cowal Hills, 34, 35, 184
Craigendoran, 117, 184
Cranston, Miss, 13
Crosbie, William, 178
Crown Hotel, Hawick, 49
Cumberland News, 150
Cumming, James, 143

Curzon, Sir Clifford, 64
Czech House, Edinburgh, 74

Daiches, Professor David, 78, 113
Daily Herald, 79, 90
Dain do Eimhir (S. McLean), 79
Dale, David, 187, 196
Dance of the Apprentices (Gaitens), 114
Danish State Radio Orchestra, 127
Darien Scheme, 199
Davaar Island, 133
David Higham Associates Ltd, 7
Davidson, John, 80, 81
Davidson, Mrs, 80
Day-Lewis, Cecil, 138
Decision, The (Musgrave/Lindsay), 140–1
Defoe, Daniel, 126
Delacroix, Ferdinand Eugène, 131
Delius, Frederick, 64, 130, 211
Dennison, Billy, 38
Dennison, Captain Bill, 38
Dent's Master Musicians Series, 64
Die Entscheidung (Musgrave/Lindsay), 140
Diss, Norfolk, 53, 55
Doak, A. M., 197
Dole, Mr, 20
Dollan, Sir Patrick, 90
Dorati, Antal, 122
Douglas, Gavin, 58
Douglas, Keith, 72, 77
"Drinan, Adam", *see* Macleod, Joseph
Drunk Man Looks at the Thistle, A (MacDiarmid), 62, 68, 97, 177
Dryden, John, 171
Dubh Hiortach, 38
Duchess of Fife, P.S., 47
Duchess of Montrose, T.S., 184
Dumbarton, 104
Dunbar, John Grieg, 194
Dunbar, William, 167
Dundee University, 132
Dunkirk, 49
Dunn, Douglas, 179
Dunoon, 34, 49
Duval, Kulgin, 75
Dvořák, Antonin, 64, 127

Eadie, Noel, 63
Ebury Street, London, 63
Edinburgh, 29, 64, 86, 101; Castle, 192; Festival, 86, 126, 131, 135, 175, 211; New Town Conservation Committee, 192, 193, 194, 196;

Society of Musicians, 136; University, 218
Edinburgh University Press, 143, 178, 179
Eindhoven, 215
Elegies for the Dead in Cyrenaica (Henderson), 90
Elg, Taina, 144
Elgar, Sir Edward, 211
Eliot, T. S., 58, 62, 79, 80, 101, 115–16, 167
Elizabeth, Queen, 45
Elmbank Street, Glasgow, 62
Endrick, River, 109
Enemies of Love, The (Lindsay), 114
Erskine, 34
Europa Nostra, 206, 207
Everyman Library, 197
Ewart, Robin (Aunt), 146
Ewart, Sir Spencer, 146
Ewing, Winifred, 204, 205
Eye, Suffolk, 54

Faber & Faber, Messrs, 35, 79, 80, 97, 101
Fairbairn, Nicholas, 174
Falconer, Dr Ronald, 152
Farquharsons of Invercauld, the, Braemar, 115
Fenby, Eric, 64
Fergusson, Sir Bernard (later Lord Ballantrae), 151
Fergusson, Sir James, of Kilkerran, 97, 98, 100, 119
Festschrift for Hugh MacDiarmid, 75
Fielding, Henry, 28
Fields, Dame Gracie, 156
Figaro House, Vienna, 208
Fingal and Comala (Lindsay), 115, 116
Finnich Malaise, by Croftamie, 116
Fintry, 107
Fir Tree Cottage, Gartocharn, 108, 113, 120
Flodden, 48
Flower, Robin, 129
For a Summer's Day Cantata (Musgrave/Lindsay), 138
Forces Music Magazine, 55, 64
Forrest, Meta, 128
Fortune Press, The, 74
Four Quartets (Eliot), 79
Francis George Scott and the Scottish Renaissance (Lindsay), 67
Fraser, G. S., 77
Fraser, Margaret, 122

Fraserburgh, 37, 91
Frederikshavn, North Jutland, 205
Freud, Sigmund, 27, 209
Frith Street, Soho, London, 63
Fyfe, Will, 13

Gaitens, Edward, 114
Gaitskell, Hugh, 156
Galashiels, 96
Garioch, Robert, 62
Gartocharn, 104, 106, 110, 113, 116, 121, 137, 163, 184
Gatehouse of Fleet, 191
de Gaulle, General, 195
General Assembly of the Church of Scotland, 133
General Strike, 1926, 13
George IV, 45
Georgian Assembly Rooms, Edinburgh, 195
"Gibbon, Lewis Grassic" (Mitchell, J. Leslie), 72, 119
Gibson, Sir Alexander, 124, 143
Gilbert, Sir W. S., 9
Gildard, Gordon, 133–4
Gill, Jack, 145
Gill, Robin, 145, 148, 149, 150, 171
Gilmour, Ian, 128
Glaister, Professor John, 155
Glasgow, 9, 13, 29, 31, 85, 94, 101, 103, 185, *et seq.*; Academy, 21, 55; Corporation, 187, 213; University, 11, 40, 93, 191, 214
Glasgow Herald, 7, 18, 41, 90, 97, 98, 99, 115, 122, 123, 128, 145, 183, 186, 202, 213, 217
Glasgow School of Art, 55
Glasgow Street, Hillhead, Glasgow, 29
Glasgow Nocturne (Lindsay), 213–14
Glasgow Treelovers Association, 187
Glasgow University Press, 179
"Glass of Pure Water, A" (MacDiarmid), 59
Glen, Duncan, 200
Glen Clovis Hotel, 68
Goddard, Scott, 64
Golden Sonata, Purcell, 24
Golden Treasury of Scottish Verse (ed. MacDiarmid), 178
Gordon, June (later Lady Aberdeen), 162
Gordon, Percy, 41, 123
Gourock, 34, 38
Gourock Ropeworks, 196
Govan, Glasgow, 194

Govan Old Parish Church, 152
Graham, Harry, 196
Grahame, Kenneth, 140
Graham, W. S., 73, 130
Gramophone, The, 155
Grampian Television, 145
Grand Hotel, Charing Cross,
    Glasgow, 18
Grant, Mr and Mrs, 19
Graves, Robert, 168
Gray, Sir Alexander, 7, 74–5, 98, 114,
    142–3
Gray, Charles, 196
Gray, John, 7
Graz, Austria, 29
Great George Street, Glasgow, 26
Great War (1914–18), 9
Great Western Road, Glasgow, 13, 93,
    190
Great Western Terrace, Glasgow, 13,
    186, 190
Great Western Terrace, 11, Glasgow,
    189, 190, 202, 203, 205, 217
Greece, 28
"Greek" Thomson, Alexander, 13
"Greenbank", Annan, 146–7
Greene, Sir Hugh Carlton, 161
Greenock, 34, 117
Grez-sur-Loing, 64
Grieg, Edvard H., 127
Grieve, Christopher, *see*
    "MacDiarmid, Hugh"
Grieve, Michael, 7
Grieve, Valda, 62, 87, 176, 179
Grimond, Jo, 156
Grimond, Laura, 198
Grützmacher, F., 55
Guardian, The, 86
Gunn, Daisy, 119
Gunn, Lieutenant-Commander
    Dermot, 7
Gunn, Dr Neil M., 7, 48, 59, 70, 103,
    114, 116, 117, 118, 119, 177
Guthrie, Tyrone, 127
Guy and Pauline (Mackenzie), 156

Haddo House, Aberdeen, 162
Hale, John, 7, 120
Hale, Robert, 119–20
Hallé Orchestra, 123
Hamilton, Iain, 126
Hamilton Terrace, Maida Vale,
    London, 63, 64
Handel, George Frideric, 57, 159
Harraby, 148

Harrison, Sydney, 120
Harvey, Marion, 94
Havelock Street, Glasgow, 61
Hawick, 49
Hay, George Campbell, 62, 172
Haydn, Franz Josef, 29, 55, 56, 122,
    210
Hazard, Patrick, 212
Hearn, Lafcadio, 30
Heads Nook, Cumberland, 163, 182,
    189
"Hector", 109
Heimskringla, 197
Helensburgh, 104
Henderson, Hamish, 90
Henderson's Stable, 17
Hendry, J. F., 77, 80, 130
Henryson, Robert, 58, 167
Henry Wood Hall, Glasgow, 20
Herbage, Anna, 64
Herbage, Julian, 64
Hero, The (G. Sackville West), 57
Heron, Robert, 100
Herring, Robert, 69, 70
Hesperus, S.S., 38
Hess, Dame Myra, 81
Highland Division, 51st, 60
Hillhead, Glasgow, 16; Burgh Hall, 18;
    Parish Church, 20
Hillington, 42, 93
Himmelpfortgrund No. 72, Vienna,
    208
Hiroshima, 84
Historic Buildings Council for
    Scotland, 190–7
History of Scottish Literature (Lindsay),
    202, 203
Hitler, Adolf, 43, 46, 65, 81
Hobbit, The (Tolkien), 140
Hodges, Desmond, 194
Hogg, James, 58
Holford, Lord, 195
"Home Sweet Home" (Bishop), 135
Hope Street, Glasgow, 58, 72
Hopkins, Gerard Manley, 90
Horn, Misses, 16
Horrocks, Lieutenant-General Sir
    Brian, 151
Housman, A. E., 23, 36, 57
Hughes, Lord, 195
Hume, Alexander, 138
Hunter, Rev. Dr John, 20
"Hurlygush" (Lindsay), 101–3
Hurn, Douglas, 174–5, 186
Hutchinson, publishers, 80

Hutchinson, Sir W. G., 142
"Hymn to Intellectual Beauty"
(Shelley), 28
Hyndland, Glasgow, 13

Independent Broadcasting Authority,
165
"Inheritance" (Bruce), 59, 91
In Memoriam James Joyce (MacDiarmid),
157
Innellan, 31, 34, 40, 42, 103, 108, 184
Inverary, 38
Inverkip, 47
Inverness, 119, 134, 198
Iona, 87, 152
Iona, S.S., 38

Jacob, General Sir Ian, 82
Jacob, Violet, 98, 100
James VI, 105
Jamie the Saxt (Maclellan), 116
Jarrolds, publishers, 119
Jeanie Deans, P.S., 184
Jedburgh Gardens, Glasgow, 88–90,
130
Jeffrey, William, 60
Joachim, Joseph, 29
Johnson, Dr, 173
Johnstone, William, 68
Jolly Beggars, The (Burns), 135–6, 139
Jones, Glyn, 175
Joyce, James, 76
Joy of Sex, The (Comfort), 87
Junior Chamber of Commerce,
Aberdeen, 193
Junior Staff College, Camberley, 57

Kailyard School, 202
Kaleidoscope, 175
Kalman, Emerich, 211
Karg-Elert, Sigfrid, 21
Keats, John, 74
Keighley, 57
Kelso, 110–12
Kelvingrove Art Gallery, Glasgow, 178
Kemp, James, 132
Kemp, Robert, 86–7, 114, 129, 174
Keppie, Jessie, 29
Keyes, Sydney, 77
Kincaid, John, 62
King, Sir Alexander, 134
King George V, T.S., 38
King, Jessie, 29
King's Theatre, Glasgow, 25
"Kinnaird Head" (Bruce), 60, 91

Kirklee Circus, Glasgow, 10
Kirkwall, Orkney, 38, 39, 197
Klein, Bernat, 159
Knox, John, 67, 79
Kreutzer, Rodolphe, 41
Kyles of Bute, Firth of Clyde, 47
Kyle, Chevalier Calloway, 73

Laing, Malcolm, 197
Lallans, 74, 78, 97, 98, 101, 118, 171, 176
Lanark County Council, 196
Langholm Academy, 67
"Largo" (S. G. Smith), 59
L'Art du violon (Cartier), 56
"Last Laugh" (D. Young), 89
Last Poems (Housman), 36
Lauder, Sir Harry, 13, 49
Laurie, John, 56, 149
Lawrence, D. H., 77, 155
League of Nations, 43
League of Nations Union, 9, 187
L'Ecole des Femmes: Let Wives Tak Tent,
86
Leggat Smith, Bill, 55
Leggat Smith, Yvonne, 55
Lehar, Franz, 209
Leighton, Kenneth, 141
Leith, 39
Leneru, Marie, 201
Lerwick, Shetland, 175, 176
Lewis, Alun, 77
Life and Letters Today, 69
Lille Vaerlose, Denmark, 205
"Linden Lee" (Vaughan Williams), 11
Lindsay, John, John Lindsay Watson,
136
Lindsay, Joyce, 87, 91, 93, 176, 182,
184, 201, 218
Lindsay, Matthew, 19
Lindsay, Maurice, birth, 9; marriage,
87; student R.S.A.M., 41; London
during war, 63; demob, 85; Jedburgh
Gardens, 88; Southpark Avenue, 93;
Gartocharn, 108; Gavin Brock, 108;
B.B.C. debut, 133; Borders, 146;
Heads Noook, 163; Return to
Glasgow, 186; Civic Trust opening,
190; Milton, 217
Lindsay, Stanley, 87
Linklater, Eric, 38, 39, 48, 59, 78, 88,
116
Liszt, Franz, 211
"Little White Rose of Scotland"
(MacDiarmid), 154
"Loch Leven" (S. G. Smith), 60

Logan, Helen, 7
Lomond, Loch, 106, 109, 145
London County Council, 195
London Mercury, 69
"London 1940" (Lindsay), 44
London Pride (James Pope-Hennessy), 82
Lookaround, 158, 163
Lorimer, Sir Robert, 183
Lovell, Sir Bernard, 176
Lowlands of Scotland, The, (Lindsay), 120
Lucca, Italy, 55, 209
Luxon, Benjamin, 139
Lyndsay, Sir David, of the Mount, 86, 126
Lynedoch Terrace, Glasgow, 9

MacBrayne, David, and Son Ltd, 31
MacCaig, Norman, 77, 80, 95, 201
MacCallum, David (actor), 108
MacCallum, David (violinist), 108
Maclay, Rt. Hon. John H. (later Viscount Muirshiel), 183, 185, 191, 193, 197
Maclellan, Robert, 116
MacClelland, Rev. H. S., 20
McClement, Robert, 214
MacCormack, John, 204
McCrone, Guy, 117
"MacDiarmid, Hugh" (also when referred to as Christopher Grieve), 7, 57–62, 67–8, 75, 80, 85, 87, 94, 97, 98, 99, 100, 102, 116, 117, 142–3, 154, 157–8, 167, 173, 175, 176, 177, 179, 188, 201, 204
MacEwan, Sir Alex, 96
MacEwan, A. D., 96
MacEwan, Tom, 190
Mackay, Neil, Lord Provost of Edinburgh, 195
Mackenzie, Sir Compton, 59, 151, 153–6
Mackie, Albert, 118
Mackintosh, Charles Rennie, 29, 189
Maclaurin, Colin, 29
Maclaurin, Elsie, 29, 73
Maclay, Jack, 183
McLean, Sorley, 79, 172
Maclehose, Mrs Agnes, "Clarinda", 86
Maclehose, printers, 79
McLeish, Archibald, 201
Maclellan, William, 57, 58, 71–3, 78, 91, 101, 114, 130, 157
McLeman, Douglas, 7

MacLeod, Rev. Dr George (later Lord), 149, 151–3
MacLeod, Iain, 156
MacLeod, Captain Jim, 51
MacLeod, Joseph ("Adam Drinan"), 60
McLeod, R. J., 80
MacNeice, Louis, 35, 167, 175
Macpherson, James, 115
Macrae, Duncan, 128
Magic Flute, The (Mozart), 209
"Magnus on Monday" (The Scotsman feature), 160
Magnusson, Dr Magnus, 7, 160
Mahler, Gustav, 65, 127, 209, 211
Main, David, 149, 151
Main, George, 115
Makartplatz, Salzburg, 207
"Malley, Ern", 78
Marks, Peter, 141
Marriage of Figaro, The (Mozart), 122, 126
Marwick, Ernest, 198
Maryhill, Glasgow, 194
Mary, Queen of Scots (Musgrave), 141
Matheson, George, 34
Matthew, Sir Robert, 191, 195
Maugham, Somerset, 147
Mavor, Dr O. H. *see* "Bridie, James"
Maxwell, Rev. Dr W. D., 20
Melville, Andrew, 67
Mendelssohn, Felix, Bartholdy, 21, 76
Meredith, George, 28, 66
Messiah, The (Handel), 57
Midsummer Night's Dream, A (Britten), 138
Millar, J. H., 202
Miller, Margaret, 191
Milton Hill, 7, 217
Miss Bishop's Primary School, 10, 11
Mitchell, Ena, 149
Mitchell, James Leslie *see* "Gibbon, Lewis, Grassic"
Mitchell, Stephen, 53
"Maurice, musician, makar, morifauld M." (D. Young), 89
Modern Scottish Poetry: An Anthology of the Scottish Renaissance 1920–45 (Lindsay), 79, 80, 98
Mod of An Comun Gaidhealach, 132
Molière (Jean Baptiste Poquelin), 86
Money, H. D. K. Lieutenant Colonel, D.S.O., 52
Money-Coutts, Alick, 53
Montague, C. E., 30
Monte Casino, 69

Montgomerie, Mr A., 99
Montrose, 68
Montrose, Duke of, 134
Moore, G. E., 77
Moore, Nicholas, 77
Moore, Priscilla, 77
Moore, Thomas, 170
Moray Firth, 39
More, Kenneth, 144
Mores, Dom, 109
More Poems (Housman), 37
Morgan, Edwin, 99, 109, 141, 178, 179
Morley College, London, 139
Moss, Stirling, 151, 153
"Mousie", 112
Mozart, W. A., 42, 44, 55, 63, 81, 122, 207, 208, 209, 210
Mr and Mrs, 148
Muir, Edwin, 38, 58, 59, 74, 178
Mull, 152
Munro, Sir Hector, 146
Munro Road, 44, Jordanhill, Glasgow, 87, 121
Murdoch, Brydon, 128
Musgrave, Thea, 121, 126, 135, 138–41, 150
Music and Letters, 55, 64, 67, 68
"Music Magazine", 25, 64, 65
Myitkyna, Burma, 82

Nagasaki, 84
National Library of Scotland, 68, 218
National Trust, 187, 193
National Trust for Scotland, 180, 192
"Native Element" (Jeffrey), 60
Nellemanns, Finne and Hanne, 127, 205
Nest of Singing Birds, A (Kemp), 86
Nethybridge, 19, 20
Nethy, River, 19
New Apocalypse Movement, 28, 76, 77, 80, 97
News Chronicle, 64
New Lanark, 196–7
Newton Place, Glasgow, 24
New Town of Edinburgh, 191, 194, 196–7
New Zealand House, London, 195
Nicols, Robert, 64
Nicol, William, 30
Nicholson, Dr Norman, 150–1
Nicolson, Harold, 56
Nielsen, Carl, 127
Noble, Elizabeth, 182
Noble, John, 182–4

No Crown for Laughter (Lindsay), 74
Nomads, The, 155
North Kelvinside School, 105
North of Scotland Hydro Electric Board, 108
North of Scotland Steam Packet Company, 39
No Scottish Twilight (ed. Urquhart and Lindsay), 72
No Star on the Way Back (N. Nicholson), 150

Oban, 38, 132, 152
O'Connor, Frank, 129
Odense, Denmark, 206
"Ode to All Rebels" (MacDiarmid), 176
O'Faoláin, Séan, 129
Officers Training Corps, 23
"Of the Day Festival" (A. Hume), 138
"O Love that will not let me go" (Matheson), 34
One Later Day (Lindsay), 171–3
Onich, Loch Linnhe, 87
Operation Neptune, 186
Operation Sealion, 50
Orkney, 36–9; Heritage Society, 198
Orkneyinga Saga, 39
Oslo, 215
Other Dear Charmer, The (Kemp), 86
Outram, George, 145
Owen, Robert, 196
Oxford, 40
Oxford Book of Scottish Verse (Ed. MacQueen and Scott), 103

Paisley, 98
Palestrina, G. P. da, 211
Palette Club, 24
Papdale House, Orkney, 197–8
Park Circus, Glasgow, 189
Park Conservation Area, Glasgow, 9
Parry, Sir C. H., 162
Parry, Marjorie, 24
Peebles, 98
Peel of Drumry, Drumchapel, 187
Pennywheep (MacDiarmid), 62, 177
Pentland Firth, 40
"Perfect" (MacDiarmid), 175
"Peter", 109
Philadelphia, U.S.A., 212
Philips, of Eindhoven, 215
Philipson, Sir Robin, 142–3
"Picking Apples" (Lindsay), 170
Picquot, Louis, 55
Pilkington Report, 166

Place of Meaning in Poetry, The
(Daiches), 78
Plymouth Brethren, 30
"Poem at Christmas" (Lindsay), 71
"Poet" (Lindsay), 169–70
Poetry Chicago, 57
Poetry London, 57, 76
Poetry Notebook, 86
Poetry Scotland, 57, 58, 59, 73, 78, 91,
153, 178, 179
Poetry Scotland One, 58
Poetry Scotland Two, 59
Poetry Scotland Three, 59, 78
Poetry Scotland Four, 94, 130
Poetry Society, Portman Square,
London, 73
Poets on Poets, 58
Poet's Pub (Linklater), 39
Points in Time (Johnstone), 68
"Pooks Nook", 163
Poosie Nansie's, 136
Pope, Alexander, 28
Pope-Hennessy, James, 82, 83–4,
120–1
Portman Square, 33, 73
Pound, Ezra, 98, 143
Prestwick, 21
Primrose, William, 29
Pringle, James, 34
Proust, Marcel, 96
Puccini, Giacomo, 139
Purcell, Henry, 24
"Pylonites", 76

Queensborough Gardens, Glasgow,
11
Queens Park, Glasgow, 45
Queen Street, 5, Edinburgh, 136

Rachmaninov, Sergei, 93
Radio Newsreel, 133
Raff, Joachim, 25, 209
Ramage, Granville, 36, 38, 39
Rankl, Karl, 124
Rantzen, Esther, 58
Rathmelton, Eire, 105
Rayment, Malcolm, 128
Rebel with a Cause (film), 175
Recorded Music Club, 55
Rees, Alan, 142–3
Regent Palace Hotel, London, 81
Reid, James Macarthur, 91, 96
Reith, Sir John, 161
Renfield Street, Glasgow, 15
Renfrew, 34

Rheinberger, J. B., 21
Richards, Grant, 80
Richards, Roydon, 24, 40
Richardson, Robin, 136, 139–40
"Riggans o' Chelsea, The" (S. G.
Smith), 130, 172
Ritter, Camillo, 29, 41, 42
*Robert Burns: The Man, his Work, the
Legend* (Lindsay), 83, 113, 136, 203
Robertson, Alec, 55–7, 64–7, 127, 211
Rockefeller Atlantic Award, 114
Rodd, Michael, 149
Roddicks (the family), 147
Rode, Pierre, 41
Rogers, W. R., 175
Rose Cottage/Corraith Gartocharn,
108, 109
Royal Festival Hall, London, 195
Royal Lyceum Theatre, Edinburgh,
135
Royal Philharmonic, 63, 108
Royal Scottish Academy of Music and
Drama, 41, 141, 155
Rubbra, Edmund, 64
Rule's, Maiden Lane, 69
Rush, Christopher, 102
Russell, Robin, 86
Russell, Ken, 65

Sackville-West, Hon. Edward, 56, 57
Sackville-West, Vita, 56
Sadler's Wells Theatre, 140
St Aloysius, Glasgow, 66
St Andrew's Hall, 13, 24, 123–5, 204
St Andrew's University, 92, 96
St Gabriel's Convent School, Carlisle,
163
St Matthew's Church, Glasgow, 25
St Rognvald, S.S., 39, 40
St Stephen's Cathedral, Vienna, 208
St Vincent Street, Glasgow, 13
Sainte Chapelle, Paris, 20
Saltire Review, The, 157
Saltire Society, The, 121, 180, 195
Salzburg, 207–8
Sandys, Duncan (later Lord Duncan-
Sandys), 190, 206–7
Sangschaw (MacDiarmid), 62, 177
Sauchiehall Street, Glasgow, 15, 62,
116
Saughton Prison, Edinburgh, 79
Saunders, R. Crombie, 100
Scenes on a Farmyard (Carroll), 12
Schikaneder, Emanuel, 209
Schimanski, Stefan, 77

Schimdt, Michael, 179
Schotz, Benno, 75, 142–3
Schubert, Franz, 128, 208, 210–11
Schumann, Robert, 42, 210
"Scotched" (A. Scott), 95
Scotland: An Anthology (ed. Lindsay), 201
"Scotland's Heritage" (lecture), 215
Scots College, Rome, 65
Scotsman, The, 7, 96, 114–15, 128, 160, 202
Scots Review, The, 96–7
Scott, Alexander, 7, 94–5, 115, 154, 172, 173, 180
Scott, Cath, 94
Scott, Francis George, 25, 60, 66–7, 75, 87, 121, 126, 144, 157–8
Scott, Sir Walter, 170, 203
Scott-Moncrieff, George, 96
Scottish Arts Council, The, 96, 178, 180
Scottish Assembly, 204
"Scottish Bards & an English Reviewer" (Barker), 109
Scottish Civic Trust, 180, 183–5, 190–4, 196–8, 202, 204, 206, 213
Scottish Co-operative movement, 196
Scottish Field, 37, 108, 120
Scottish Life and Letters, 92, 121, 137
Scottish Literary Journal, 102
Scottish Lyrics (F. G. Scott), 67
Scottish National Academy of Music, 41
Scottish National Orchestra, 20, 124
Scottish National Party, 89, 154, 155, 204
Scottish Opera, 124, 126, 141
Scottish Orchestra, 13, 24, 42, 123–5
Scottish Poetry, 179–81
Scottish Poetry 9, 179
Scottish Renaissance Movement, 58, 178, 202
Scottish Review, The, 7, 96, 113, 180
Scottish Trades Union Congress, 133
Seasons, The (J. Thomson), 217
Sekers, Sir Miki, 162
Selected Poems (Sir Alexander Gray), 75
Serif Books, 101
Sev'cik, Otakar, 29
Seven Journeys, The (Graham), 73
Sforza, Count, 195
Shakespeare, William, 28, 113, 125, 138, 167, 171
Shapinsay, Orkney, 38
Shapiro, Karl, 72

Shawcross, Sir Hartley (later Lord), 185
Shawe-Taylor, Desmond, 211
Sheffield, 69
Shelley, P. B., 28
Shostakovich, Dmitri, 211
Shropshire Lad, A (Housman), 36
Sibelius, Jean, 127
Silver Branch, The (Gunn), 129
Sinclair, Donald, 80
Sinister Street (Mackenzie), 156
Sitwell, Sir Oswald, 69, 70
Skerryvore, 38
Skye, 17
Smith, T. Dan, 159
Smith, Harry S., 196–7
Smith, Mrs Hazel Goodsir, 7
Smith, Iain Crichton, 132, 172, 201
Smith, Jean Taylor, 128
Smith, Dr Marion Goodsir, 129
Smith, Sydney Goodsir, 58, 59, 60, 62, 74, 92, 97–8, 101, 114, 129, 172
Smollett, Tobias, 28
"Snip", 111–12
Snow Warning (Lindsay), 171, 201, 206
Sorlin, François, 195
Soutar, William, 51, 61
Southpark Avenue, 13, Glasgow, 93, 94
Spain, 55
Spender, Sir Stephen, 138
"Spem in Alium" (Tallis), 42
Spohr, Louis, 41
Springburn, Glasgow, 194
Squire, Sir John, 69
"Stars like Thistle's Roses Flower" (MacDiarmid), 68
Stephens, James, 137
Stevenson Hall, Glasgow, 75, 127
Stevenson, R. L., 28, 121
Stewart, Andrew, 92, 144
Stewart, Ian, 128, 129
Stewart, Misses, School of Music, 11
Stirling, 87
Stolz, Robert, 29
Stones of the Field (R. S. Thomas), 90
Stornoway, 17
Story, Lieutenant Colonel H. H., 52
Stony Limits and Other Poems (MacDiarmid), 177
Strathclyde Regional Council, 214
Strauss, Johann, 209
Strauss, Richard, 65, 206, 210
Stronsay, Orkney, 36, 37

Suite of Bairnsangs, A (Musgrave/ Lindsay), 118
Sullivan, Sir Arthur, 128, 211
Sutherland, James, 115, 136
Swan, John, 63
Swanky, Mrs, 54, 55
Swilly, Loch, 105
Swinburne, Algernon Charles, 28
Symonds, Joe, 159

Tail o' the Bank, by Greenock, 34
Tales of the Borders (ed. Wilson), 139
"Talking with Five Thousand People in Edinburgh" (MacDiarmid), 60
Tallis, Thomas, 41, 42
Tambimuttu, Meary J., 57, 75–6
Taylor, Dr A. B., 39
Taylor, Kenneth, 140
Taylor, Wilfred, 96, 115
Tchaikovsky, P. I., 127, 128, 211
Teddington, 156
Temple, Dr "Teddy", 23
Tennyson, Lord Alfred, 170
Thackeray, W. M., 28
Thatcher, Margaret, 146
That's Life, 58
Theatre Royal, Glasgow, 141
"These Two Lovers" (Lindsay), 170
Thirty-five Scottish Songs (F. G. Scott), 121
Thirty-nine Steps, The (film), 144
This Business of Living (Lindsay), 200, 201
Thistle and the Rose, The (MacEwan), 96
Thomas, Dylan, 73, 76, 130, 175
Thomas, R. S., 90
Thomson, Alexander ('Greek'), 189, 217
Thomson, Derick, 172
Thomson, Harold, 138–9
Thomson, Roy (later Lord), 142
Thorndyke, Dame Sybil, 151, 153
Thornton, Joe, 18
Thorpe Davie, Cedric, 114, 135
"Three Measures" (Drinan), 60
Tiefland (d'Albert), 18
Tilty Mill House, Great Easton, 71
Time will knit (Urquhart), 72
"Toby", 216
Todd, Mr and Mrs, fruiterer, 17
Todd, Ruthven, 7, 70–2, 80
Tolkien, J. R. R., 140
Tomorrow's World, 149
Town House, Stranraer, 192
Trade Unions, 13, 84, 97, 141, 212

Treece, Henry, 76, 80
Trenton, U.S.A., 212
Trial by Jury (Gilbert and Sullivan), 24
Trinity Church, Glasgow, 20
Trojans, The (Berlioz), 117
Trollope, Anthony, 121
Tully, Ironmonger, 17
"Two Memories" (MacDiarmid), 59

U. F. Church, Innellan, 34
Under the Eildon Tree (S. G. Smith), 74, 101, 130, 131
Union of the Crowns, 199
Urquhart, Fred, 72, 101
Urquhart, Sir Thomas, 131
U.S.A., 212

Vaughan Williams, R., 162
V. E. Day, May 1945, 83
Verdi, G., 134, 135
Via Boccherini, Lucca, 209–10
Victoria Park, Glasgow, 12
Vienna, 208
Viotti, G. B., 41
Vittoria, Tomas Luis da, 211
Vivaldi, Antonio, 211
Voice of Ariadne, The (Musgrave), 141
Voice of Scotland, The (ed. MacDiarmid), 89
Voices of Our Kind (ed. Lindsay, 2nd edition Cameron), 213

Wagner, Richard, 42, 65, 210
Walk in the Sun, A (film), 72
Wallace, Lucille, 64
Walton, Sir William, 42, 138
Warr, Reverend Alfred, 20
Warren, Colonel Victor, 54
Watson, Roderick, 179
Waverley Novels (Scott), 28
Wax Fruit (McCrone), 117
Webster, Miss, 18
Westbourne Church, Glasgow, 87, 217
Western Front, 10
West Nile Street, Glasgow, 15
Westwater, R. H., 130
Widor, Charles Marie, 21
White Horse Inn, The (Benatzky), 29
White Horseman, The, 77
Whitehouse, Mary, 161
White Man's Saga (Linklater), 38
Whittaker, W. Gillies, 41–2, 138
Wightman, Harold, 128
Wilkie, Grocer, 16
Wills, Christine, 63

Wills, John, 63

Wilson, Charles (later Sir Charles), 189, 191

Wilson, C. A., 22

Wilson, Noble, 136

Wilson, Mrs Norma, 213

Wimberley, Major General Douglas, 60, 61

Wind in the Willows, The (Grahame), 140

Wolfe, Curtis, 191

Wood, H. K., 91

Woodcock, George, 156

"Woodlands", Heads Nook, 163

Wordsworth, William, 167

Wright, Professor Esmond, 143

Yeats, W. B., 154, 188

"Yet hae I silence left, the croon o' a" (MacDiarmid), 68

Yorke, Susan, 102

Young, Professor Douglas, 7, 58, 62, 79, 80, 89, 94–8, 99, 100–2, 114, 117, 163

Young, Mrs Hella, 7

Zwemmer's, Bookshop, 70